IMAGES
of America

TUSCARAWAS COUNTY OHIO

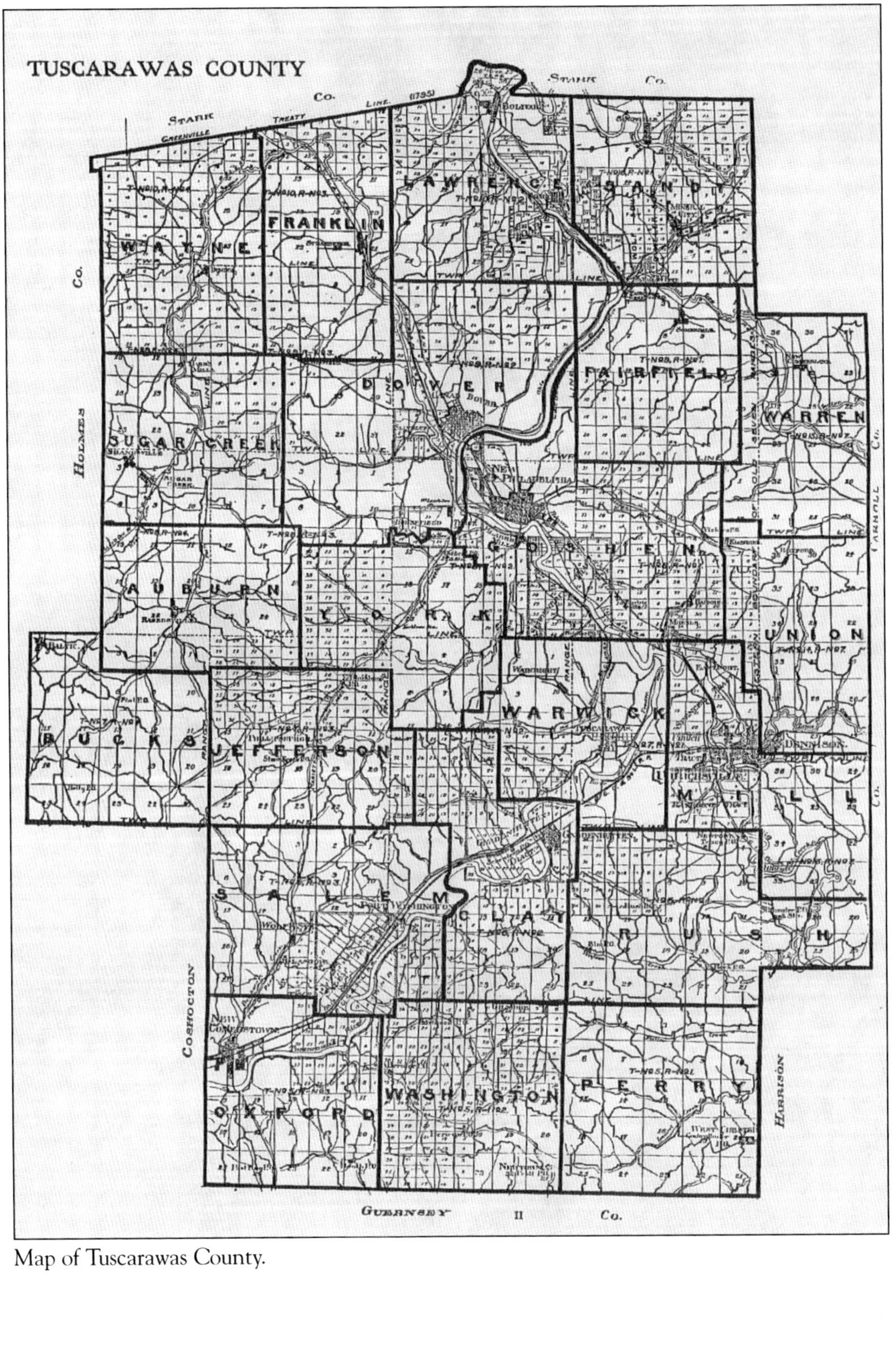

Map of Tuscarawas County.

IMAGES
of America

TUSCARAWAS COUNTY OHIO

Fred Miller

ARCADIA
PUBLISHING

ISBN 978-0-7385-0740-8

Published by Arcadia Publishing
Charleston, South Carolina

Printed in the United States of America

Library of Congress Catalog Card Number: 00106893

For all general information contact Arcadia Publishing at:
Telephone 843-853-2070
Fax 843-853-0044
E-mail sales@arcadiapublishing.com
For customer service and orders:
Toll-Free 1-888-313-2665

Visit us on the Internet at www.arcadiapublishing.com

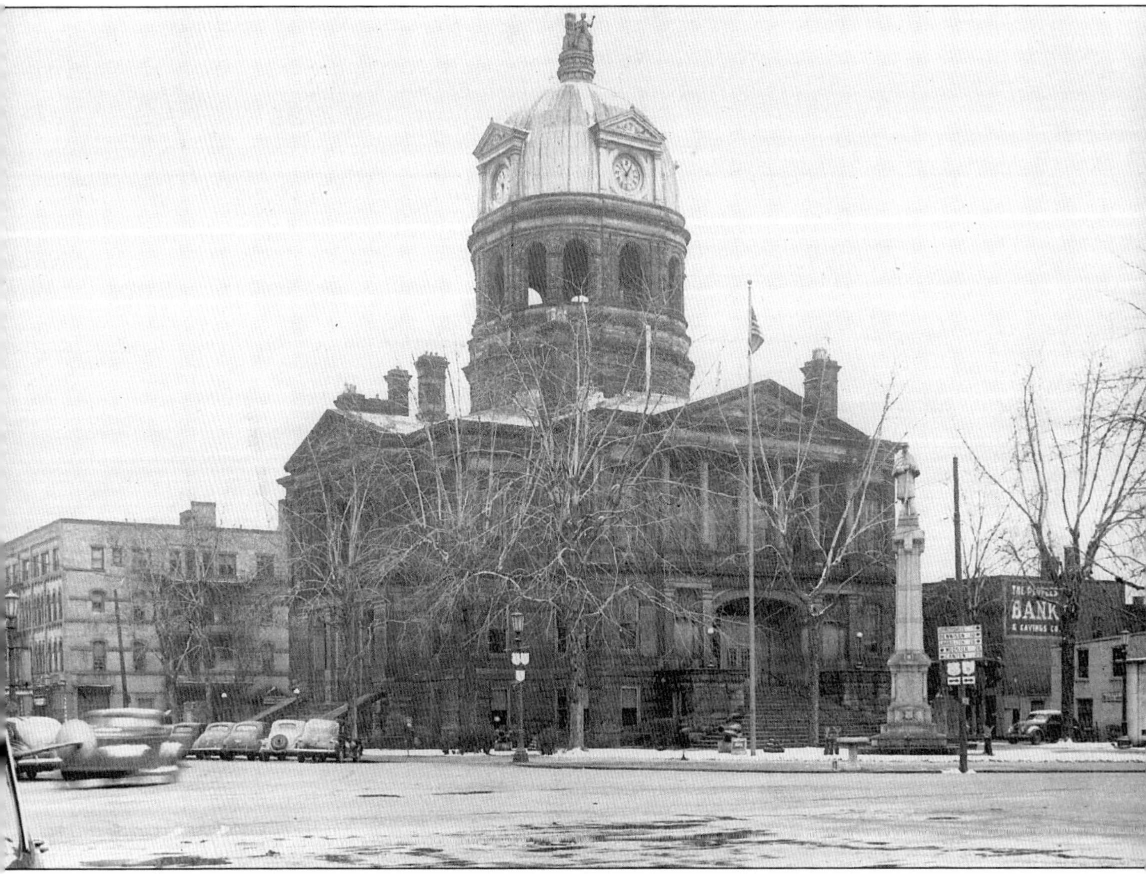

Tuscarawas County Courthouse.

Contents

ACKNOWLEDGMENTS

The Tuscarawas County Historical Society appreciates the donations of the pictures from the following collections: Wes Green, Joe Charlton, Thomas Hamilton, Pede Meese, Wilma Herman, Ivan DeWitt, George Freightling, Dan Fait, Bertha Geiser, the *Times Reporter*, Robert Shoemaker, Mildred Pearch, Rich Geib Jr., Loretta Coutts, Peg Stewart, Anna Debevec, Joe Davis, Dr Terry Miller, Ted Findley, Dr. Michael Gramly, Verna Maurer, Emma McDonald, Martin Keck, and Dorothy Mehok. Without these most generous donations, the pictorial record on Tuscarawas County would not have been possible. The Society extends most sincere thanks for their most generous donation.

The author wishes to thank the late Henry Hagloch for his work entitled *The History of Tuscarawas County, Ohio, to 1956*. I am indebted to this resource for many of the finite details in the research of the pictures and the writing of the captions. The author extends a most generous thank you to Dr. Earl P. Olmstead, President Emeritus of the Tuscarawas County Historical Society and Curator of the Tusc Kent Archives for his vast knowledge of the stories and events of Tuscarawas County and for his untiring dedication to the collection of these photographs. These past four years I have learned so much from my dear friend and colleague. The author is grateful to the officers and trustees of the Tuscarawas County Historical Society for providing the support to undertake this project and for the resources to see the project through to its fruition. Lastly, to my dear wife, Becky, I am eternally grateful for the time she has kindly given me to complete this labor of love.

This book is the result of all of the above named individuals, and if I have missed anyone, my most sincere apologies.

INTRODUCTION

Tuscarawas County, Ohio, was formed from the much larger Muskingum County in March of 1808, just five years after the formation of the State of Ohio in 1803. The Tuscarawas River, which nearly bisects the county, was also originally known as the Muskingum River. The word Tuscarawas is derived from an Indian word that means "open mouth." This river played a major role in the formation of the Ohio Country during the last half of the eighteenth century.

Moravian missionaries came to the area via the rivers and the Moravian Trail to begin the long and arduous process of Christianizing the Delaware Indian and establishing the Villages of Schoenbrunn (1772–1777), Gnadenhutten, Salem, and New Schoenbrunn. They first visited the site of the present-day Bolivar and the village of Gelekemepachunk (Newcomerstown), the Delaware Indian capital. With the construction of the only Revolutionary War fort in the Ohio Country (Ft. Laurens—1778–1779), and the Greenville Treaty Line crossing the northern border of the county, the area is rich in late eighteenth century drama of frontier American history, especially as it pertained to the development of the Ohio Country.

In the nineteenth century, the valley was witness to many significant social and economic events that opened the county to rapid growth and development. The first major event was the settling of 5,500 acres of prime real estate in the northern part of the county by the Separatist Society of Zoar, a pietistic group of Germans (three hundred members) who came to America pursuing religious freedom in which to practice a social and economic program known as Communalism. Leader Joseph Bimeler established the Society in the year 1817. The group grew and prospered until the year 1898, when it elected to dissolve.

Three additional major economic measures that shaped nineteenth century Tuscarawas County included the bisecting of the county by the Ohio Erie Canal in 1825, the crisscrossing of the county via the railroads in the late 1850s, and the Industrial Revolution in the late 1880s. Iron ore, coal, and clay, which were abundant in the hills of Tuscarawas County, played a most important role in the development of the county economically, but more importantly, in the settlement of the county by many nationalities. Although the canal, railroad, and clay and coal mining have run their course, today, we find the beloved Tuscarawas Valley looking ahead to a healthy economic future at the beginning of the twenty-first century.

Where the Ohio Erie Canal and the railroads provided a most important avenue for commerce, trade, and tourism in the nineteenth and early twentieth centuries, Interstate 77, which was built in the late 1950s and early 1960s, provided the same for the late twentieth and early twenty-first centuries. Industries have an important link to the outside world. The county also provides its business and industry leaders with a local venue for higher learning—the Tuscarawas Campus Kent State University, which provides the training for many of the latest technology and business acumen so vital in the twenty-first century global world economy. Many of the industries have reached the worldwide markets and are prospering in a very competitive market.

Images of America: Tuscarawas County, Ohio, captures—through picture and word—the story of the development of Tuscarawas County from 1761 through the late 1980s. The reason we stopped with the late 1980s was the fundamental fact that our collection of pictures at the Tusc Kent Archives unfortunately ends at that time. We wish we had more pictures to chronicle the later twentieth century. Perhaps the publication of this book will foster donations of pictures of the later twentieth century to our permanent collection.

When selecting the pictures for this book, the author attempted to cover the history of Tuscarawas County within the confines of the resources at the Tusc Kent Archives. A most sincere attempt was made to be as comprehensive as possible of the total county. Our collection is very limited regarding a few areas of Tuscarawas County, and we welcome photographs of any and all communities.

We hope you enjoy this pictorial history of Tuscarawas County, Ohio.

One

The Early History of Tuscarawas County

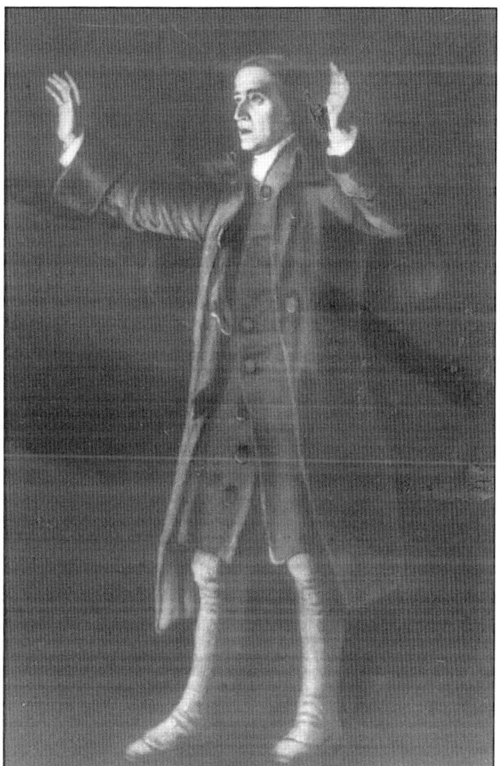

David Zeisberger. David Zeisberger, a leader of the Moravian missionaries among the American Indians of the middle and late eighteenth century, made his first visit to what is now Tuscarawas County in 1771, and in 1772, founded the first church and first schoolhouse and established the first codified set of laws in what was then known as the Ohio Country. During the turbulent years of the Revolutionary War, David sought permission of the Moravian church in Bethlehem, Pennsylvania, to move his flock from Pennsylvania to this region. In March of 1772, he found the Big Spring and called the town Schoenbrunn, which means "beautiful spring." David Zeisberger was 50 years old when he began this mission.

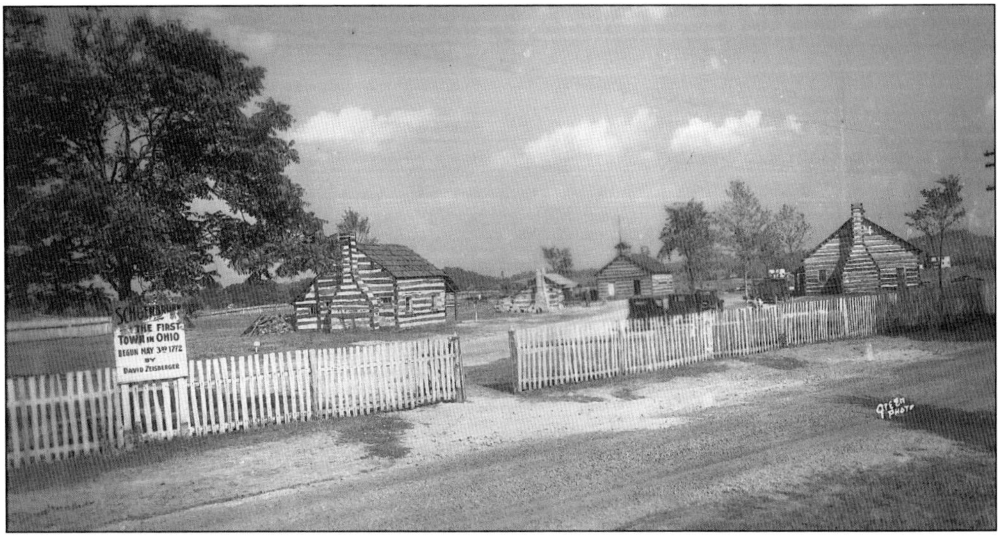

SCHOENBRUNN 1928. The above photograph taken in 1928 shows the completed restoration of the Village of Schoenbrunn undertaken by the Tuscarawas County Historical Society and the Ohio Historical Society. The Tuscarawas County Historical Society was founded in 1921 for the express purpose of locating the ancient village of Schoenbrunn. Using maps from the Moravian Historical Society in Bethlehem, Pennsylvania, work began, and the village was completed in 1928.

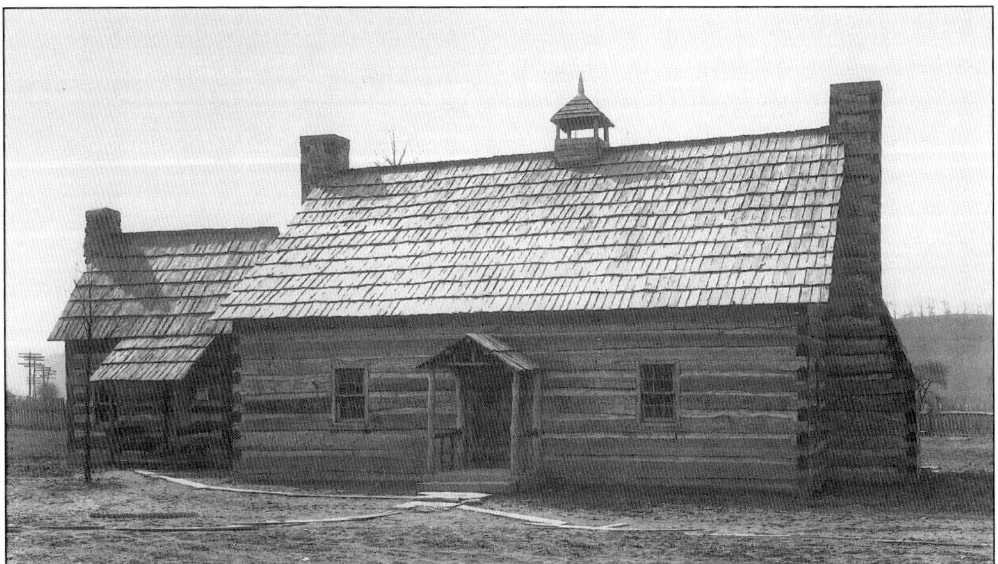

SCHOENBRUNN CHURCH 1928. The reconstructed church at Schoenbrunn is pictured here after it was located and then restored in 1928. David Zeisberger, Moravian missionary to his beloved Delaware Indians, founded this village of three hundred in 1772. His diaries recounted the trials and tribulations of his flock during these very troubling times in American history, but the church was the central meeting place in which he passed on the Christian faith to his people. The Village of Schoenbrunn lasted from 1772–1777, when he was forced to move the remaining loyal members to Lichtenau, near the present town of Coshocton, Ohio. The church was burned to the ground in 1777 to prevent its desecration.

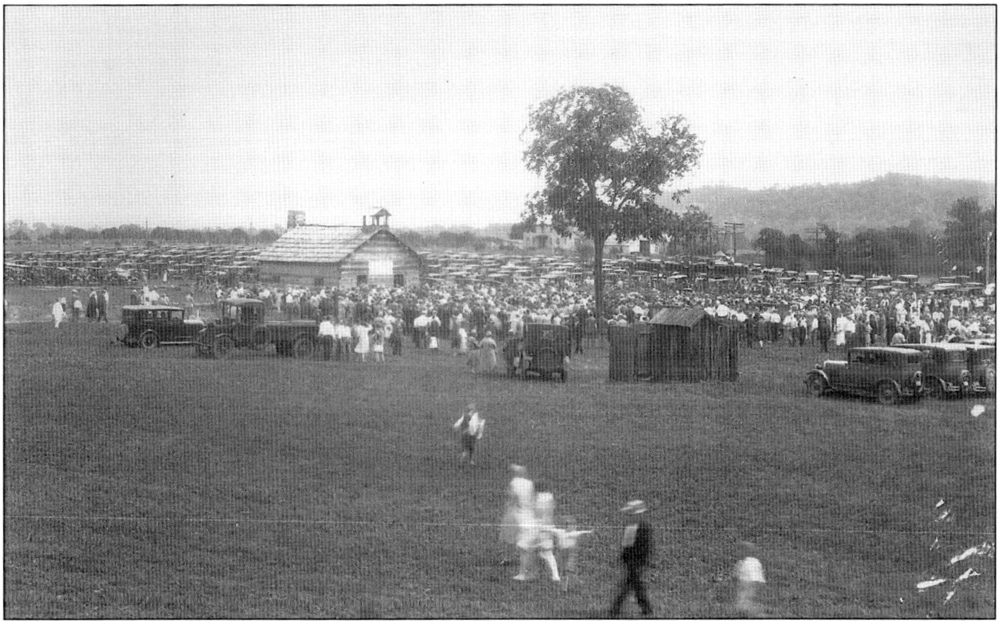

SCHOENBRUNN GATHERING 1928. This photograph depicts the gathering of many interested people at the dedication of the church in 1928. The rest of the village has not been restored at the time of this dedication. The newspapers printed special editions reviewing the history of this revered site.

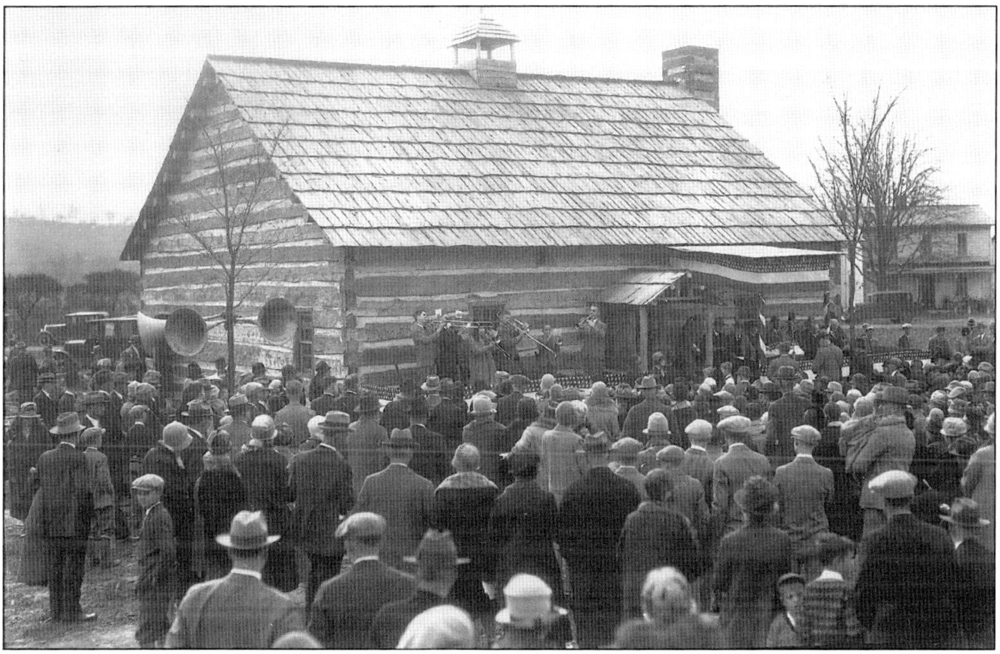

SCHOENBRUNN CHURCH DEDICATION. A Moravian brass ensemble plays selections for the gathered masses in this 1928 picture. The traditional "Love Feast" is conducted at Easter sunrise in the restored village, and a special candlelight Christmas Eve Service features a brass ensemble from the local Moravian churches each year. The restored church is usually filled (300) to capacity for these annual events.

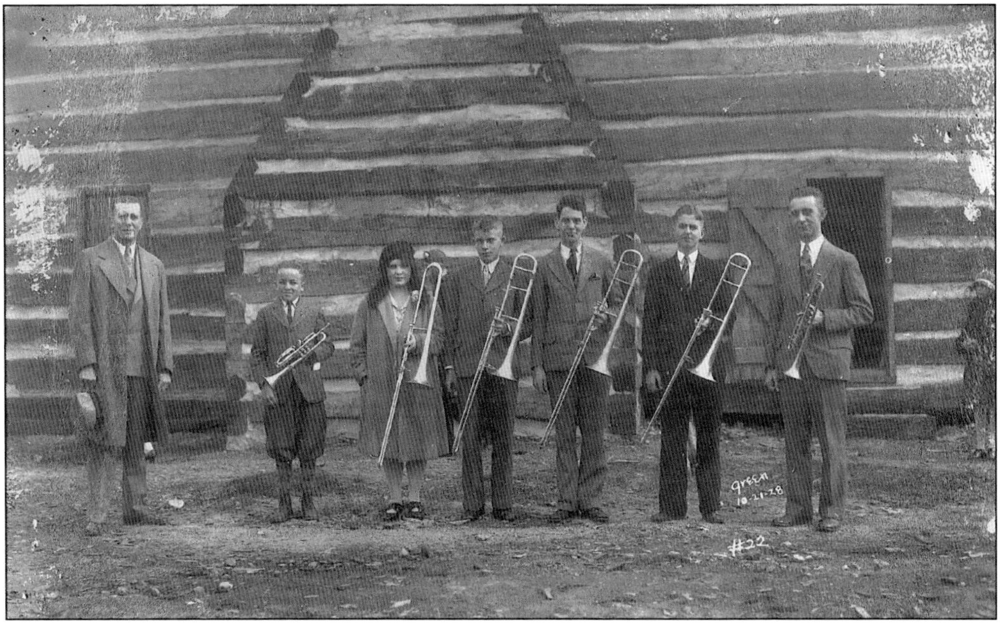

THE BRASS CHOIR. The official portrait of the brass choir was taken before their performance at the dedication of the church. This photograph was taken at the site of the reconstructed church.

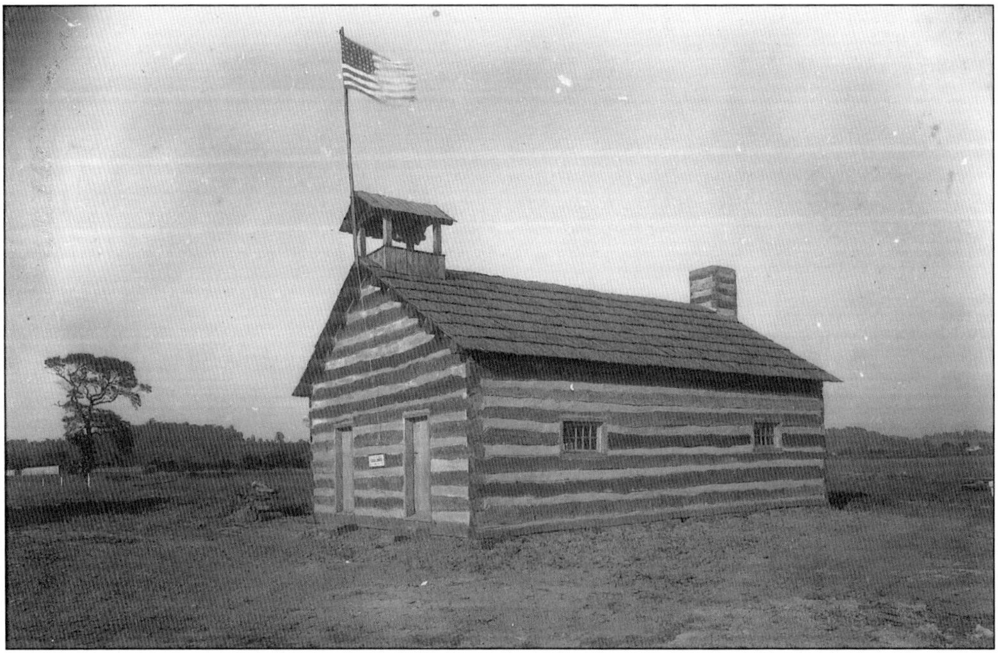

SCHOENBRUNN RECONSTRUCTED SCHOOLHOUSE. The Schoenbrunn schoolhouse, of simple but sturdy construction, has become an important symbol in pioneer history. The reconstructed schoolhouse was the first in the Ohio Country. John Heckewelder, who had come to the Ohio Country in 1751 as an educator, came along with missionary David Zeisberger as the first schoolteacher in the Ohio Country. Daily instruction as well as bringing the gospel to the Delawares was the goal of the missionary and teacher.

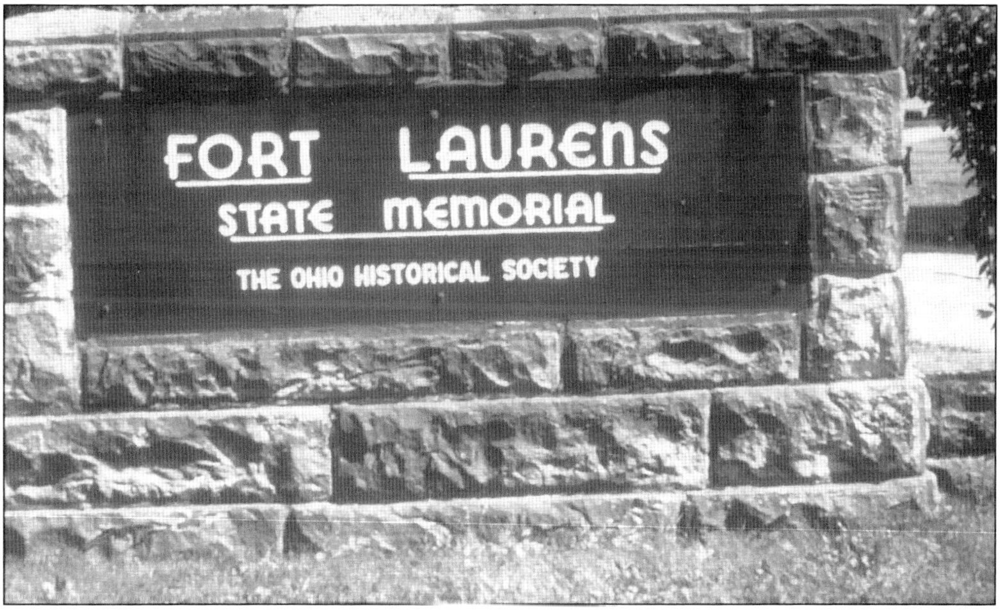

FORT LAURENS SIGN. The entrance to the site of Fort Laurens was built in the late 1930s as a part of the many federal economic recovery programs. The Ohio Historical Society secured the site at the turn of the twentieth century in order to preserve the area of the only Revolutionary War fort to be built in the Ohio Country. Several archeological excavations have been conducted at the site over the years.

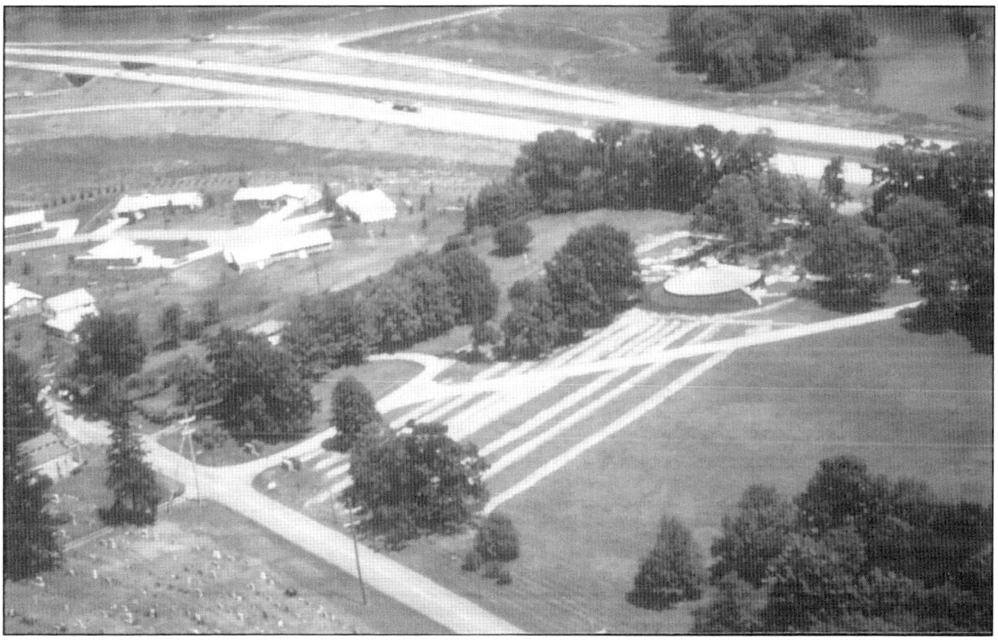

FORT LAURENS DIG. This picture is an aerial view of Dr. Michael Gramly's archeological excavation of Fort Laurens in 1972–1973. The long brown strips running from the country road toward the Ohio Historical Society Museum indicate attempts to locate the mass grave. Recently completed Interstate 77 is visible at the top of the picture. The Ohio Erie Canal in the late 1820s and Interstate 77 in the 1960s were constructed on a portion of the fort.

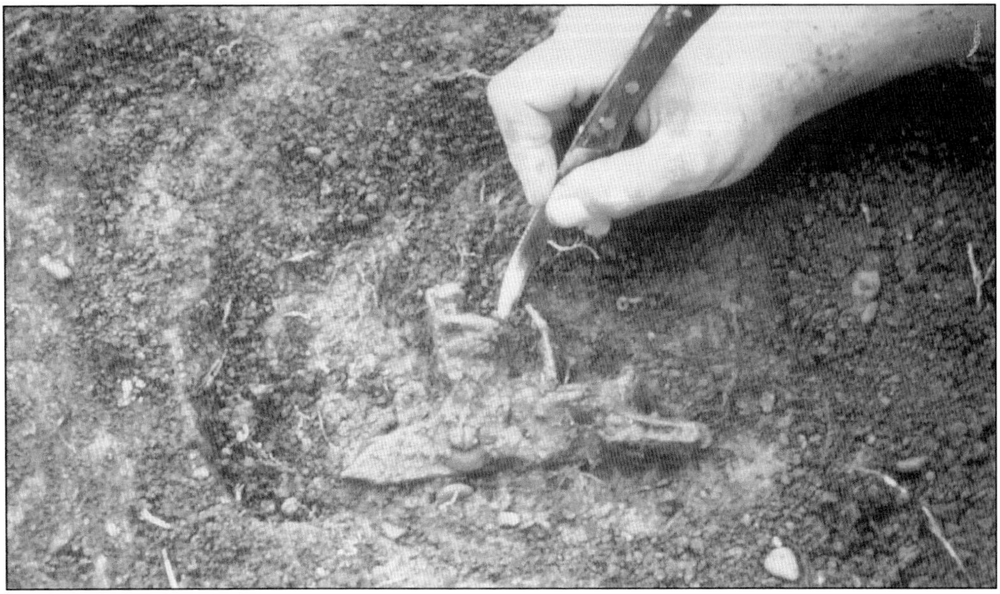

Fort Laurens Hand/Bones. The integral details associated with any archeological excavation are displayed in this photograph. The ground is reverently searched for any artifact. When an item of interest is located, the delicate piece is painstakingly examined, recorded, and preserved. If found to be significant in recording the history of the site, the artifact is carefully removed and taken to be further cleaned, inspected, and preserved.

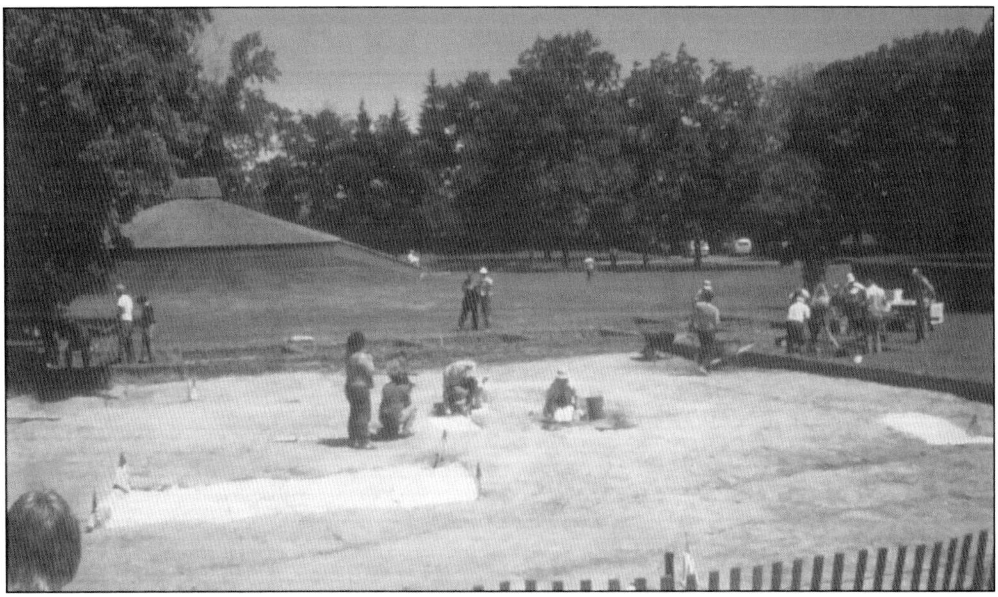

Fort Laurens Burial Site. The site of the massed grave at Fort Laurens was first secured, and then the work began in earnest with only those associated with the archeological party permitted in the dig site. The archeological site was opened for daily public observation with renowned historian Major Tom Pieper (Kings 8th Regiment recreated) presenting daily commentary on the history of the fort. An honor guard representing the 8th Pennsylvania and the 9th/13th Virginia Regiments (recreated) was mounted at all times at the site. The Ohio Historical Society's Museum is in the left background of the picture.

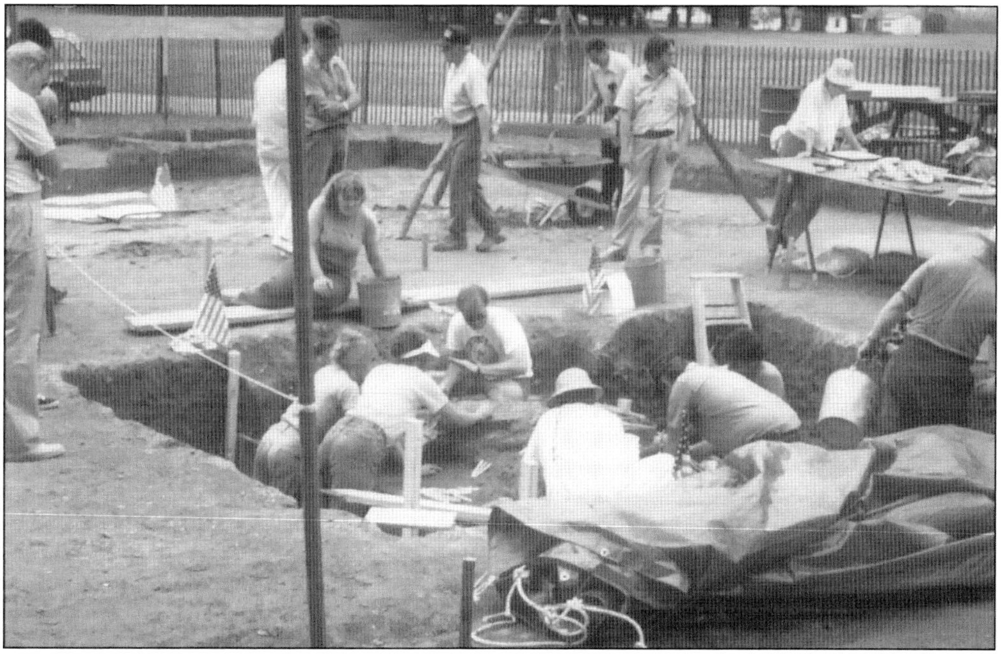

FORT LAURENS BURIAL SITE. The work of the dig had reached a fevered pitch as is evidenced by this photograph. The main burial site of the 15 soldiers was about to be uncovered. The work was slow and arduous, but minute detail work takes time, experience, and backbreaking effort—usually under a hot sun. As the work progressed, daily reports were relayed to the local newspapers, and the crowds increased as Dr. Gramly and his team had reached their objective.

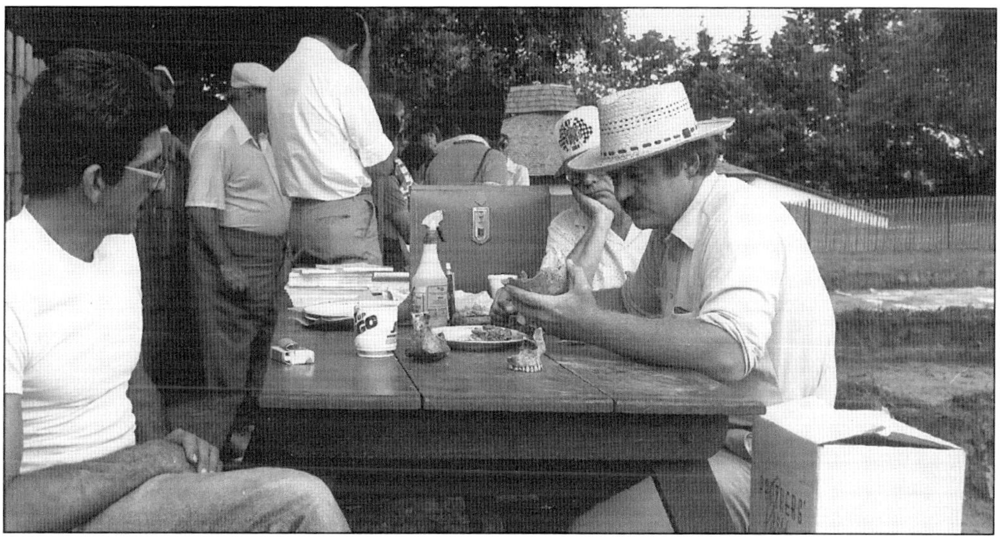

DR. MICHAEL GRAMLEY. Dr. Michael Gramley, archeologist (pictured near right in the photograph), takes a much-needed break for nourishment and rest. Yet even while eating, the talk continued about the work (see the jawbone near Dr. Gramly's plate.) After his work was completed in the field, a massive amount of work continued until his final book on the archeological explorations at Fort Laurens was completed in 1999. The Tusc Kent Archives has received as a donation from Dr. Gramly—his photographic record and field notes of the various digs at Fort Laurens.

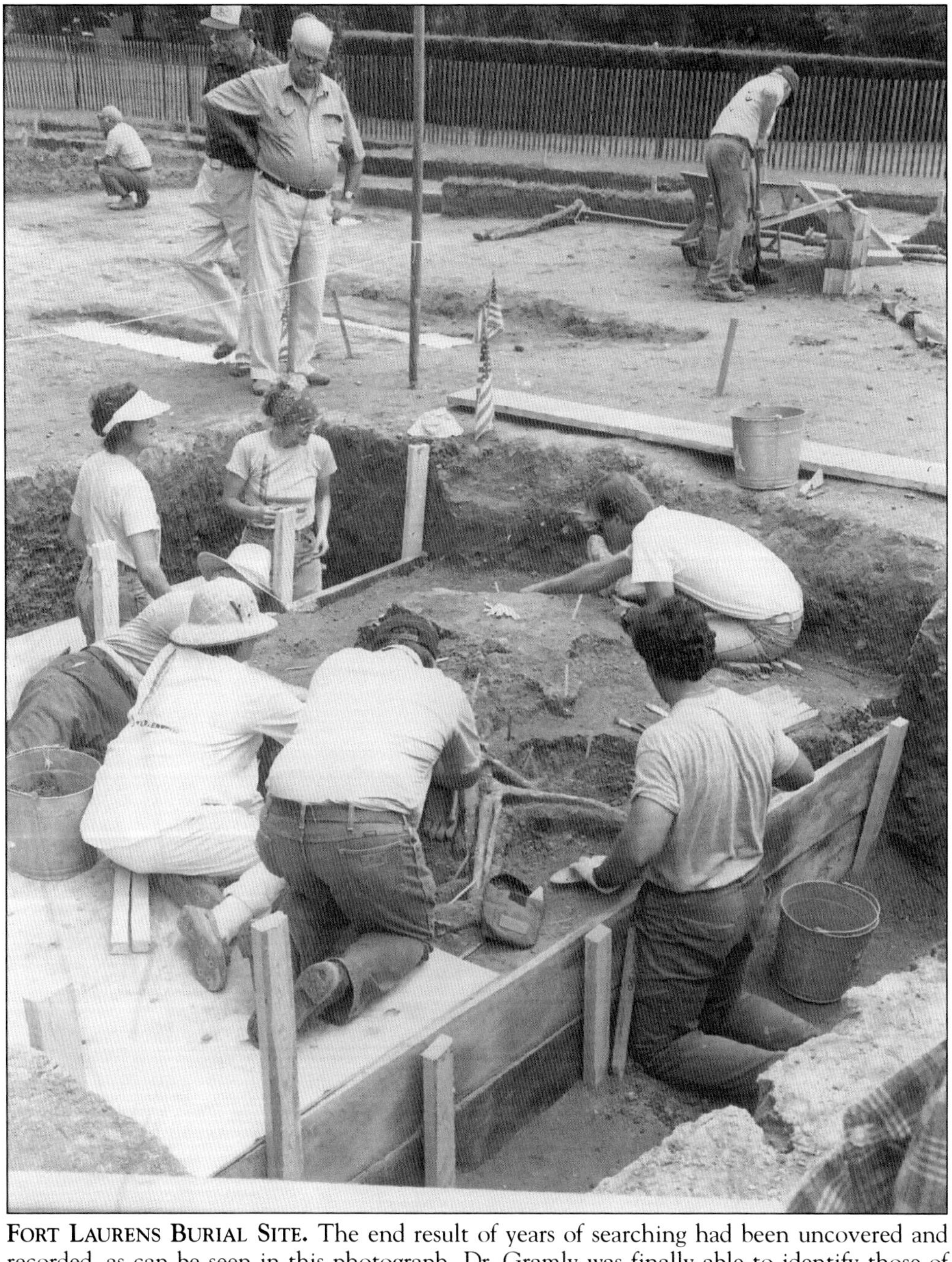

FORT LAURENS BURIAL SITE. The end result of years of searching had been uncovered and recorded, as can be seen in this photograph. Dr. Gramly was finally able to identify those of the mass grave. The fieldwork of 1972, 1973, 1986, and 1987 uncovered many significant facts and a great number of artifacts relating to Fort Laurens, and the Ohio Historical Society properly preserved all. After the 1972–73 explorations, which located the exact site of Fort Laurens between 1778–1779, a tomb for the unknown soldier of the Revolutionary War was impressively dedicated on June 26, 1976. The Tuscarawas County Historical Society is deeply indebted to Dr. Gramly and all who worked in unearthing the details behind this important piece of Ohio history.

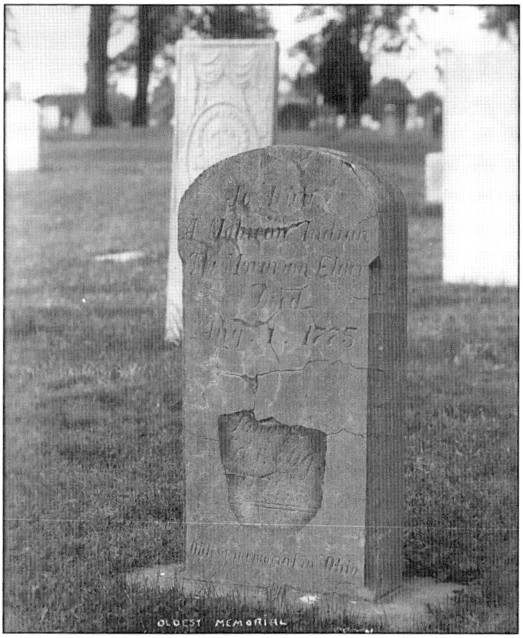

GNADENHUTTEN MEMORIAL. The two photographs on this page are reminders of the infamous massacre that occurred on March 8, 1782. The unsuspecting Indians had returned from the northwest area of the Ohio Country to gather in the corn from about 300 acres they had to abandon when taken captive in the fall of 1781. Because of raids by other Indians into Pennsylvania, a counteroffensive was made by militiamen who came upon the followers of Zeisberger harvesting the corn along the banks of the Tuscarawas River near their home of Gnadenhutten. Trusting peoples, they were massacred in what has been described as "one of the blackest deeds of frontier history" by writer Henry Hagloch. The remains of the 90 Christian Indians who died that year were interred in a common grave that is marked by these monuments which were dedicated in 1882, the centennial of the massacre. A grandson of John Heckewelder had attended that service.

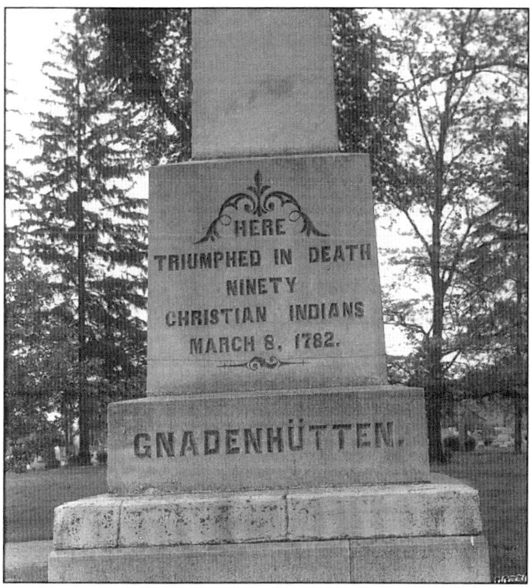

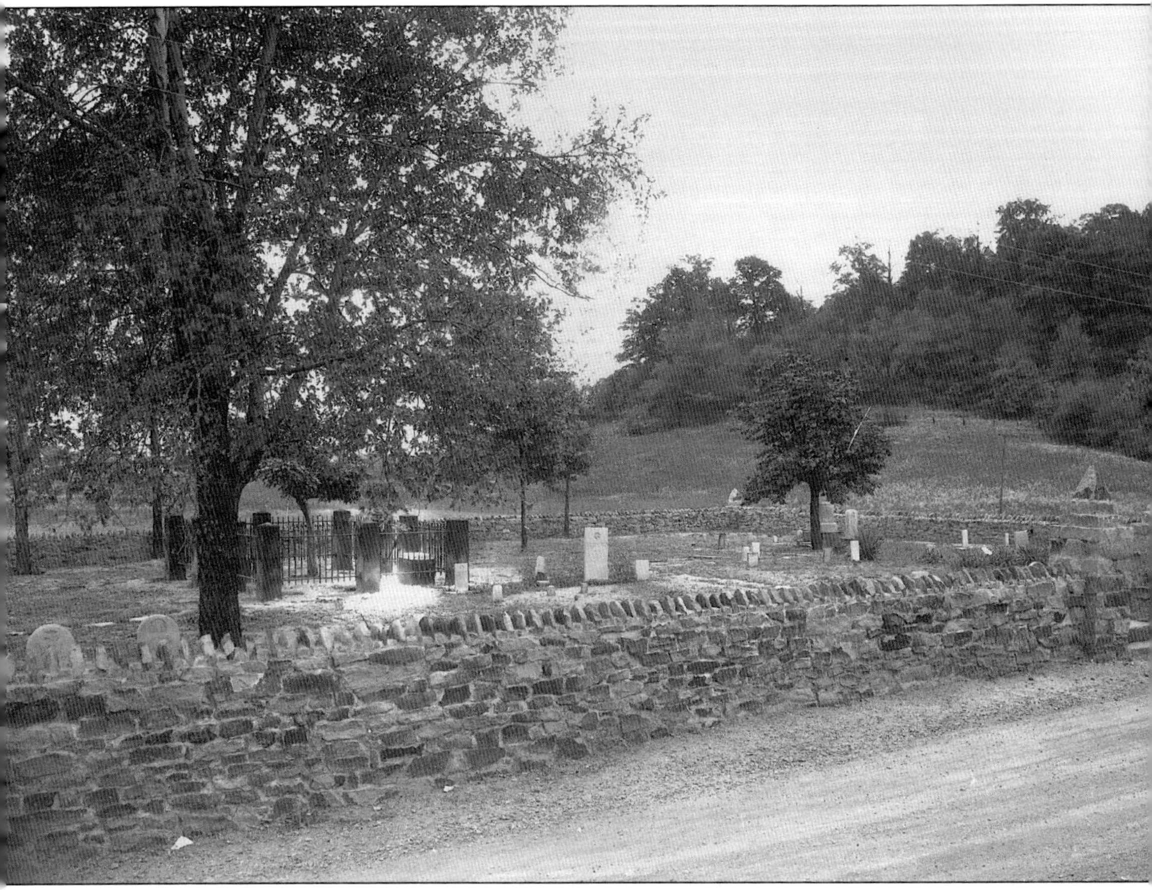

GOSHEN CEMETERY. Dr. Earl P. Olmstead has exhaustingly recorded and preserved the history of missionary David Zeisberger. In his book, *Blackcoats Among the Delaware*, Dr Olmstead records the final mission at the Village of Goshen, begun in 1798. David Zeisberger is buried on this small peaceful site. His grave is inside the fenced-in portion of the burial grounds. Goshen completes the circle and binds the contribution of his influence in the Ohio Country. In 1909, the Northern Provincial Elders of the Moravian Church erected the cemetery walls around the cemetery. Since 1997, the Tuscarawas County Historical Society has undertaken the cemetery as a special project with assistance from the Rosenberry Foundation. The crumbling walls were repaired and special permanent markers have been erected denoting the names of the people buried at this site.

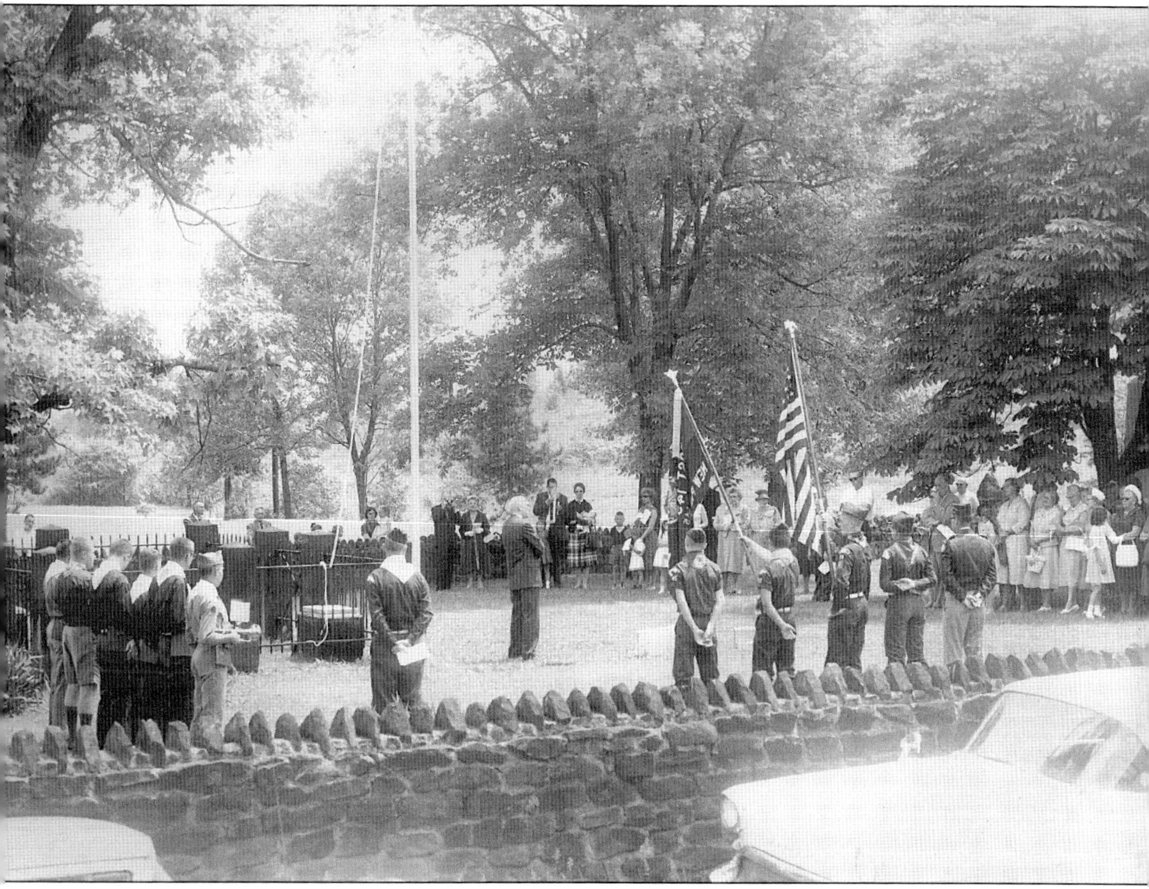

GOSHEN CEMETERY. This rare photograph records the 150th anniversary of the founding of the Village of Goshen by David Zeisberger. In 1798, 78-year-old David, his wife Susan, and 33 converts made the arduous journey by canoe to this site that had been prepared by John Heckewelder. The converts had been in Fairfield, Ontario, Canada, and longed to return to the Tuscarawas Valley. Ted Finley (now deceased), a well-known local historian and the first president of the Ohio Canal Society, is shown in the photograph delivering the keynote speech about this important place in Ohio frontier history.

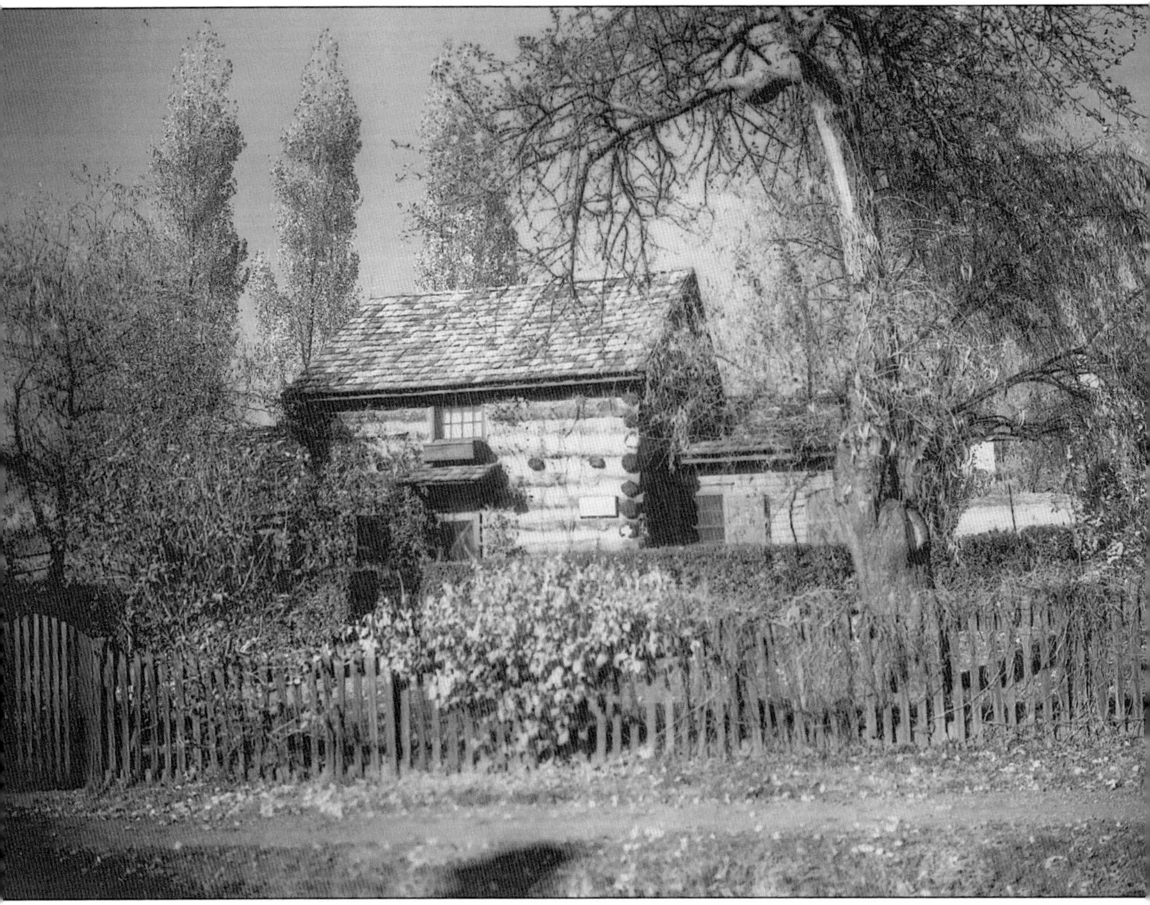

BIMELER CABIN. The Separatist Society of Zoar was founded on 5,500 acres in the northern portion of Tuscarawas County, Ohio, in 1817. As with many of the early pioneers, these individuals came to America because it was the "land of opportunity." The three hundred Zoarites came in search of religious freedom. Befriended by the Society of Friends in England and in Philadelphia, money was secured by Joseph Bimeler from the Friends and paid to Godfrey Haga, a businessman in Philadelphia, for the right to purchase 5,500 acres of military land in Tuscarawas County. A contract was written that the money would be paid back within 10 years. Bimeler and a few men came to Tuscarawas County in the fall of 1817, built this cabin in which to live, and then began the task of preparing a place for the remaining group in Philadelphia. The privately owned cabin still stands in the Village of Zoar.

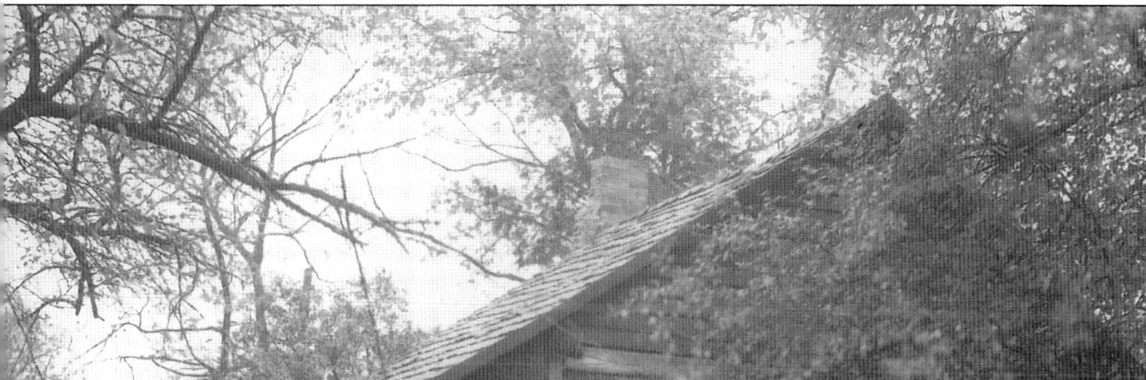

GUNN CABIN. Alexander Gunn, a wealthy businessman from Cleveland who had many friends of high esteem and was a personal friend of the Whitney's of New York City and a world traveler, found refuge in the community of Zoar during his later life. Visiting the village for the first time in 1879, he became enamored with the locale and its peoples. His diaries tell of his happiest times when he was with his friends in Zoar. Some feel that Gunn's influence in the village helped lead the Society toward its final demise. After the dissolution of the Society, he purchased this home and the famed brewery. Gunn died in Germany in 1901 and was brought back to Zoar where he was buried on a hill overlooking his brewery.

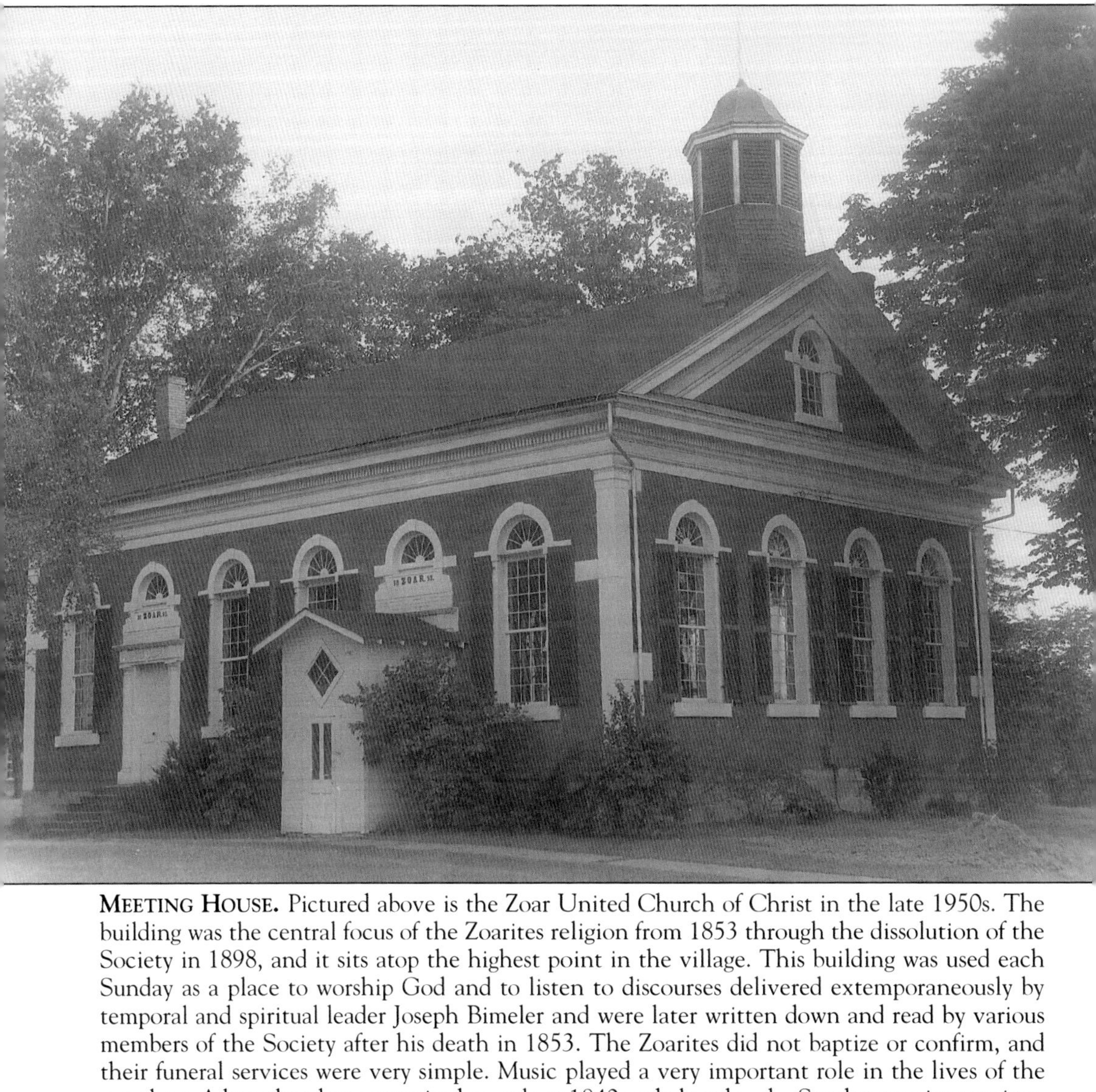

MEETING HOUSE. Pictured above is the Zoar United Church of Christ in the late 1950s. The building was the central focus of the Zoarites religion from 1853 through the dissolution of the Society in 1898, and it sits atop the highest point in the village. This building was used each Sunday as a place to worship God and to listen to discourses delivered extemporaneously by temporal and spiritual leader Joseph Bimeler and were later written down and read by various members of the Society after his death in 1853. The Zoarites did not baptize or confirm, and their funeral services were very simple. Music played a very important role in the lives of the members. A brass band was organized as early as 1840 and played at the Sunday evening services. A train from Cleveland brought a beautiful pipe organ in 1873, which is still in use today.

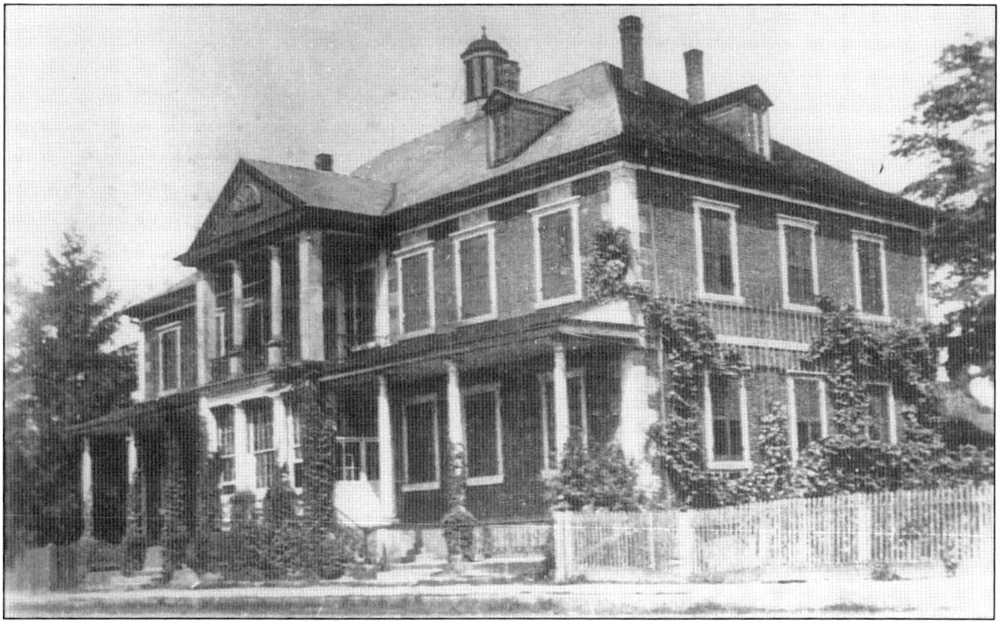

NUMBER ONE HOUSE. The House Number One or Kings Palace, as it was formerly known, was originally built as a home for the senior citizens of the Society. The older members rejected that idea, and it became the home of leader Joseph Bimeler and his family. This magnificent structure was the central focus of life in the village. Workers would get their orders from the porch, and the magazine where the members came to select necessary items for their families was located behind the building.

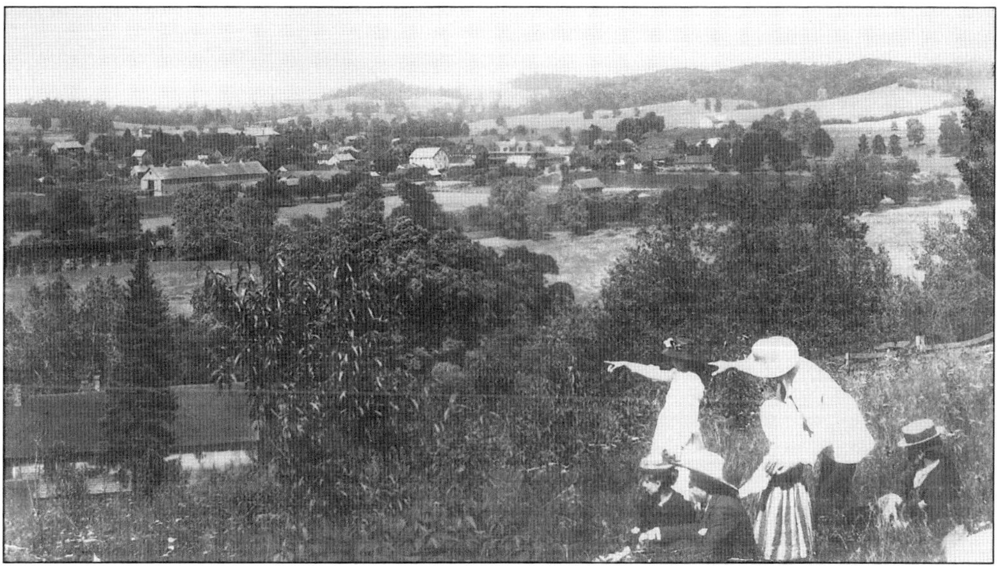

BIRDSEYE VIEW OF ZOAR. A photographer around the turn of the twentieth century captured a family outing on the hillside south of the Village of Zoar. It appears in this photo that the father and his daughter are pointing out the Canal Hotel, which is to the lower left in the picture. This hotel, built by the Zoarites in the early 1830s, served passengers on the Ohio Erie Canal which ran below the structure. Today this building is again utilized as an eating establishment called the Inn on the River.

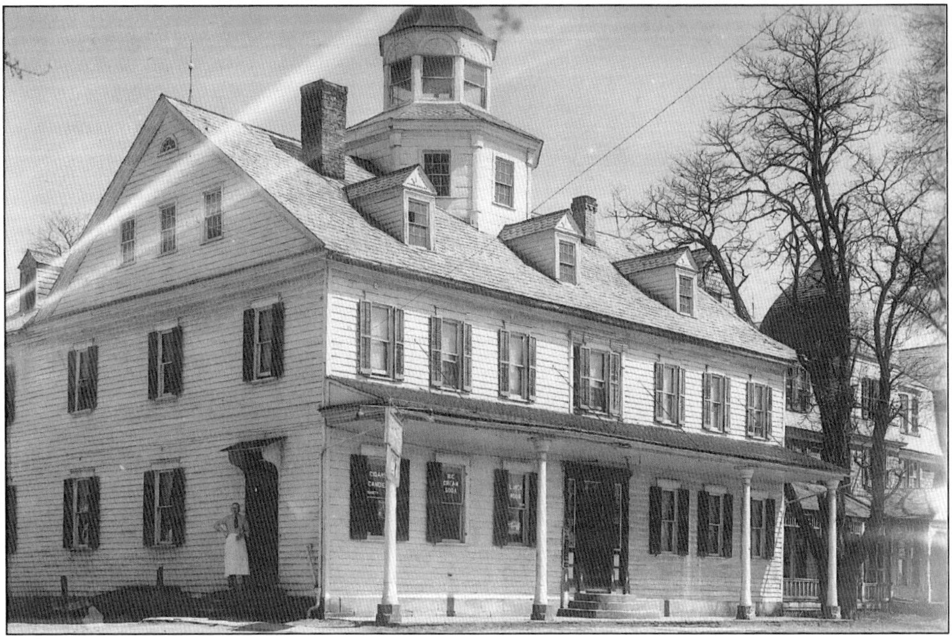

Zoar Hotel. This photograph taken of the Zoar Hotel in the early 1900s shows the original building built in 1833 and the Victorian addition of the 1890s. Almost from its inception, the village became a magnet for visitors. To some extent, they were thought to be one of the reasons for the breakup of the Society. The Zoarites began to capitalize on the visitors. Prominent visitors to this fine establishment were U.S. Senator Mark Hanna, President William McKinley and members of his Cabinet, and wealthy businessman Alexander Gunn of Cleveland, Ohio.

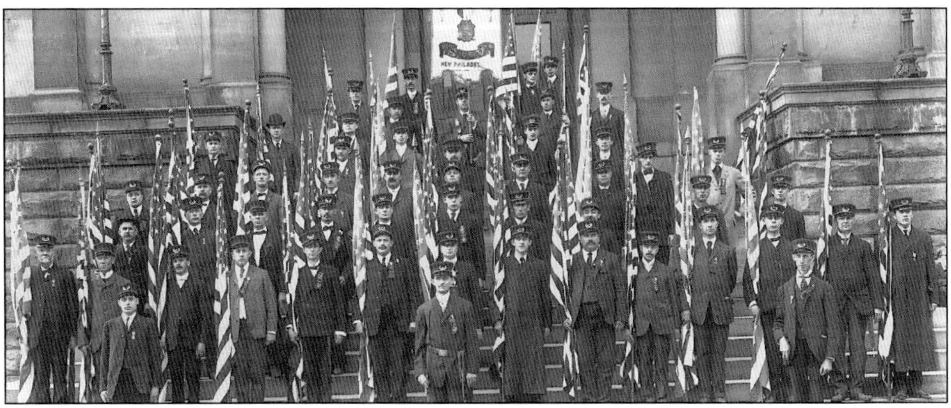

GAR Sons on the Steps of Tuscarawas County Courthouse. Members of Tuscarawas County formed their own regiment (51st) for the Ohio Voluntary Infantry during the Civil War from 1861 through 1865. Other groups with members from Tuscarawas County were the 80th, 87th, 107th, 126th, 129th, 161st, 178th, and 185th, including some in the 12th Ohio Calvary. A few joined as one-hundred-day enlistees, while others served for the four-year duration. Most served in the battles of the South including the battles of northern Georgia, the Battle of Atlanta, and the campaign in Tennessee before being mustered out in Texas. Camp Meigs was organized at the Tuscarawas County Fairgrounds. After their service, they formed into an organization called the Grand Army of the Republic (GAR) and gathered on the steps of the Tuscarawas County Courthouse for their annual picture.

Two

A History of Transportation in Tuscarawas County

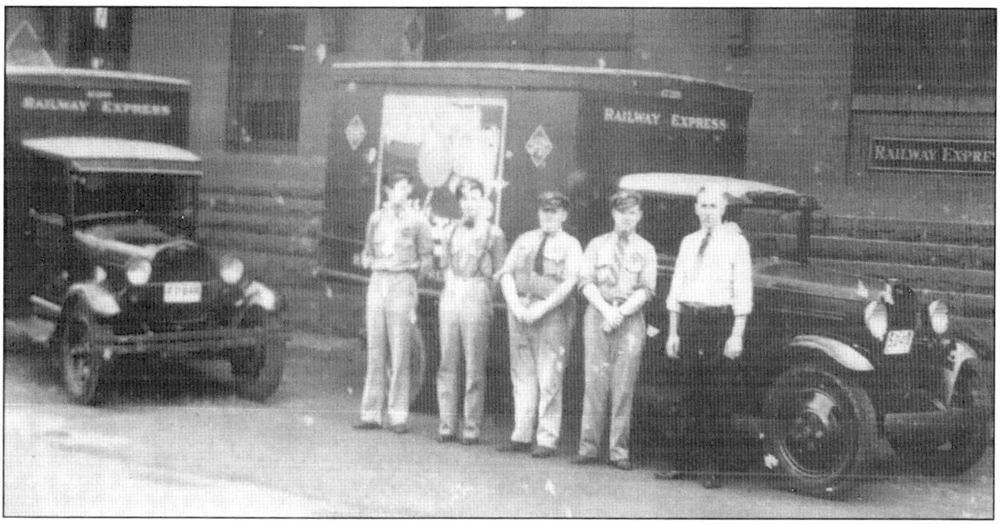

Railway Express at Dennison Railroad Depot. The history of transportation in Tuscarawas County, like many counties in the Midwest, followed a pattern from animal paths to Native American and Fur Traders and Trappers paths, which led to the faster Ohio Erie Canal, and eventually improved roads for horse and buggy. The invention of the Iron Horse took over very quickly for the slower canal movement. Even this was bypassed for the quicker Interstate system by which individual wants and needs could be better accommodated. The picture shown is of the Railway Express at the Dennison Railroad Depot, which combined the era of the railroad and individual service to our homes and businesses. The picture was taken in 1937 and shows Agent Frank Page, along with drivers Herb Still, Jerry O'Brien, D. Gezzi, and L. Carrother.

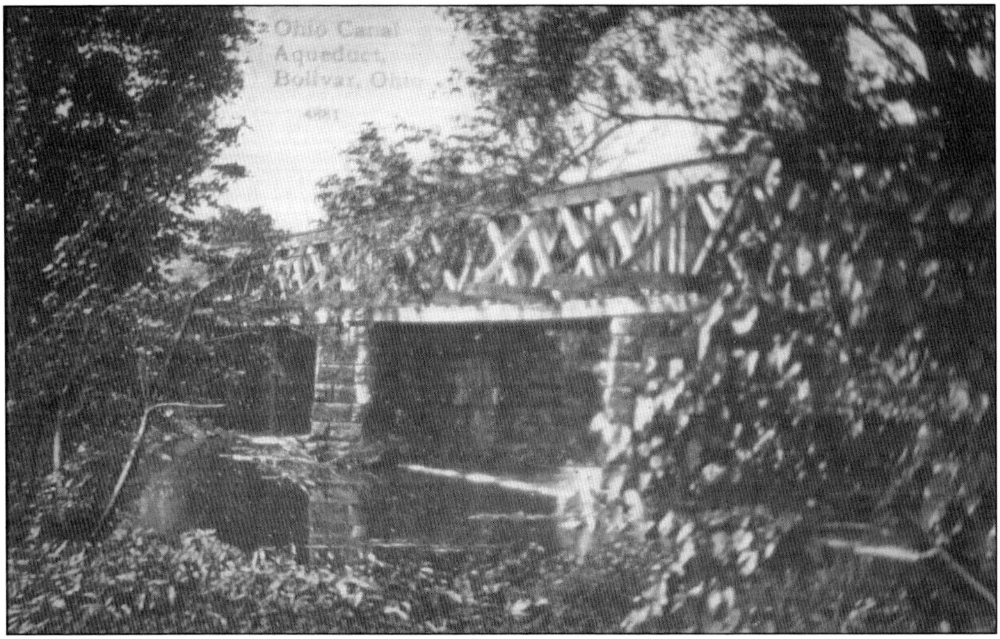

TWO PICTURES OF THE BOLIVAR AQUEDUCT OHIO ERIE CANAL. The two pictures on this page show the rather unique invention of providing a waterway above and across another waterway—called an aqueduct. Used as far back as the Roman period in history, the above means of crossing a barrier was used a great deal in the construction of the Ohio Erie Canal. Both pictures are used since they represent an aqueduct for the Ohio Erie Canal at the west end of the village of Bolivar and an aqueduct at the center of the village of Bolivar which carried the Sandy Beaver Canal to its end point from the Ohio River in the east. The Ohio Erie Canal entered Tuscarawas County at Bolivar and transverses the county through the villages and towns of Zoar, Canal Dover, New Philadelphia, Lockport, Blakes Mill, Goshen, Trenton, Lock Seventeen, Port Washington, and Newcomerstown. From Newcomerstown it entered Coshocton County on its way to the Ohio River.

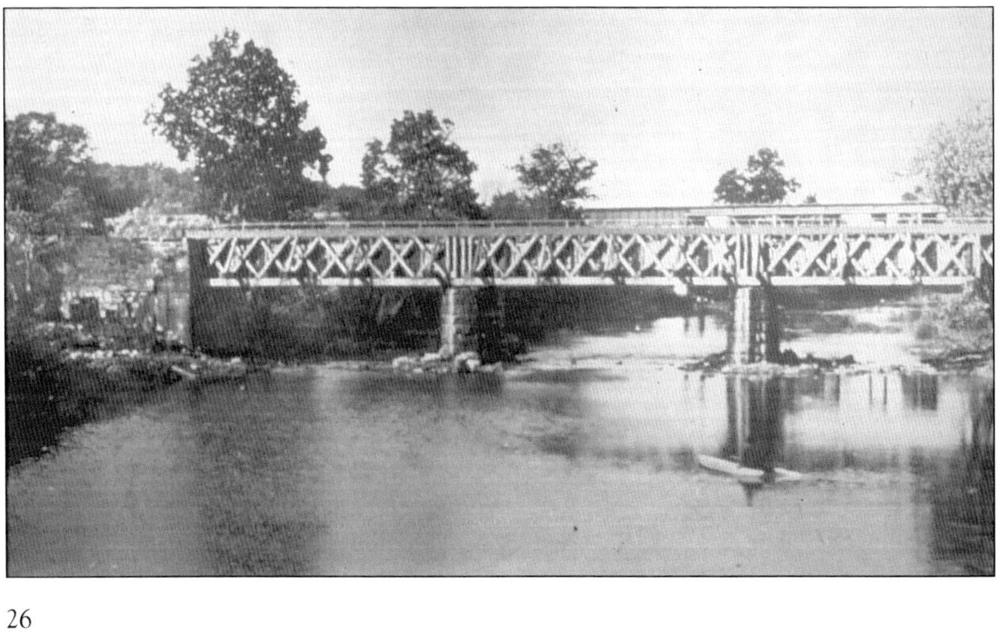

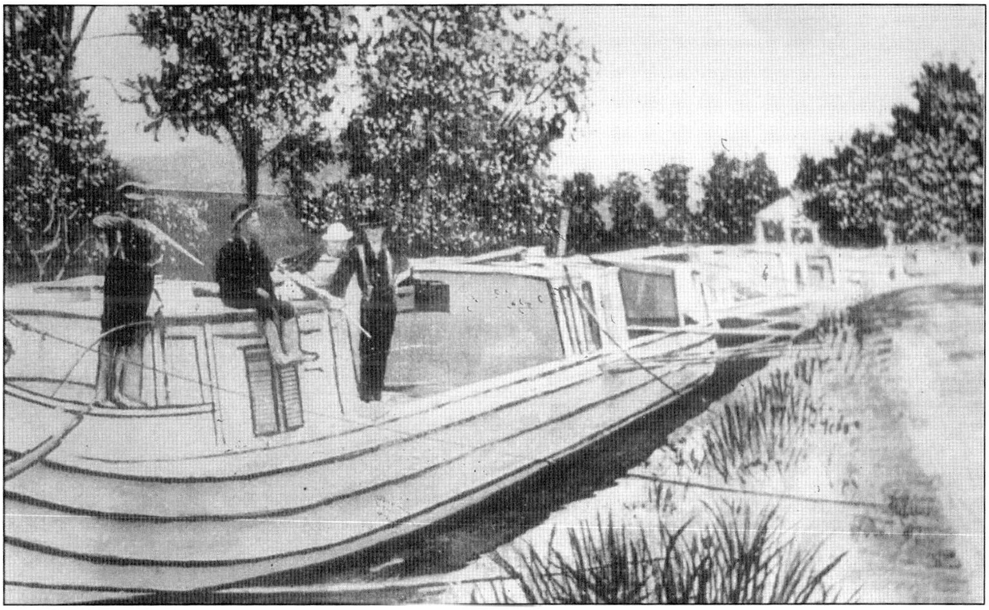

OHIO ERIE CANAL AT BOLIVAR. Workers on a packet spend some free moments shooting at muskrats along the banks of the canal. Muskrats and other varmints created a legitimate problem for the canal in that they dug holes which caused fresh outs in the canal. These fresh outs would drain the water from the canal into the river, basin, or fields adjoining the canal.

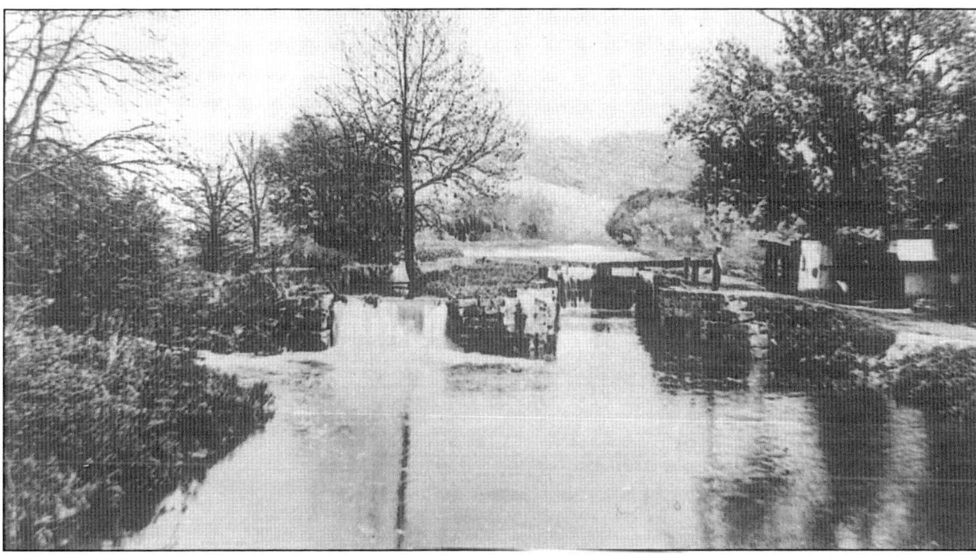

JONES LOCK ABOVE CANAL DOVER, OHIO. The Ohio Erie Canal depended on a locking system to traverse the hilly terrain of eastern Ohio. This picture shows Jones Lock, named for the lock keeper. His home is located to the right of the picture. The process of moving from one elevation to another was performed by either entering the lock and then waiting for the water in the lock to be lowered until the level at the other end was reached, and then opening the lower end and proceeding on their way, or by entering a lock and then filling the lock, thereby raising the boat to the higher level. This took time, and with the many boats on the canal, many battles ensued between the deck hands as to who would get into the lock first—sometimes with the winner of the fight having first choice.

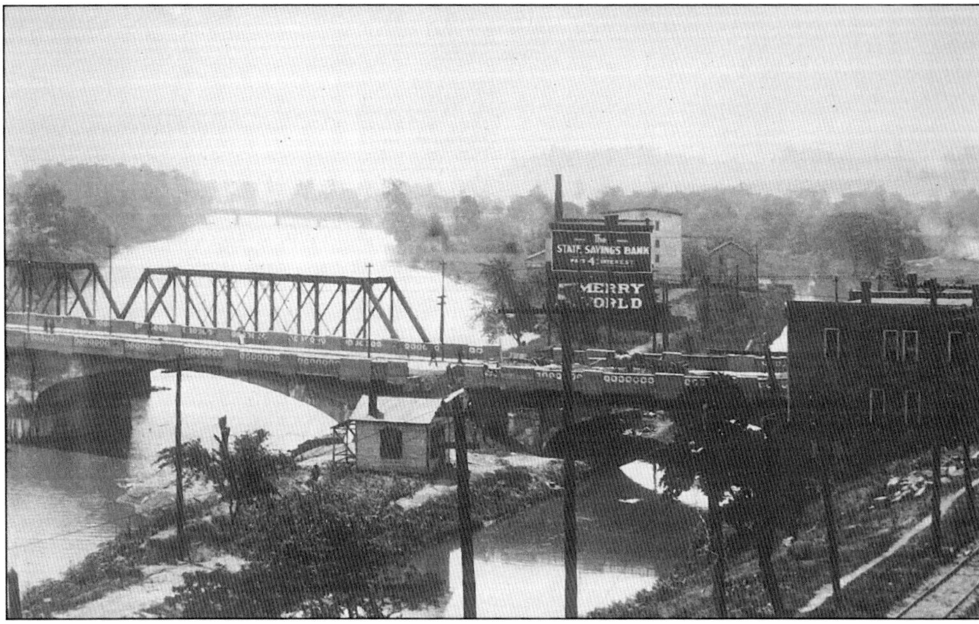

Canal Dover Toll Both. The only toll booth on the Ohio Erie Canal was located near the Factory Street bridge over the Tuscarawas River in Canal Dover, Ohio. Here tolls were collected on the goods that were carried on the Ohio Erie Canal through Tuscarawas County. In villages and towns along the canal, businesses and factories were quickly built to use this new resource to the outside world. The buildings quickly became advertising signs, similar to the billboards along the highways today.

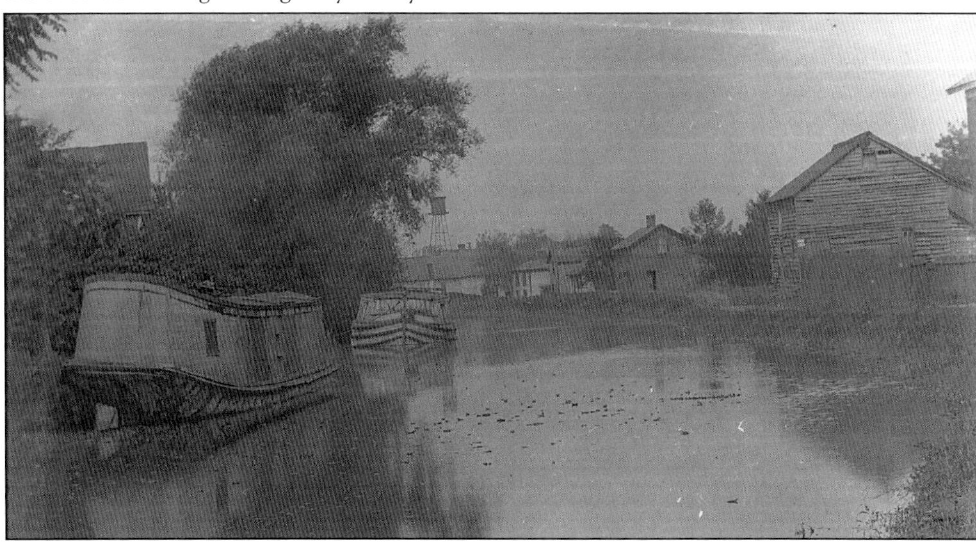

Lockport. The south side of New Philadelphia was known in the early days as Blakes Mill and Lockport. New Philadelphia contained a lateral canal, which began above where the Super K-Mart store is located today and came around past the Gradall Manufacturing Company. Many mills and factories sprang up along this lateral. The picture depicts the canal at Lockport near Lock 13 looking west. Most people who traveled on the canal would use this location for embarking or disembarking from the canal boats. Lock 13 is still visible from State Route 416, and the Tuscarawas County Historical Society marked Lock 13 with an Ohio Historic Marker.

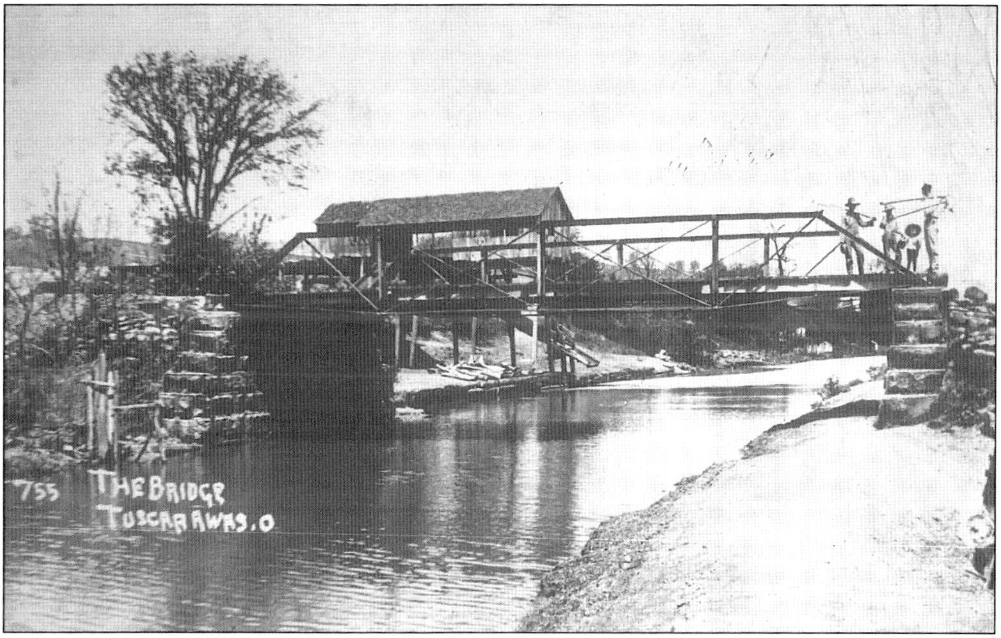

THE BRIDGE OVER THE OHIO ERIE CANAL AT TUSCARAWAS. The canal at times inconvenienced residents and farmers from going about their daily chores, therefore, a bridge was necessary at various places. Near the town of Trenton, now the Village of Tuscarawas, we witness such a bridge.

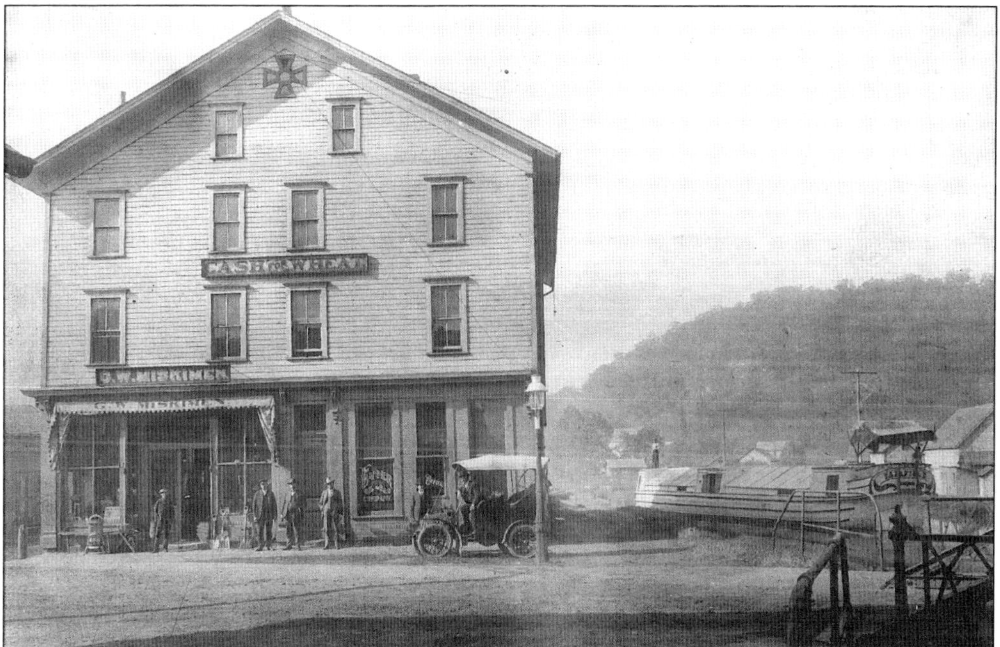

NEWCOMERSTOWN ON THE OHIO ERIE CANAL. The building in this picture still stands today and is known as the Eureka Hardware Store in Newcomerstown. Entering this building today is like taking a time-warp journey into the days of the canal period. The building was known as the Miskimen General Store during the canal period.

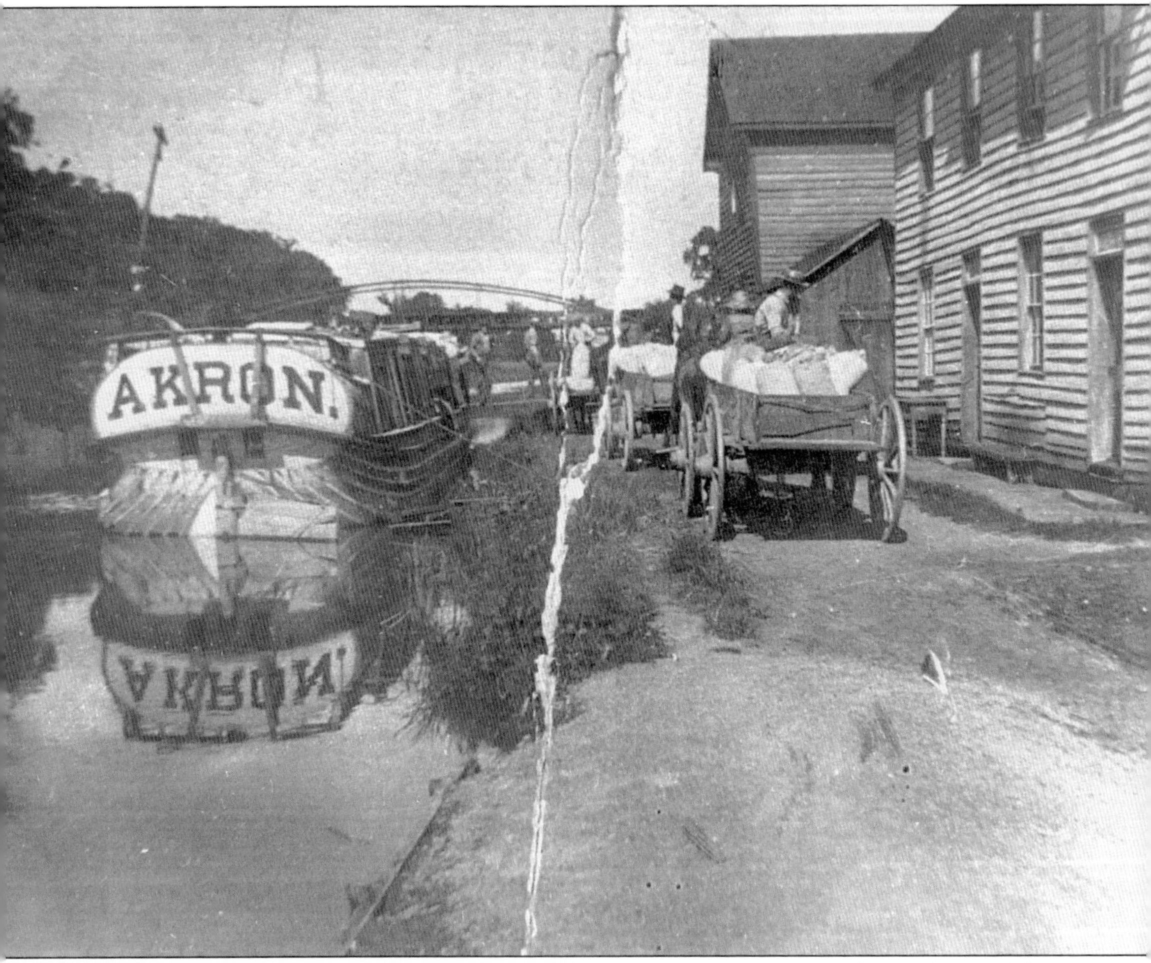

WAITING TO LOAD AT LOCK SEVENTEEN. This extraordinary picture shows the local farmers waiting to load their cash crop onto a canal boat at Lock Seventeen. The area around this lock had beautiful level fields most suitable for raising corn, wheat, and other cash crops that could be easily shipped on the canal to the larger cities to the north and south. Lock Seventeen was so named because it was the seventeenth lock south of Akron. There are still structures today at Lock Seventeen that remind us of the heyday of this "Silver Ribbon" through Tuscarawas County. Just north of Lock Seventeen, the families and businessmen earned their living by transporting coal from the small family "groundhog holes" and from the larger mines of Wainwright and Goshen. The villages and cities of Tuscarawas County grew and prospered because of the Ohio Erie Canal.

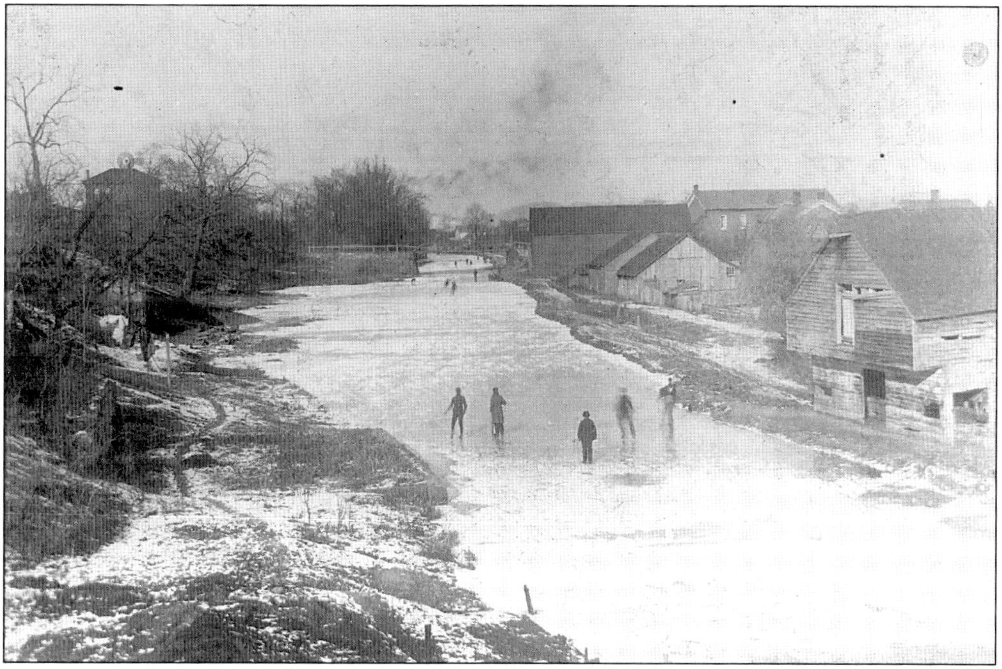

ICE SKATING ON THE CANAL. The winters of Ohio brought snow, cold temperatures, and frozen conditions on the canal, ponds, lakes, streams, and the Tuscarawas River for at least three months. A favorite pastime of that era was swimming in the canal or ice-skating. This picture, which came from a stereoptic photograph, was taken near the town of Tuscarawas.

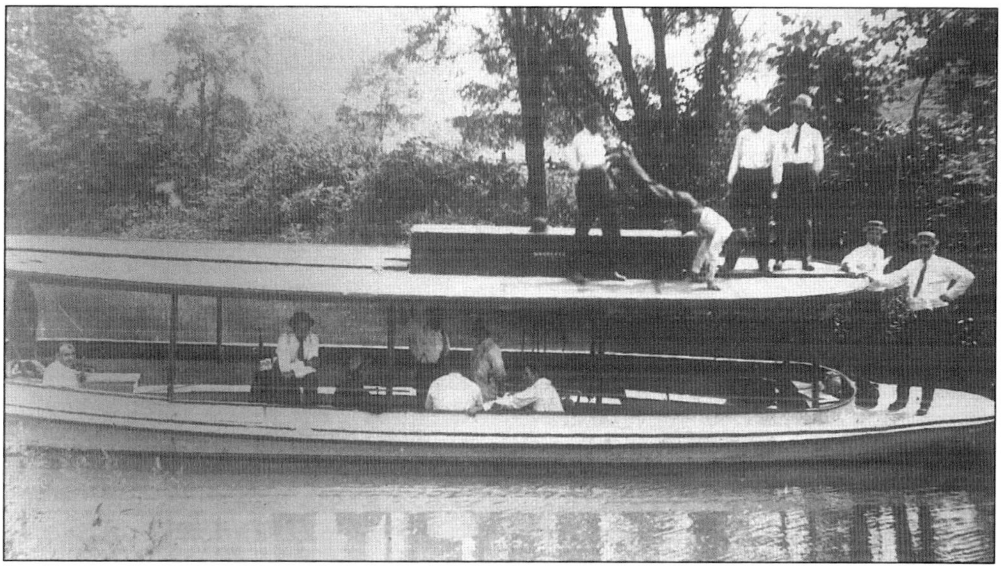

CANAL PASSENGER BOAT NEAR CANAL DOVER, OHIO. This lively photograph depicts the fun times of the canal period. On summer afternoons, the folks would pack up a picnic basket and travel the canal to the various recreation points including Yankee Dan's Island just north of Canal Dover, the quaint Village of Zoar which catered to the many travelers and picnickers in the various groves in and near the town, or Springer's Park on the west end of New Philadelphia, to name just a few.

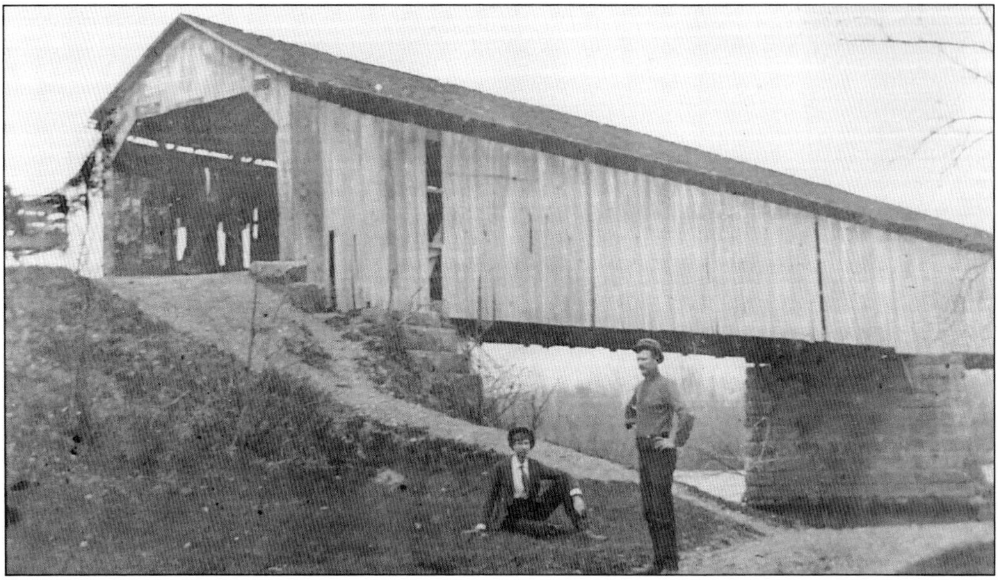

Blicktown Bridge, New Philadelphia, Ohio.

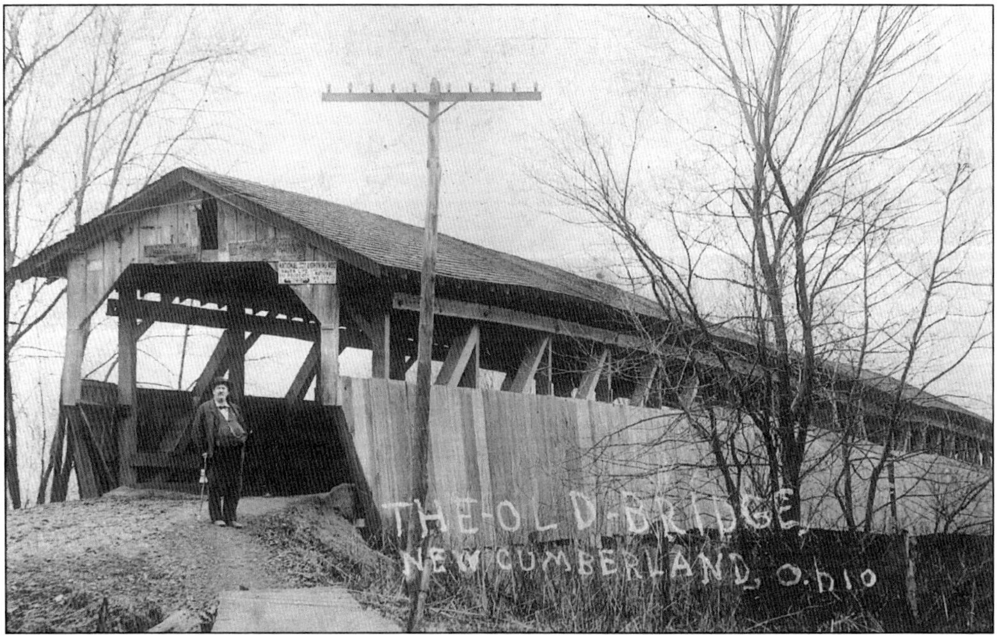

New Cumberland Bridge. During the very early days of the existence of the county, ferry boats were the only way to cross the streams and rivers. Licenses for providing this service had to be obtained from the county commissioners. Because the county had a natural supply of good hardwoods, various farmers, who were excellent builders of barns, contracted with the county commissioners to build covered bridges across the rivers and streams. From the 1820s through 1936, there were 89 fine structures dotting the landscape of the county. Today there are none. Dr. Terry Miller in his book *Covered Bridges of Tuscarawas County* has provided the reader with the greatest details on each of the bridges. The builder of the New Cumberland Bridge, shown in the lower photograph, was a civil war prisoner of war at the famous Andersonville prison in Georgia.

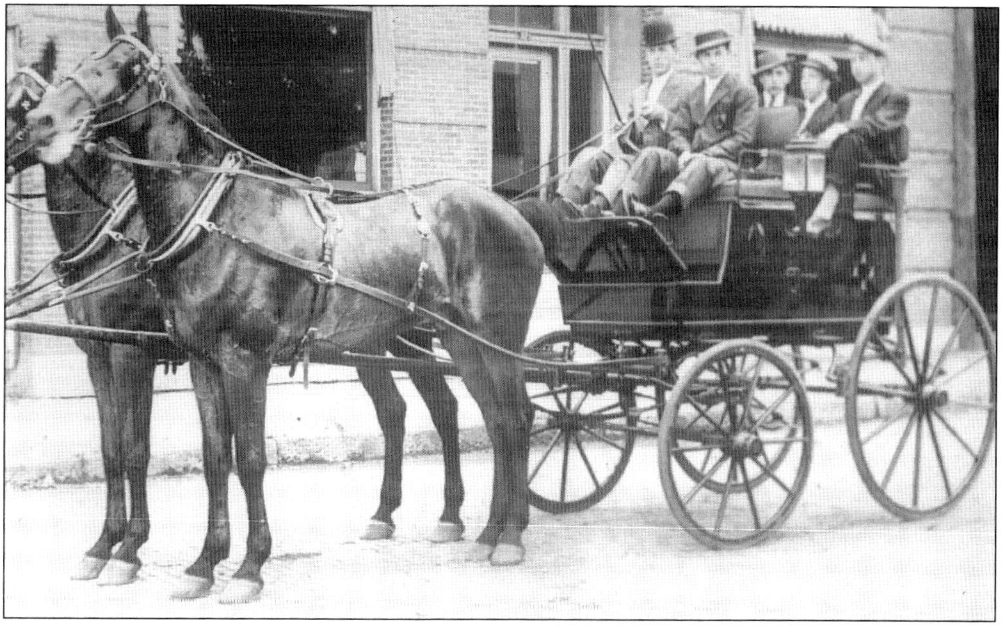

A Grand Ride in Uhrichsville. Ed Uhrich had many fines horses and carriages, and in this photograph taken in Uhrichsville in 1909, five young men are on an outing. This mode of transportation was just beginning to be phased out, for the automobile was beginning to gain in popularity throughout the nation. Pictured in the photograph are Ed Uhrich, Art Cummings, Neil Peoples, and Kellie Cox.

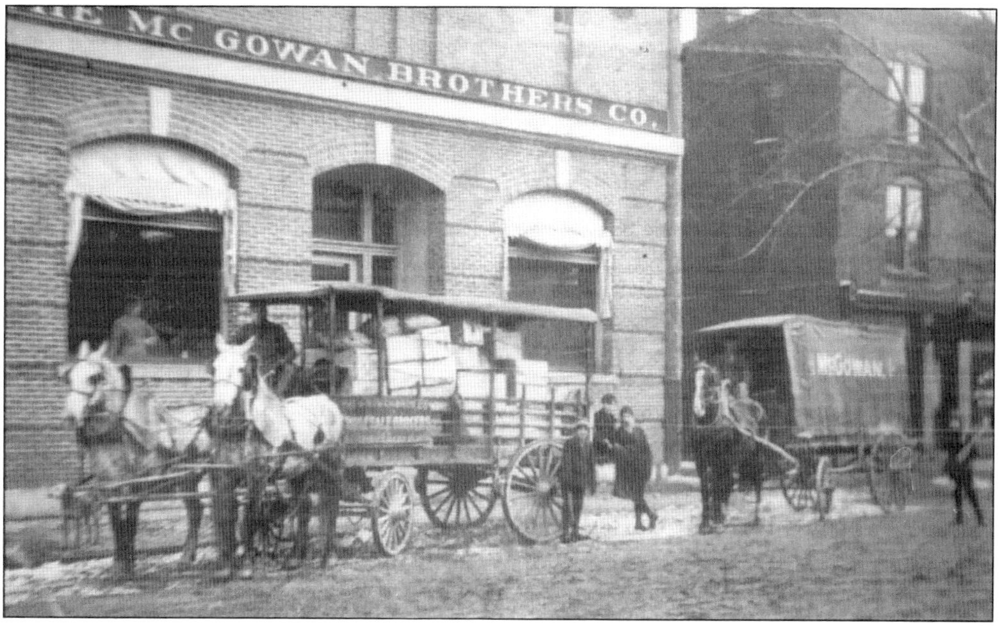

Early Transport of Goods Uhrichsville 1907. Today we find our highways packed with 450-horsepower tractor-trailer rigs hauling necessary products to our stores, factories, and businesses. At the turn of the twentieth century, we had just one or two horse-powered vehicles. In front of the McGowan Brothers store in Uhrichsville, the workers are waiting to move the goods to their delivery sites.

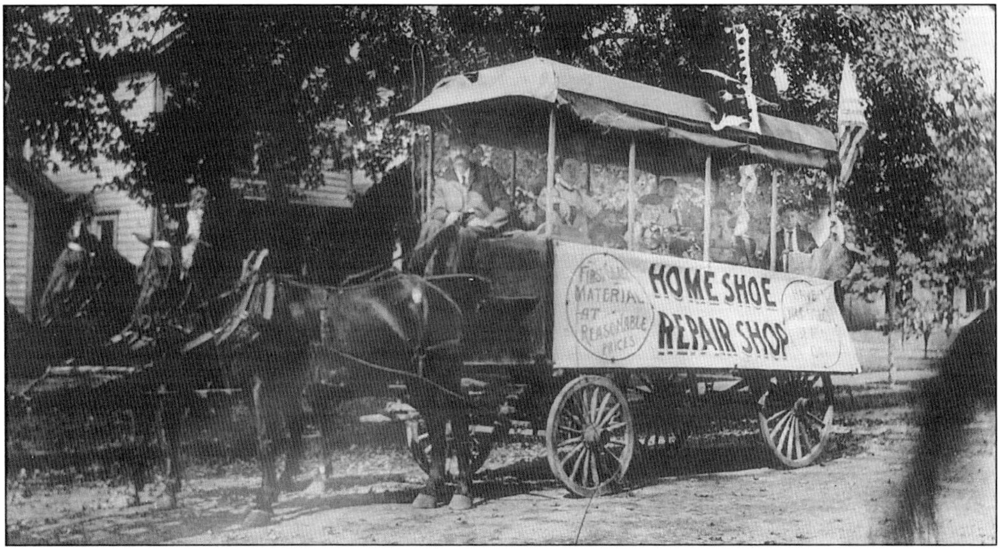

SHOE REPAIR WAGON IN UHRICHSVILLE, OHIO. William Donaldson operated a shoe repair shop in Uhrichsville from the late 1800s until the 1930s. Gathered for a parade, William Donaldson has a three-hitch wagon for transporting many people in the parade. As with all astute business people who refuse to let a golden opportunity to advertise slip by, he had a sign made advertising his business along the parade route.

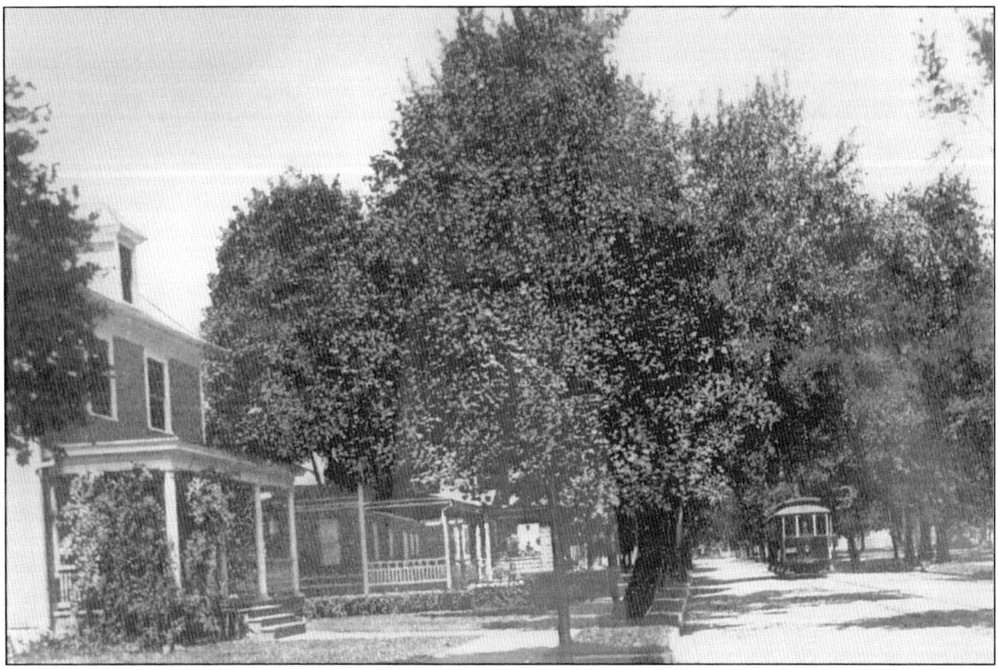

STREETCAR ON A STREET IN NEW PHILADELPHIA, OHIO. During the mid-1800s, the iron horse era began. Passenger train service eventually replaced the trip to the various cities via canal boat. There were 44 depots in Tuscarawas County at one time. However in 1903, the interurban service began competing against train travel. You could travel from Uhrichsville to Cleveland via the Interurban line. This photograph shows a streetcar running down the middle of the street in New Philadelphia, Ohio.

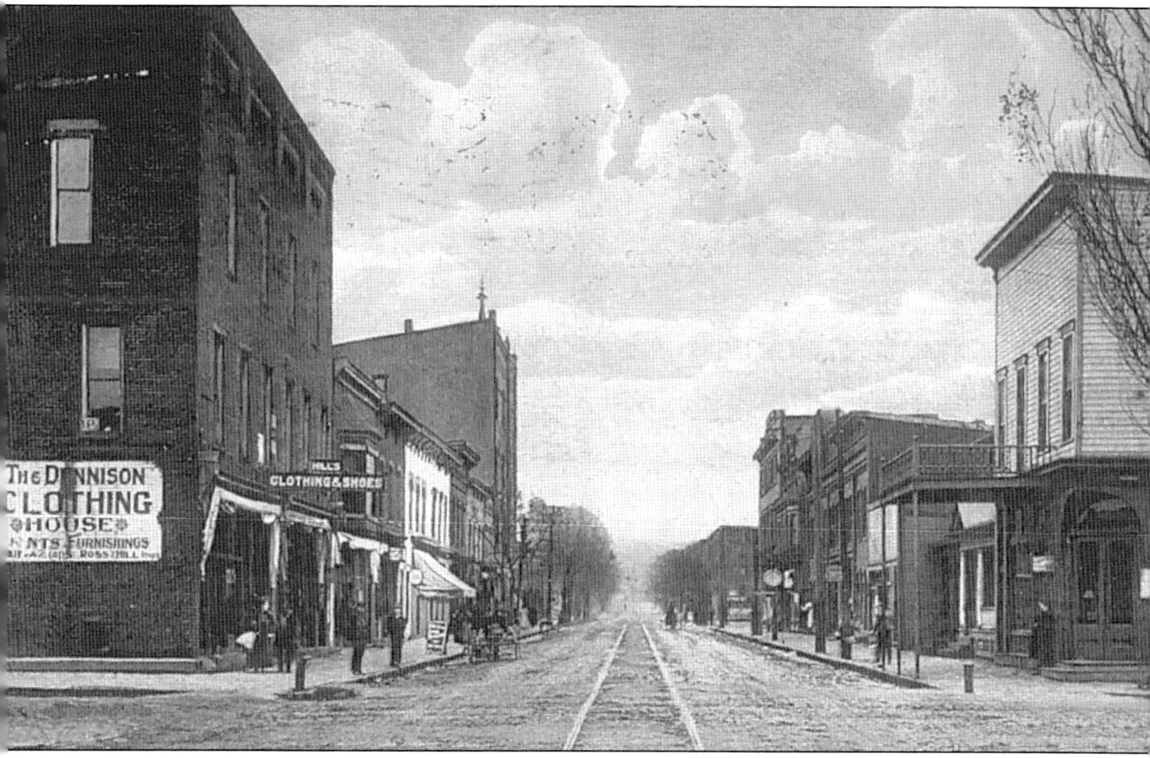

DENNISON, OHIO 1907. Dennison, Ohio, was a booming town between the 1880s and 1920s. This postcard scene of Dennison in 1907 depicts a town with many large buildings for that time and the interurban line running down the middle of the unpaved street. The impact of the railroad was the catalyst for the great economy, many jobs, and a phenomenal population increase. The Pennsylvania Railroad Company established Dennison as its halfway point between Pittsburgh and Columbus. Thousands of workers were employed at the rail yards. The PHAC, an athletic group of the company, staged an athletic event in 1920 with upwards of 20,000 athletes competing in many events. The town would later serve its country during World War II when it operated the famous Dennison Canteen from 1942 through 1946.

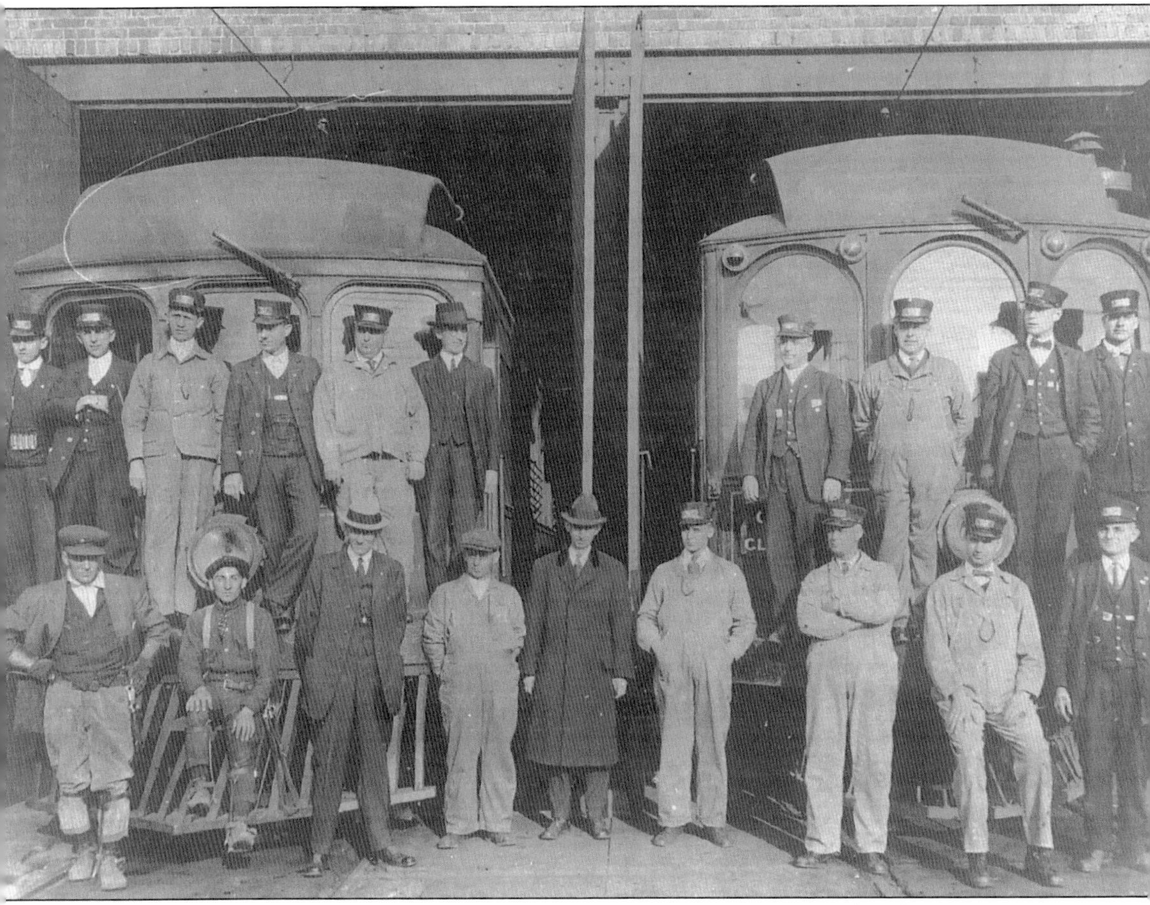

CAR BARN IN DOVER, OHIO, 1918. The Northern Ohio Traction and Light Company was a company located in Cleveland, Ohio, that extended the lines from that city to Uhrichsville, Ohio. Perhaps the most notable employee of that company was none other than Wendell Wilke, the Republican nominee, who ran against Franklin D. Roosevelt in the 1940 election. Fares were only 15¢ for a ride from Dover to Uhrichsville. This 1918 photograph was taken of the car barn in Dover, Ohio. The men in the picture are, from left to right: (back row) Harry Rausch, Harry Green, Curt Benson, Harry Patterson, Heber Patton, Roy Cox, Roy Van Lane, Cliff Loos, Irvin Stauffer, and Mr. Boyer; (front row) William Whitten, unidentified lineman, Charlie Porter, Charlie Krebs, Roy Kennedy, district manager wearing the Chesterfield hat, Milton Walters, Bill Baker, Frank Davidson, and Orin Mohn. The company ceased operation in Tuscarawas County in 1929.

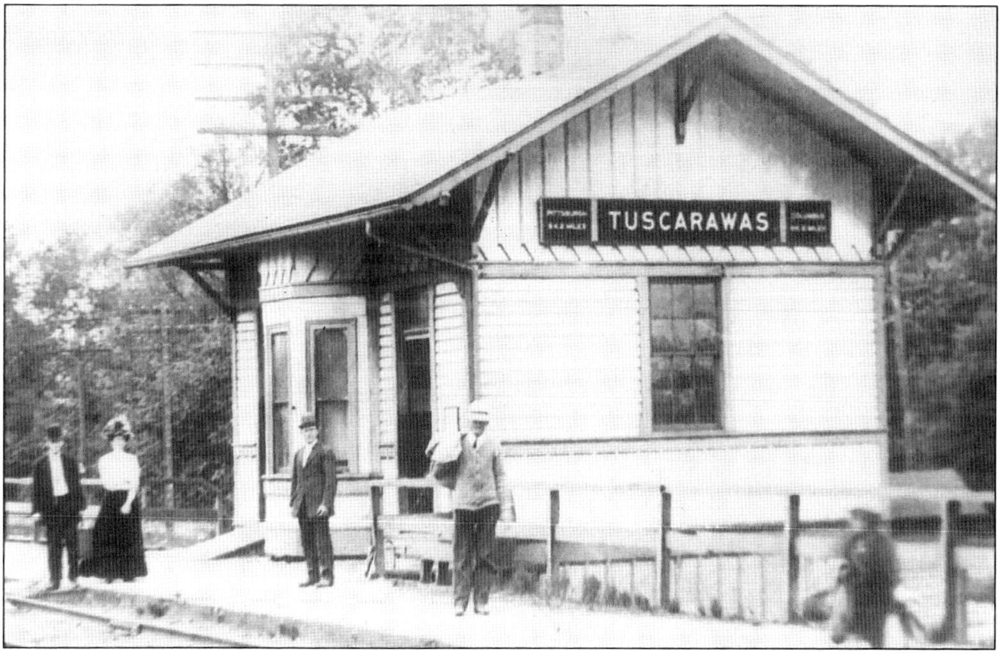

TUSCARAWAS RAILROAD DEPOT. The next seven photographs illustrate the influence of the railroad in Tuscarawas County. Practically every community had a railroad depot. The communities that were not located on the interurban line utilized the railroads as a means of travel. At the depot you could purchase your ticket or pick up items which had been shipped by railway express. Weekly time schedules were published in the newspapers.

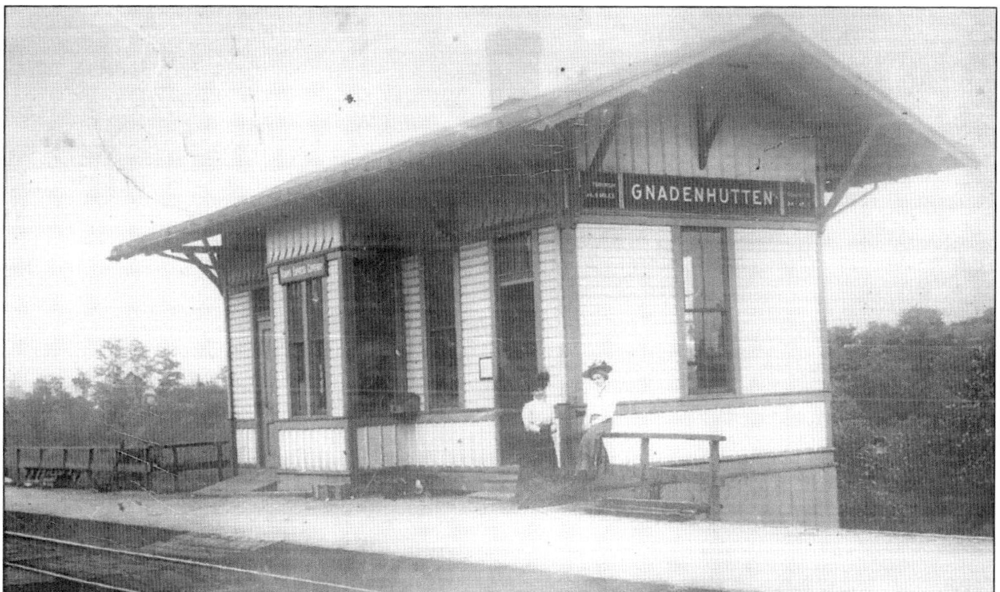

GNADENHUTEN RAILROAD DEPOT. This village was situated beside a major rail line—the Pennsylvania—which was a very busy track. Many passenger trains passed along this village from Columbus, Ohio, to Pittsburgh, Pennsylvania. Two very fashionable ladies are seen awaiting the next train for a shopping trip to the city or perhaps to visit friends.

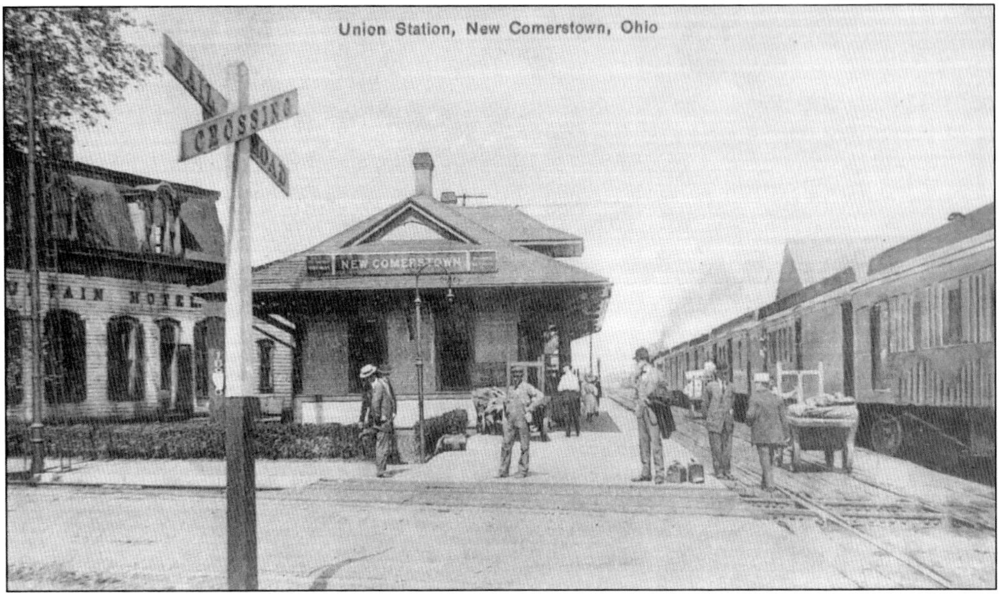

NEWCOMERSTOWN RAILROAD DEPOT. Another very busy depot in Tuscarawas County was located in the town of Newcomerstown, Ohio. In 1939, one of the most famous citizens of the county boarded a train for a trip to Cooperstown, New York. Denton True Young boarded the train from this depot at Newcomerstown and traveled to his induction into the Baseball Hall of Fame. Cy Young died in 1955. His funeral was conducted in Newcomerstown, and his body was interred in the church cemetery in the town of Peoli.

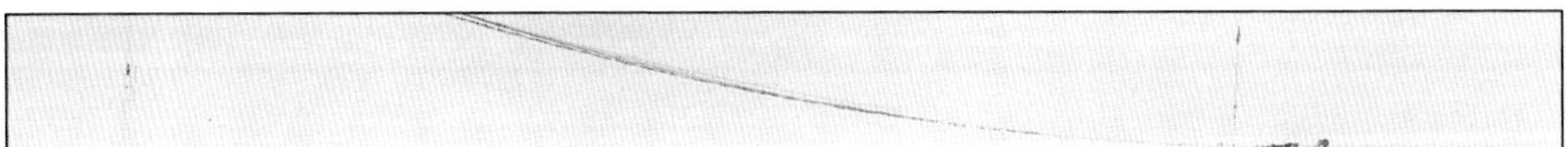

DOVER FREIGHT STATION PENNSYLVANIA RAILROAD. This large freight station was located near the former toll booth on the Ohio Erie Canal. Located at the corner of Tuscarawas Avenue and Front Street in Dover, Ohio, it was near many of the businesses and factories of this very busy town. Today this location serves as a parking lot, due to the demise of the railroad industry in the county.

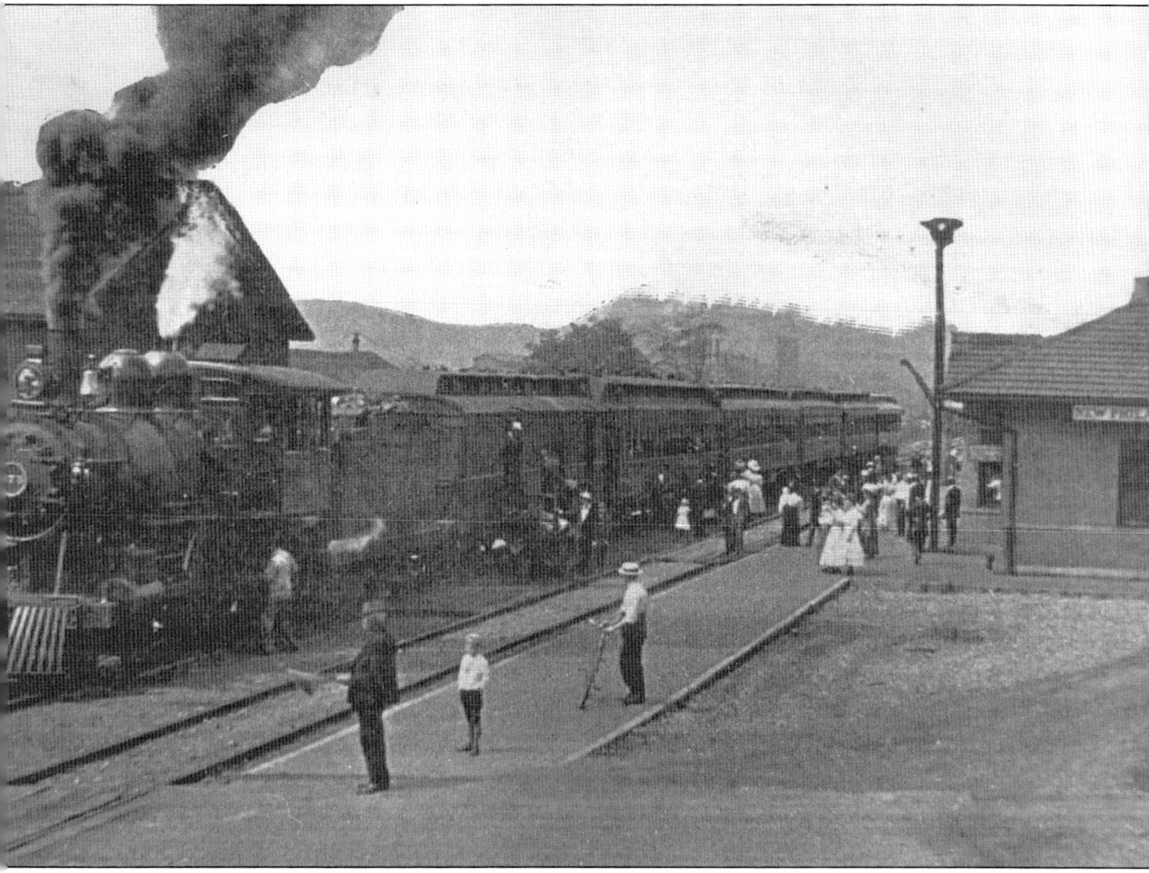

Baltimore & Ohio Railroad Depot New Philadelphia, Ohio. This great photograph taken from a postcard in the late 1900s illuminates a period when it was most fashionable to ride the rails. Men dressed in white shirts, suits, and ties, and ladies in very beautiful dresses are shown waiting to board the train or to welcome a loved one home from a journey. I wonder how many looked so fresh after their journeys with the open car windows in summer combined with the black ash of the smokestack? The building to the left of the train was the Ladel Company, later to become the Joy Manufacturing Company. Today this company, called the New Philadelphia Fan Company, has its products in mines and subways throughout the world.

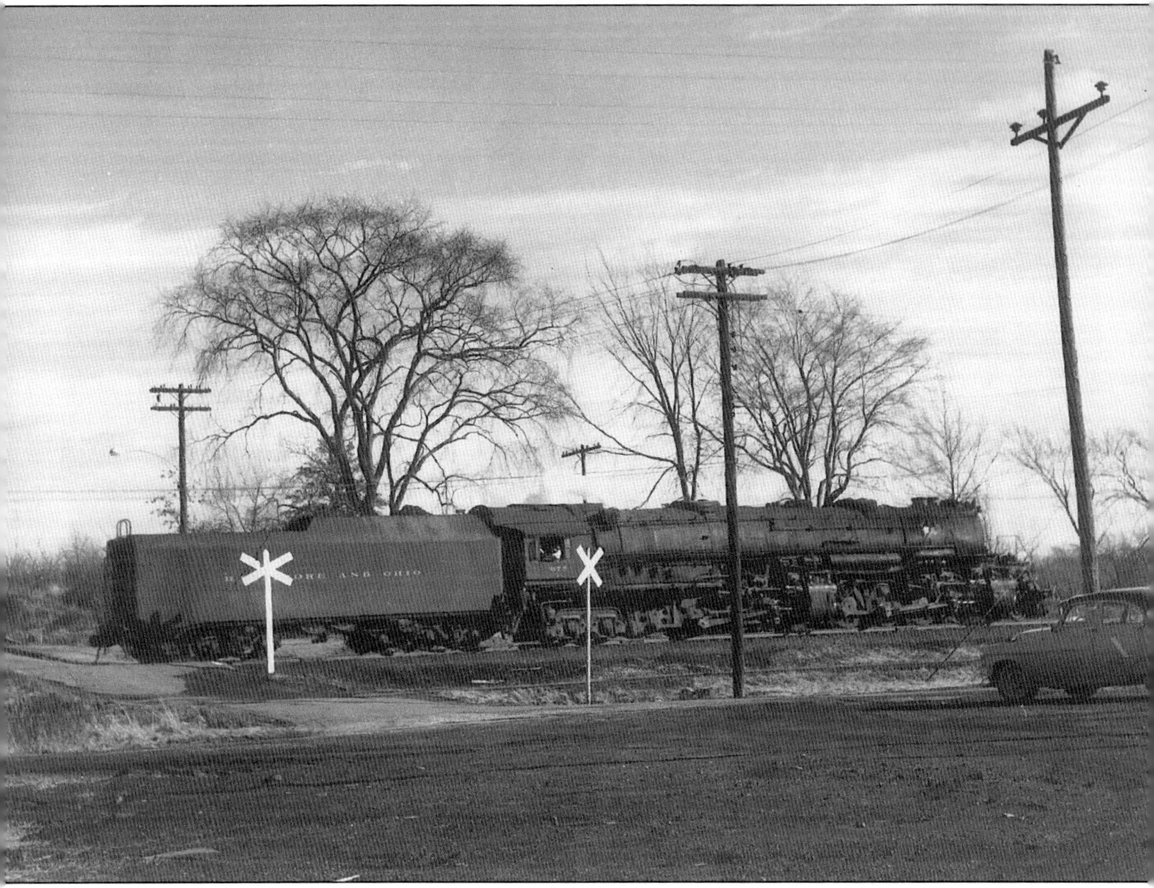

Steam Train in Dover, Ohio. The late Ed Maurer of New Philadelphia, Ohio, heard that the last working steam train was about to pass through Tuscarawas County in the 1950s. He took his camera to the crossing at 15th Street in Dover, near the Dover Chemical Company, and shot this picture, thus preserving a great moment for the county. The train was backing into the chemical side yard to pick up a load of cars. The diesel, which began service in the 1930s, was fast becoming the engine of preference for faster service and easier maintenance.

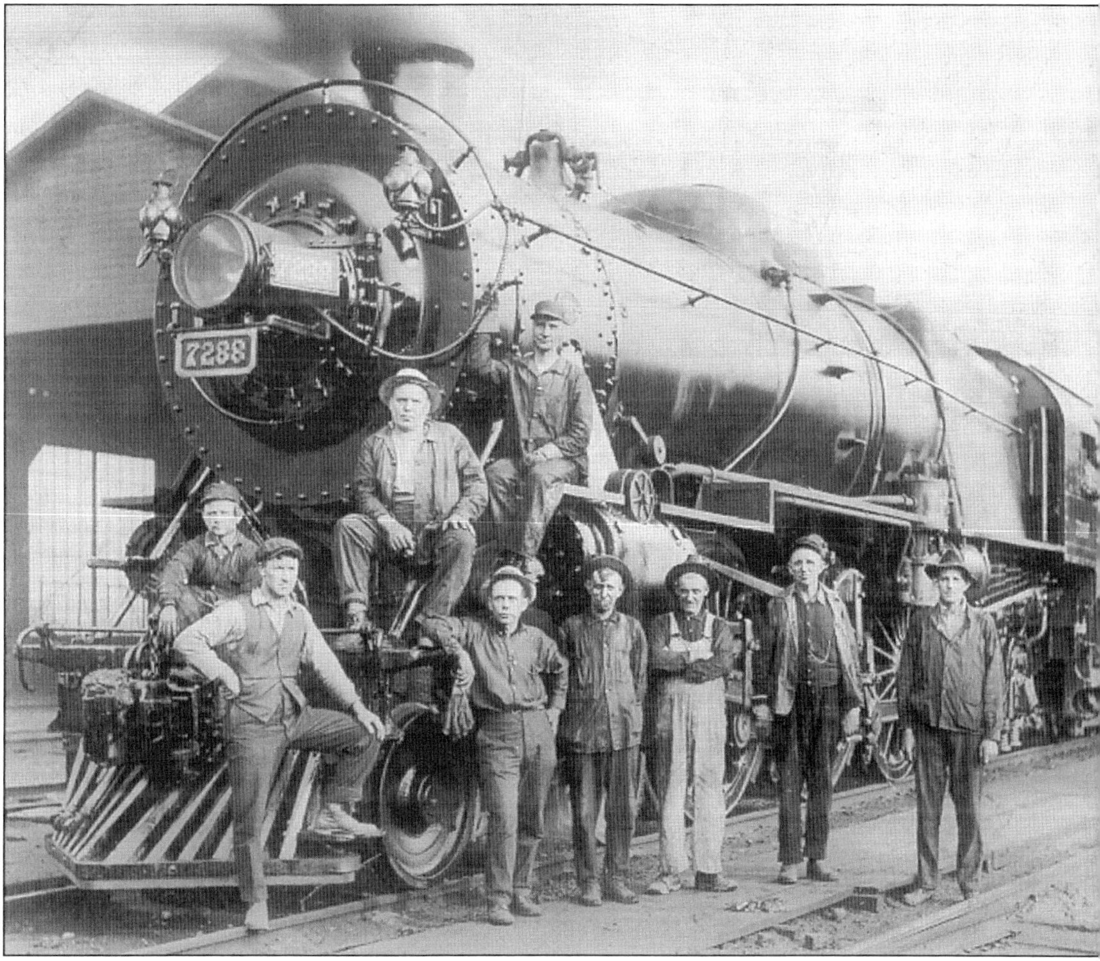

Railroad Crew at Dennison Yard. The crew identified working on steam engine *7288* at the Dennison Rail Yard included Tom Haley, Mr. Shaffer, Mr. Himes, Al Gump, John Albaugh, John George, and Mr. Schwab. In order to keep the engine in good repair, the men worked at a very demanding task. All parts to the engine were heavy and required backbreaking efforts by the men. It was also dangerous work—not for the timid. Besides the clay and coal fields nearby, the railroad was one of the biggest employers in Dennison at the turn of the twentieth century.

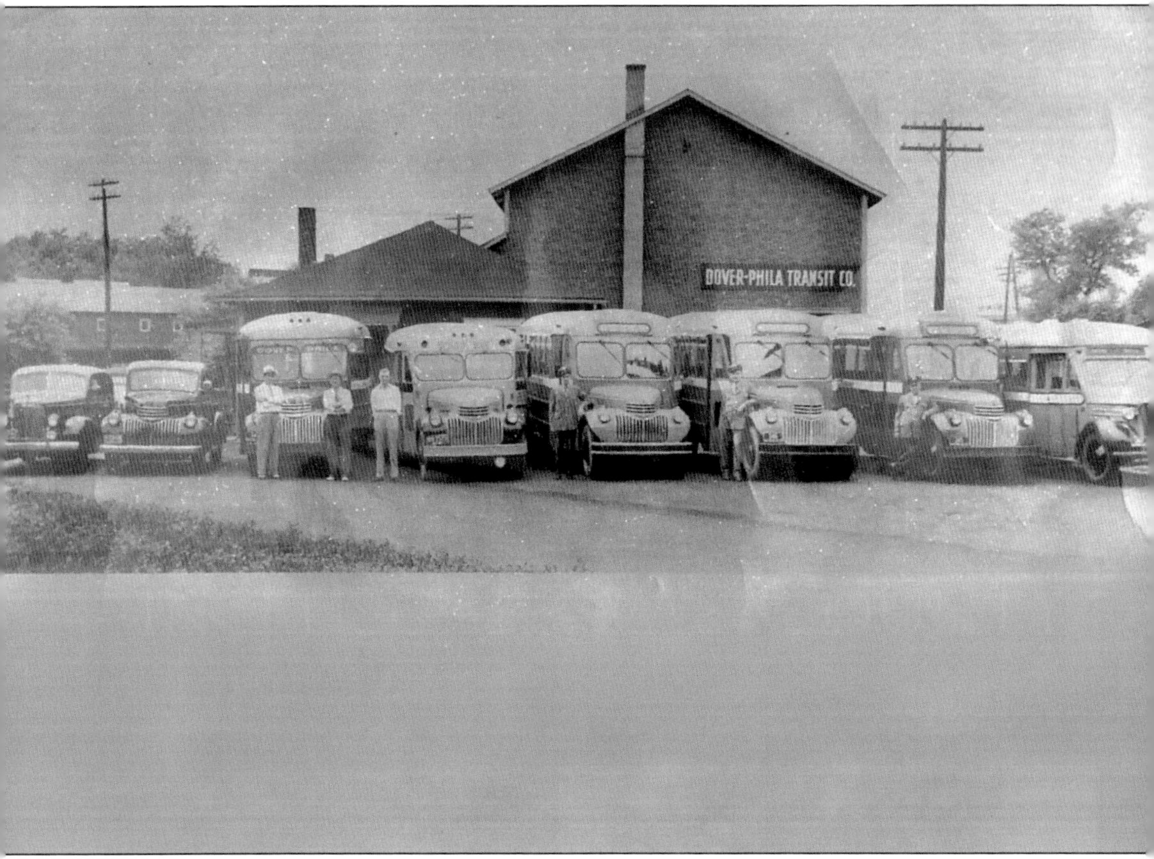

BUS TRANSPORTATION SYSTEM LATE 1940S. The Dover New Philadelphia Transit Company, located on Fourth Street near the beginning of the Boulevard in New Philadelphia, provided bus service throughout the cities of Dover and New Philadelphia from the 1940s through the 1960s. Regular daily routes were run on the major streets of the cities. The company provided school transportation in the two cities at one time. However, that soon gave way to the schools purchasing their own bus fleets and drivers. Along with the regular bus service, they had a comfortable bus for longer trips in which they would transport the athletes to away games. Your author remembers many trips during the late 1950s on this bus. Compared to the regular bus, this was true luxury. Newcomerstown had the Red Eagle Bus Lines during this same period, which took people to Cleveland or Columbus, Ohio.

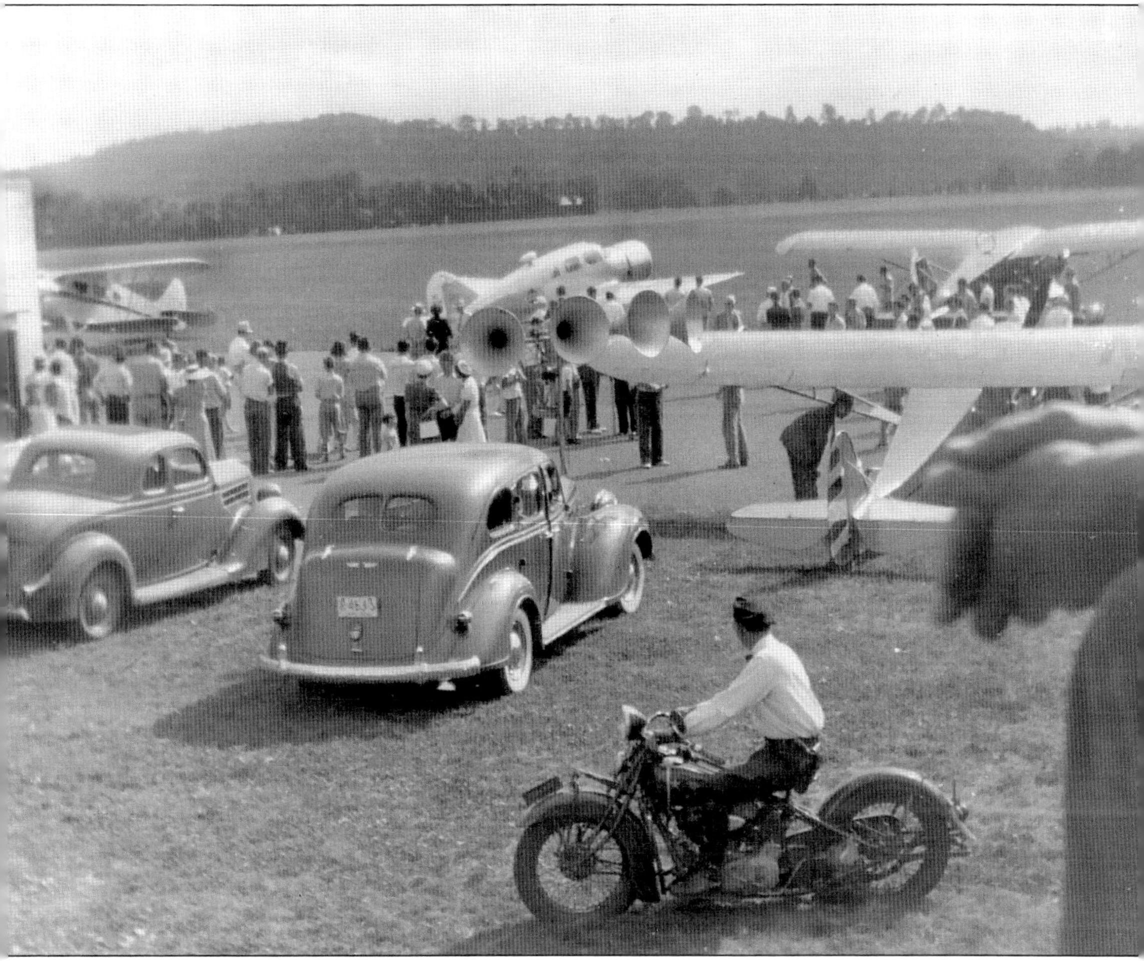

AIR SHOW AT HARRY CLEVER FIELD. The late 1920s found a man by the name of Harry Clever with a vision of a different form of transportation. A pilot and flight instructor, he encouraged the construction by New Philadelphia officials of an airport on the east side of the city at what was then known as Schoenbrunn. Senator John Glenn, decorated war pilot and astronaut, began his flight instruction under the tutelage of Harry Clever at this field while a student at Muskingum College. The photograph shows an air show at the field in the 1940s. This image is very interesting in that it shows several of the newer aircraft of that period along with the automobiles and the city policeman on his motorcycle.

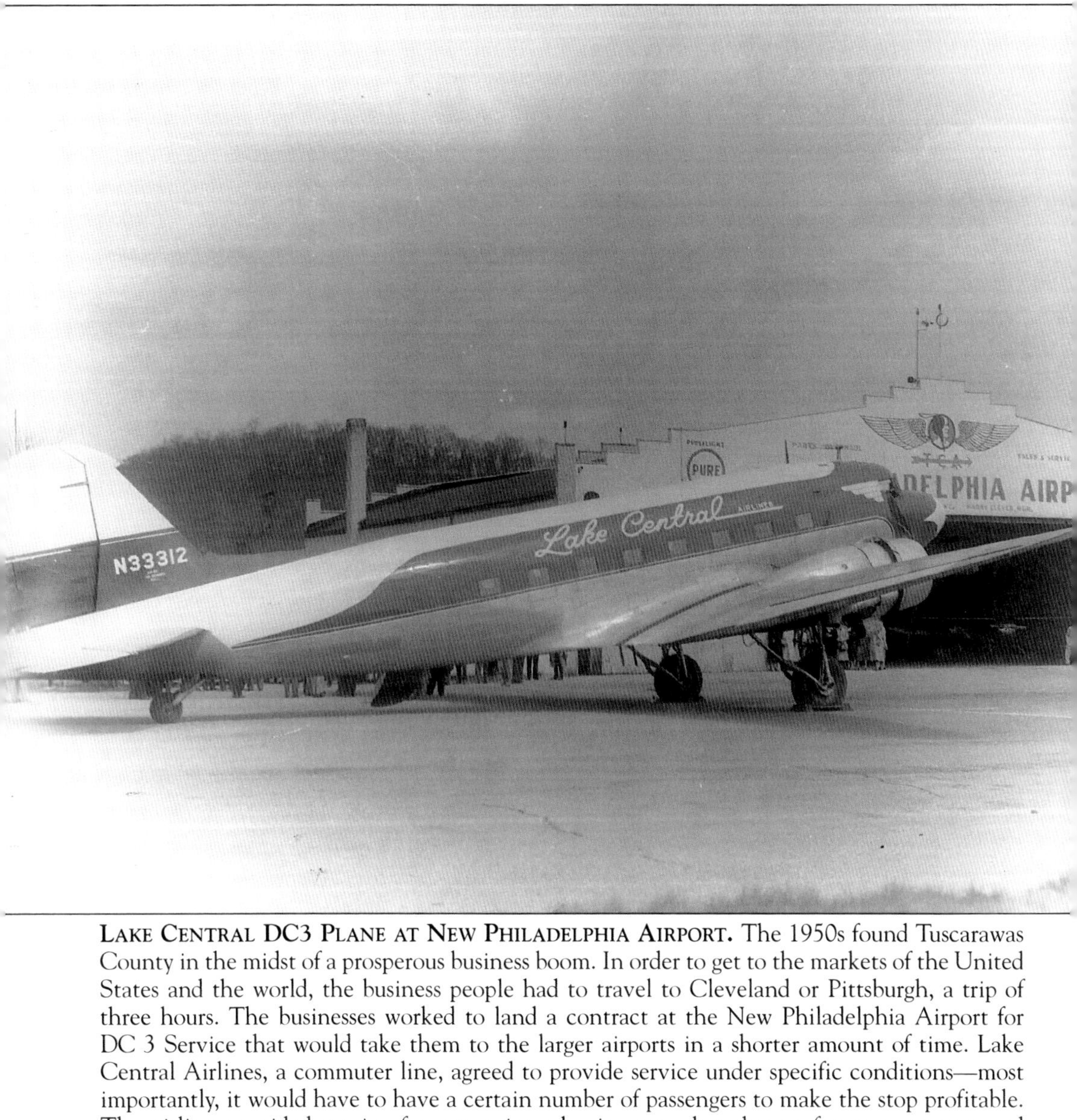

Lake Central DC3 Plane at New Philadelphia Airport. The 1950s found Tuscarawas County in the midst of a prosperous business boom. In order to get to the markets of the United States and the world, the business people had to travel to Cleveland or Pittsburgh, a trip of three hours. The businesses worked to land a contract at the New Philadelphia Airport for DC 3 Service that would take them to the larger airports in a shorter amount of time. Lake Central Airlines, a commuter line, agreed to provide service under specific conditions—most importantly, it would have to have a certain number of passengers to make the stop profitable. The airline provided service for approximately six years, but due to fewer passengers and decreased service, they ended the contract in 1959.

Three

Business and Industry in Tuscarawas County

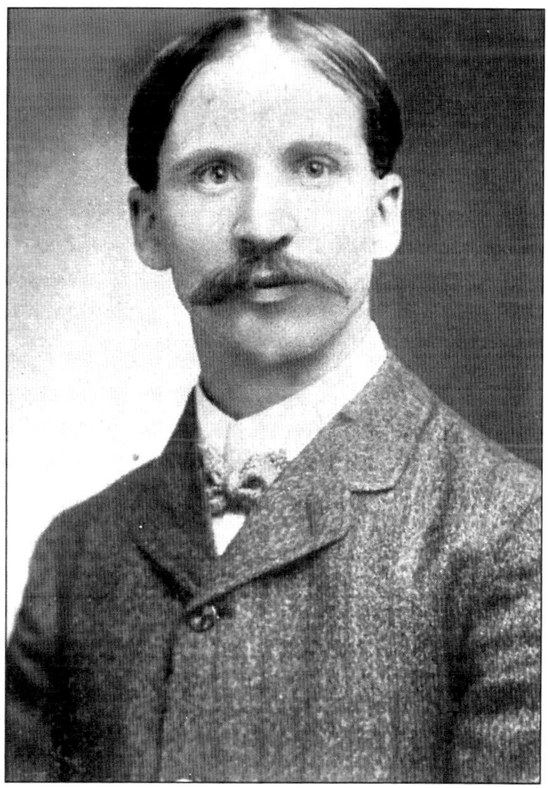

WES GREEN. The Tuscarawas County Historical Society has been indebted to Wes Green, a businessman and photographer in New Philadelphia, Ohio, who provided the Society with many of the photographs in this collection through his son-in-law, Bob Foutz. The generosity of the Dover-New Philadelphia *Times Reporter* in donating their 3,000 negatives of the 1950s and 1960s to the Tusc Kent Archives has greatly helped to provide many of the business and street scenes in the county. Thank you Wes, Bob, and the TR.

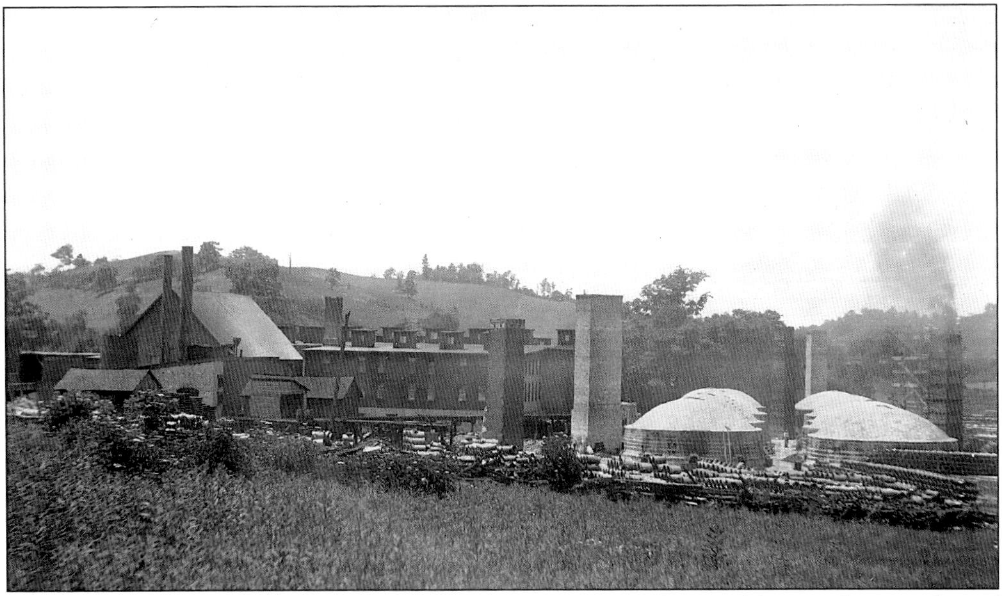

Robinson Graves Clay Co. The title "Clay Capital of the World" was the moniker of the area of Tuscarawas County along its eastern border from Dennison in the north through Uhrichsville, Stillwater, Gnadenhutten, and Port Washington, to Newcomerstown in the south. Sewer pipe and brick plants were scattered along Route 36. This picture depicts the Robinson Graves Clay Plant which began operation on July 25, 1903.

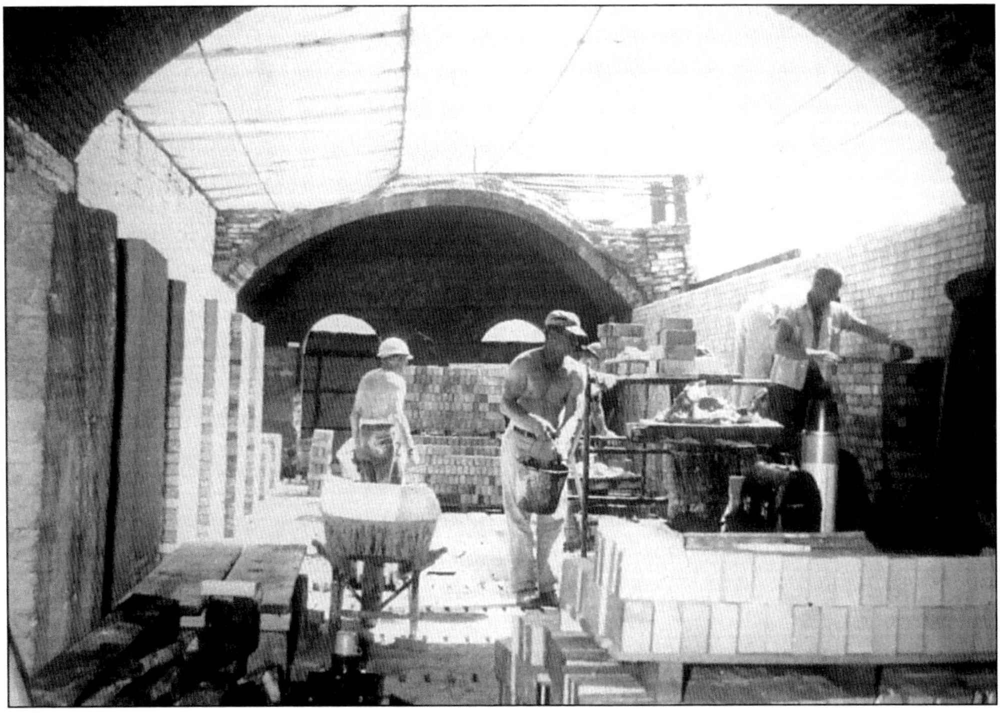

Preparing the Bricks for Firing. This interior picture of the men preparing the raw brick for firing was taken at the Belden Brick Plant near Port Washington, Ohio. This was tedious backbreaking work.

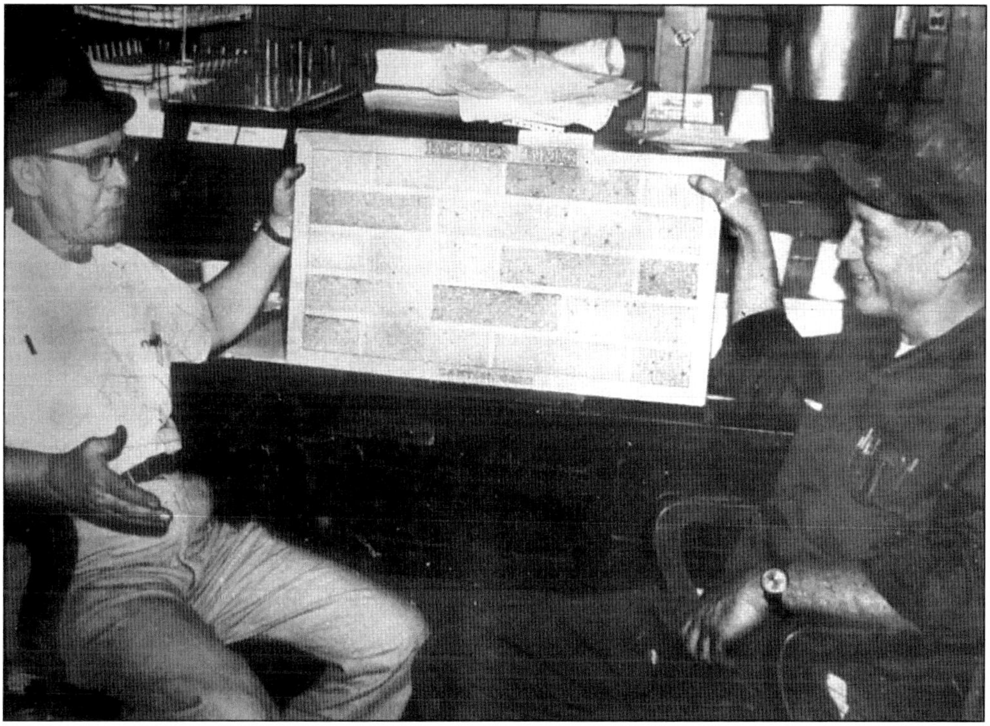

BELDEN BRICK PLANT AT PORT WASHINGTON. Don David and Don Roth are pictured discussing the color and type of brick that has been planned for addition to the production schedule.

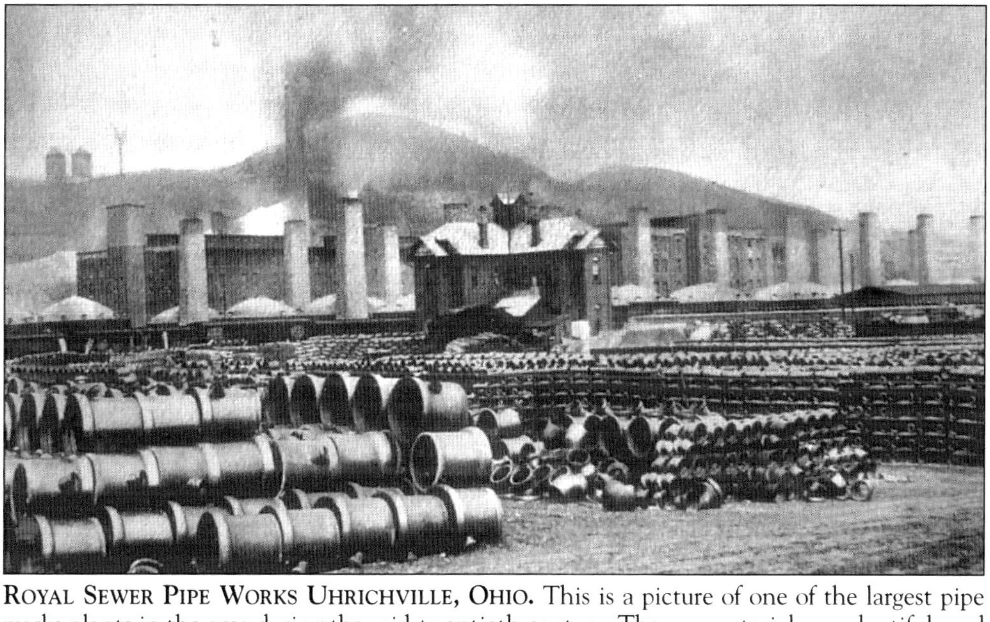

ROYAL SEWER PIPE WORKS UHRICHVILLE, OHIO. This is a picture of one of the largest pipe works plants in the area during the mid-twentieth century. The raw material was plentiful, and the product had a ready market in the removal of wastewater from cities and towns. However, the discovery of polymers, coupled with a cheaper production of plastic pipe, caused the sewer pipe industry to fall on hard times. The brick industry continues to thrive in the county.

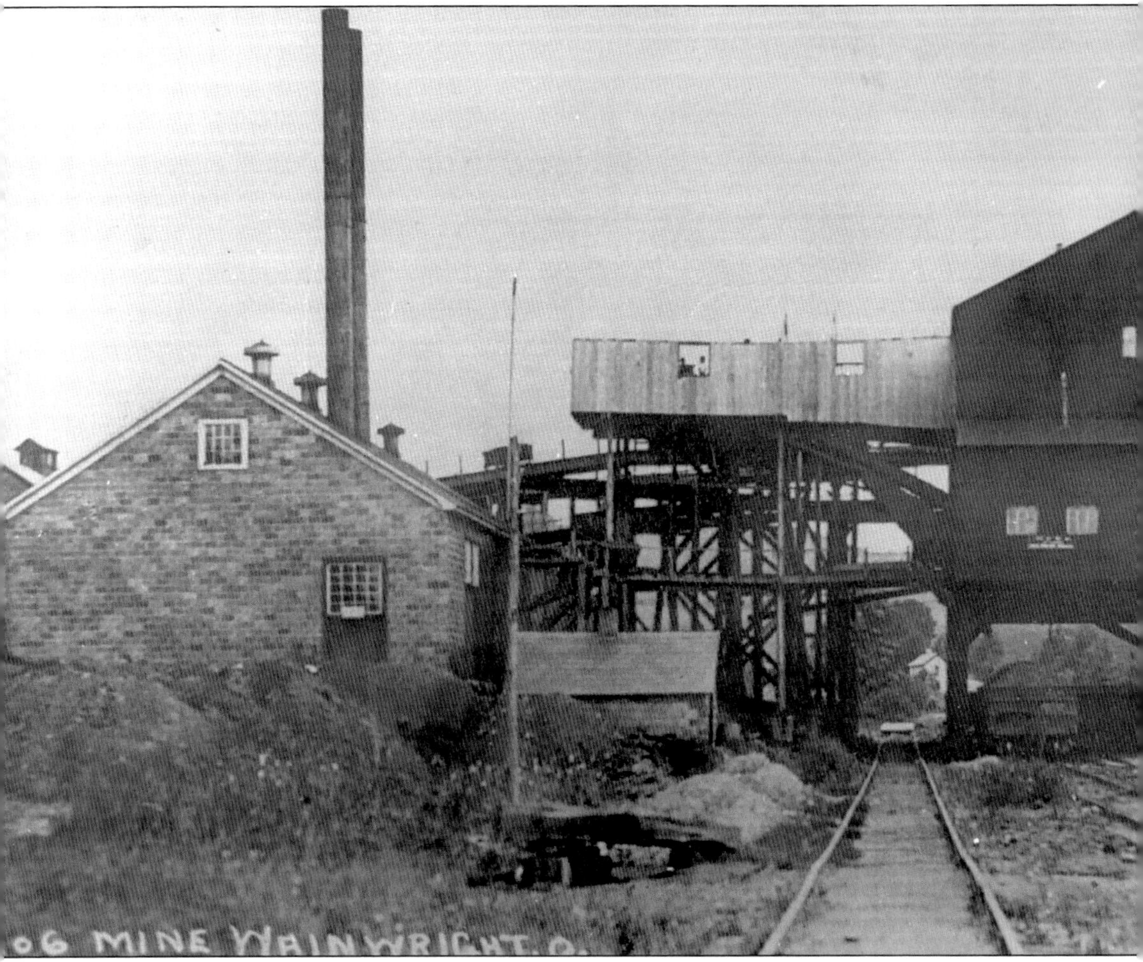

WAINWRIGHT COAL TIPPLE WAINWRIGHT, OHIO. Coal was discovered to be plentiful in the hills of Tuscarawas County in the late nineteenth century. There were many "Groundhog Holes" by farmers who would dig partially into the hillside and scratch out enough coal for their own use or to sell to neighbors. However, Tuscarawas County was known for its big deep mines. Today there are no underground mines in operation. The coal industry is based on strip mining, but even that is beginning to wane due to the many restrictions on the burning of coal. Thousands of middle-European immigrants came to the valley and began working in these underground mines. A businessman from Massillon, Ohio, established this mine in Wainwright. He came to the small valley and built many homes for the employees. There was a general store owned by the mine company for the miners and their families.

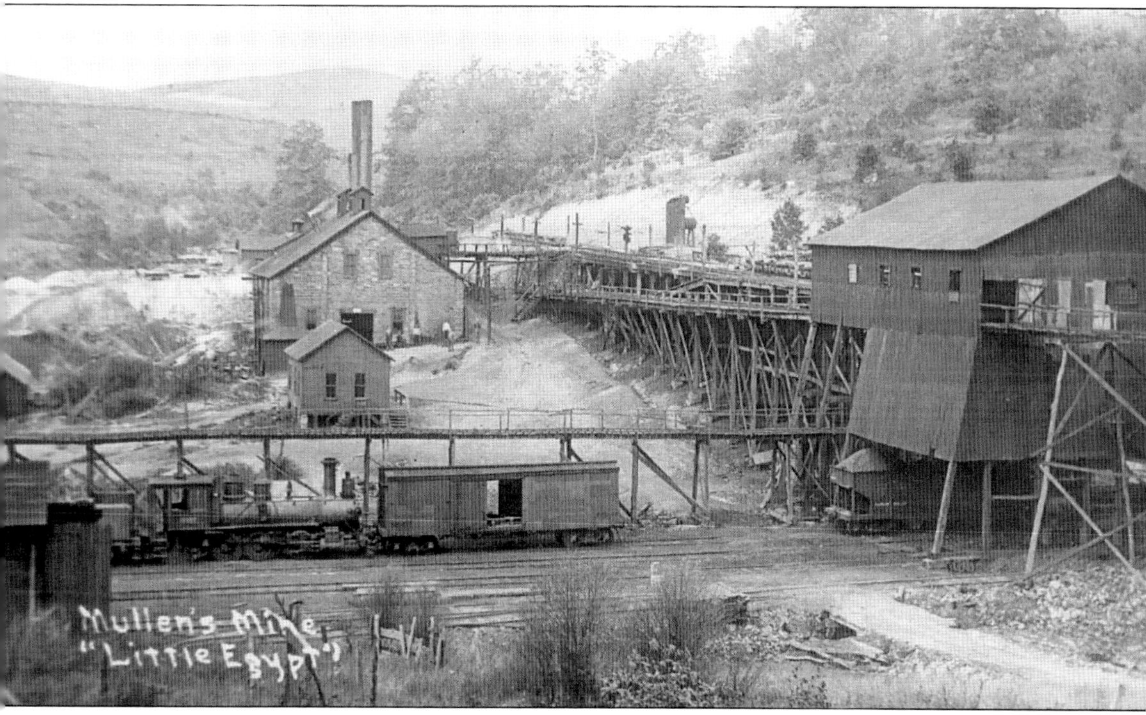

MULLINS COAL TIPPLE EAST OF NEW PHILADELPHIA, OHIO. To the east of New Philadelphia lay perhaps the best coal seam in Tuscarawas County. This mine, the Mullins, in what was called "Little Egypt," was an excellent provider of coal. Railroads would build feeder or switch lines at the site of the mine to better facilitate the removal of the coal to the markets. The work of being a coal miner was dirty, difficult, and dangerous. Without the technology of today, there were numerous accidents that claimed the lives of many miners.

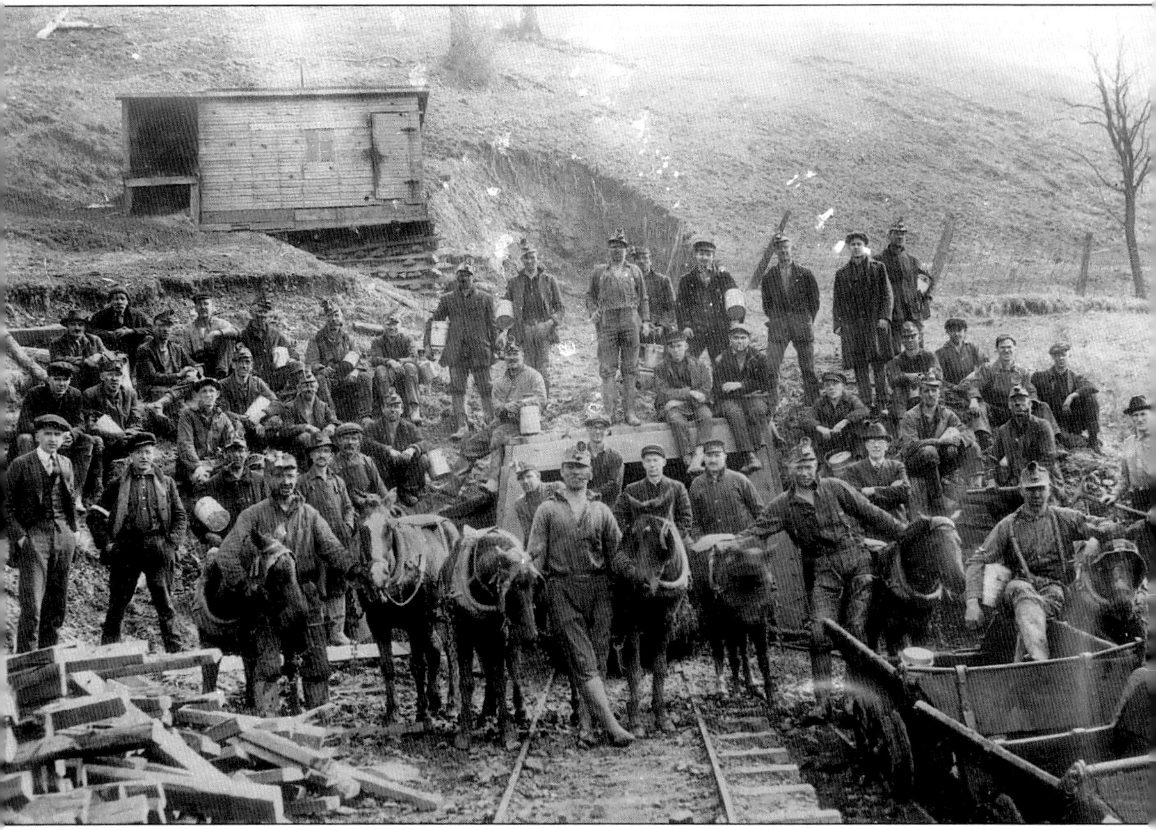

JOHN MARCHESI COAL MINE. The number of coal miners is quickly diminishing due to death. These were the common men and women, the unheralded people, who made the lives of those living in Tuscarawas County and throughout the state more comfortable. John and Mary Marchesi had immigrated to America shortly before the turn of the twentieth century. John was born in the Tyrol section of Austria. They moved to the Oldtown area south of New Philadelphia and opened the mine in Possum Hollow which is pictured here. Their son, John Jr., was born in 1899, and is visible on the far left dressed in business clothes with his hands in his pocket. He died shortly after this picture was taken at the young age of 29 of peritonitis. John Sr. is pictured in the second row on the right just behind the pony, hands folded, wearing a hat.

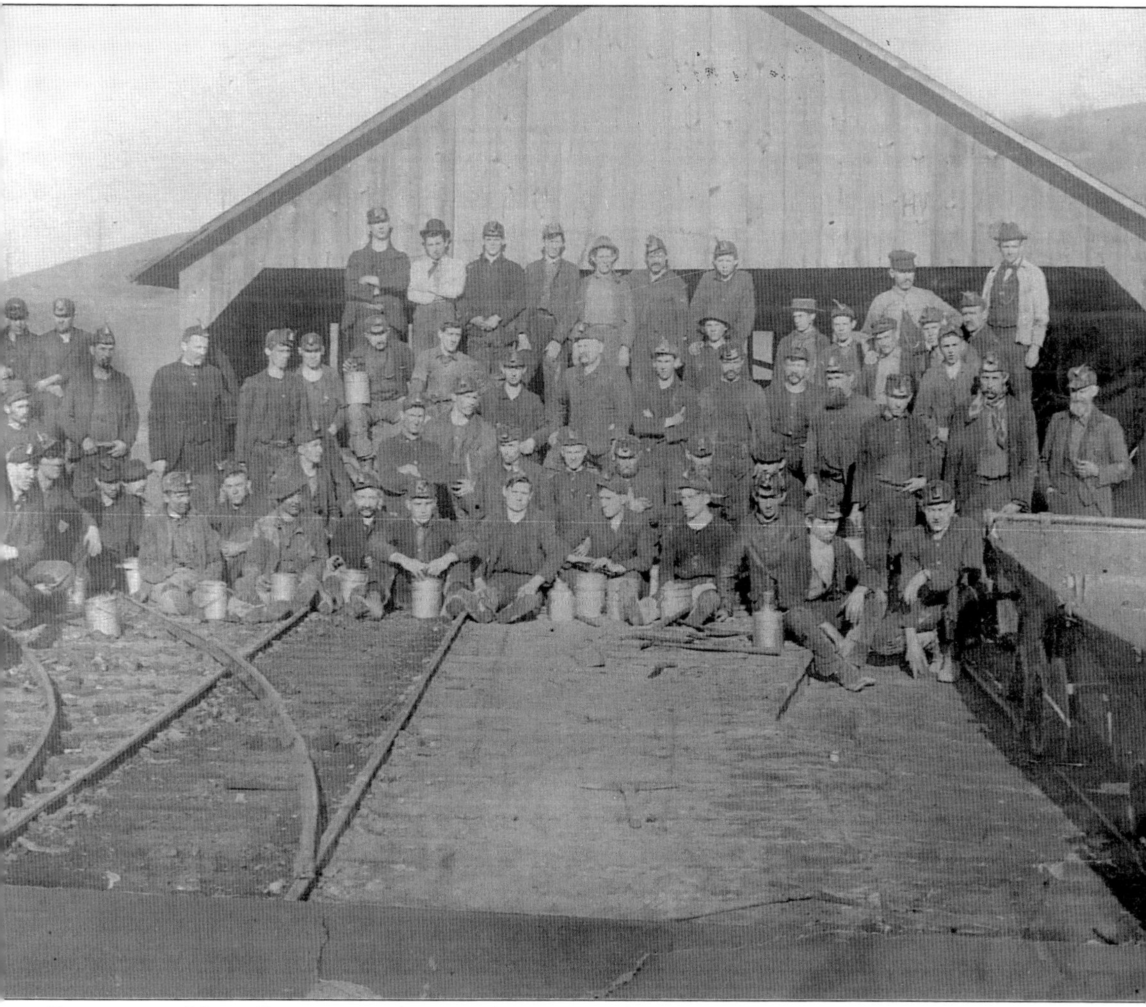

BROCKHILL MINE BARNHILL, OHIO. This group of miners was captured on film before descending into the mine for another day of backbreaking labor. The mine was in the coal-rich hills near the town of Barnhill, Ohio. Armed with their headlamp and bucket for a noontime meal, they would slowly descend into the shaft to begin their assigned work. A mine car, which would transport the miners into the mine, can be seen at the near right in the picture.

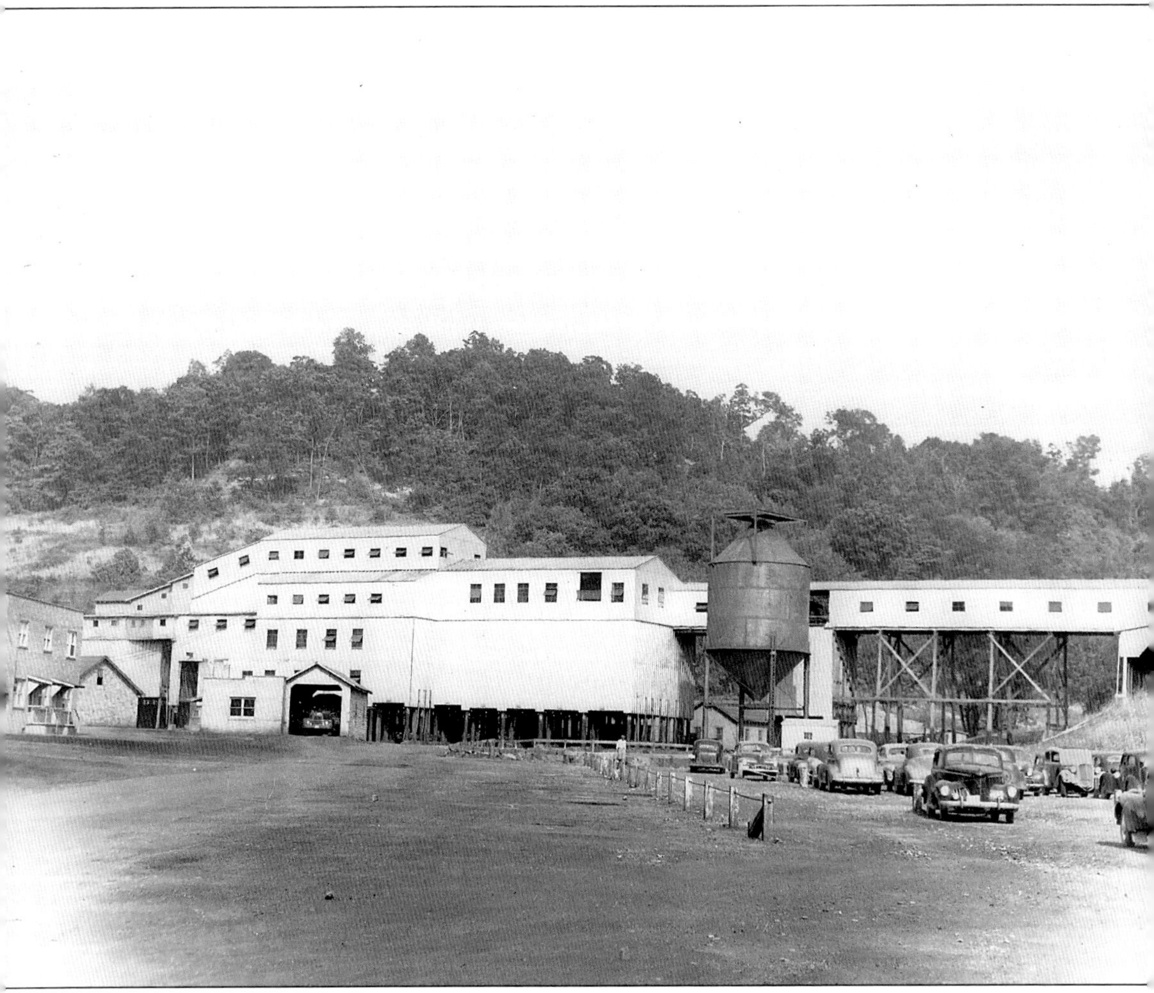

MIDVALE MINE IN THE LATE 1950S. This is one of the last pictures we have of the mine tipple at the famous Midvale Mine, perhaps the largest and longest-lasting mine in the county. The Rutledge family owned the mine for a number of years, but toward the end, the Pittsburgh Plate Glass Company of Pittsburgh, Pennsylvania, purchased it. The mine closed its operations in 1972 after a disastrous fire destroyed the plant. Mining was important to the economics of the county for almost a century. Many families have relatives who once worked either in the mines or for the mining companies. With the establishment of the gas fields and the ease of using this resource for heating and cooking, the general public moved away from its reliance on coal. Today, only the coal seams lying close to the surface are mined in a process called strip mining.

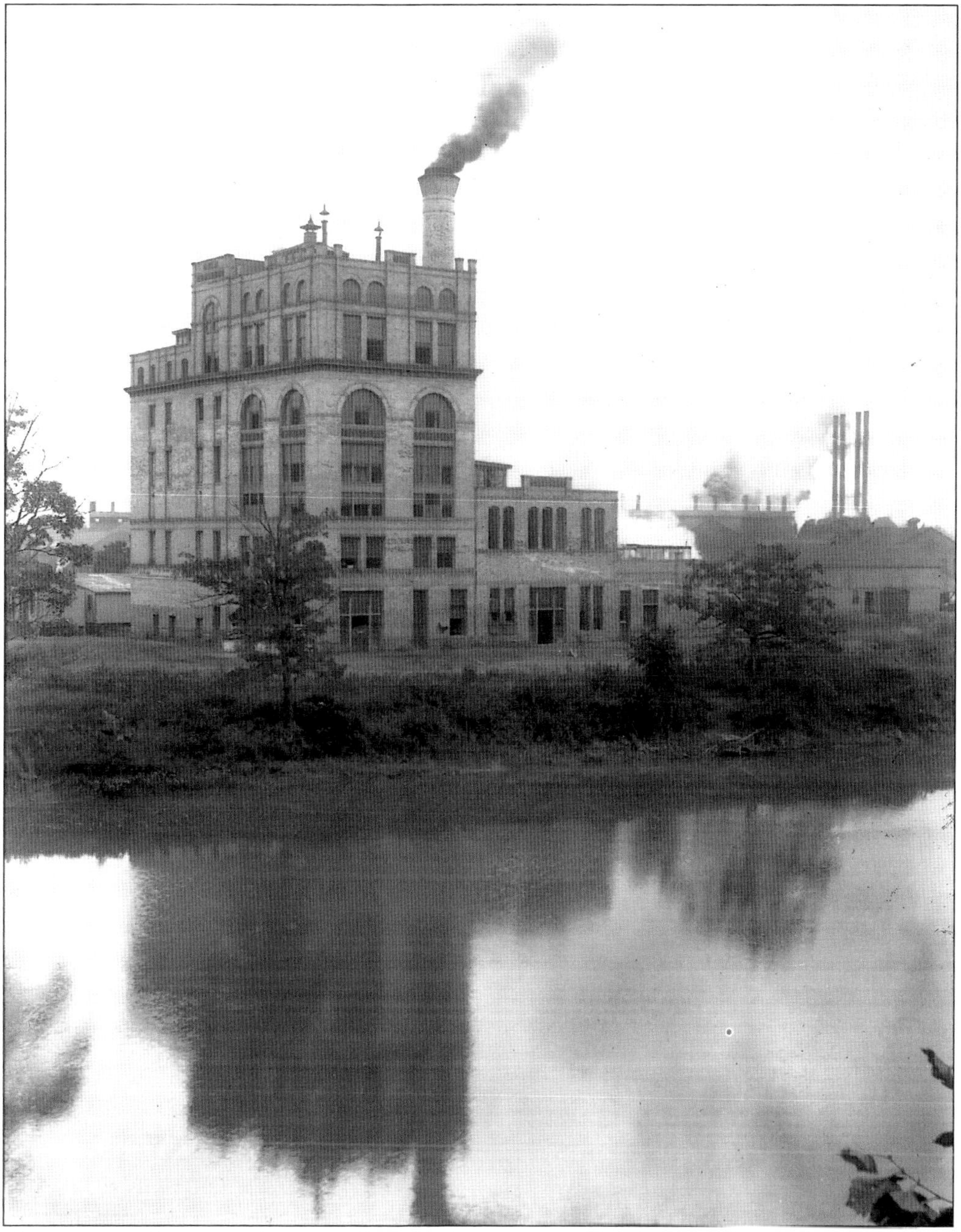

TUSCARAWAS BREWING COMPANY DOVER, OHIO, 1907. The settling of Tuscarawas County in the very early days was mostly performed by German and Swiss immigrants. Having been raised in a culture where they relied on the brewing of beer and ale, as they arrived in their new home in America, the brewmasters began the business of producing beer and ale on a large scale. Most brewmasters and their employees were trained in Munich, Germany. In Dover, there were two major breweries. An extensive ice plant was added to this brewery in 1906. The remnants of both breweries are still visible along the Tuscarawas River near downtown Dover. The industry began its decline when the issue of Prohibition began in the early twentieth century.

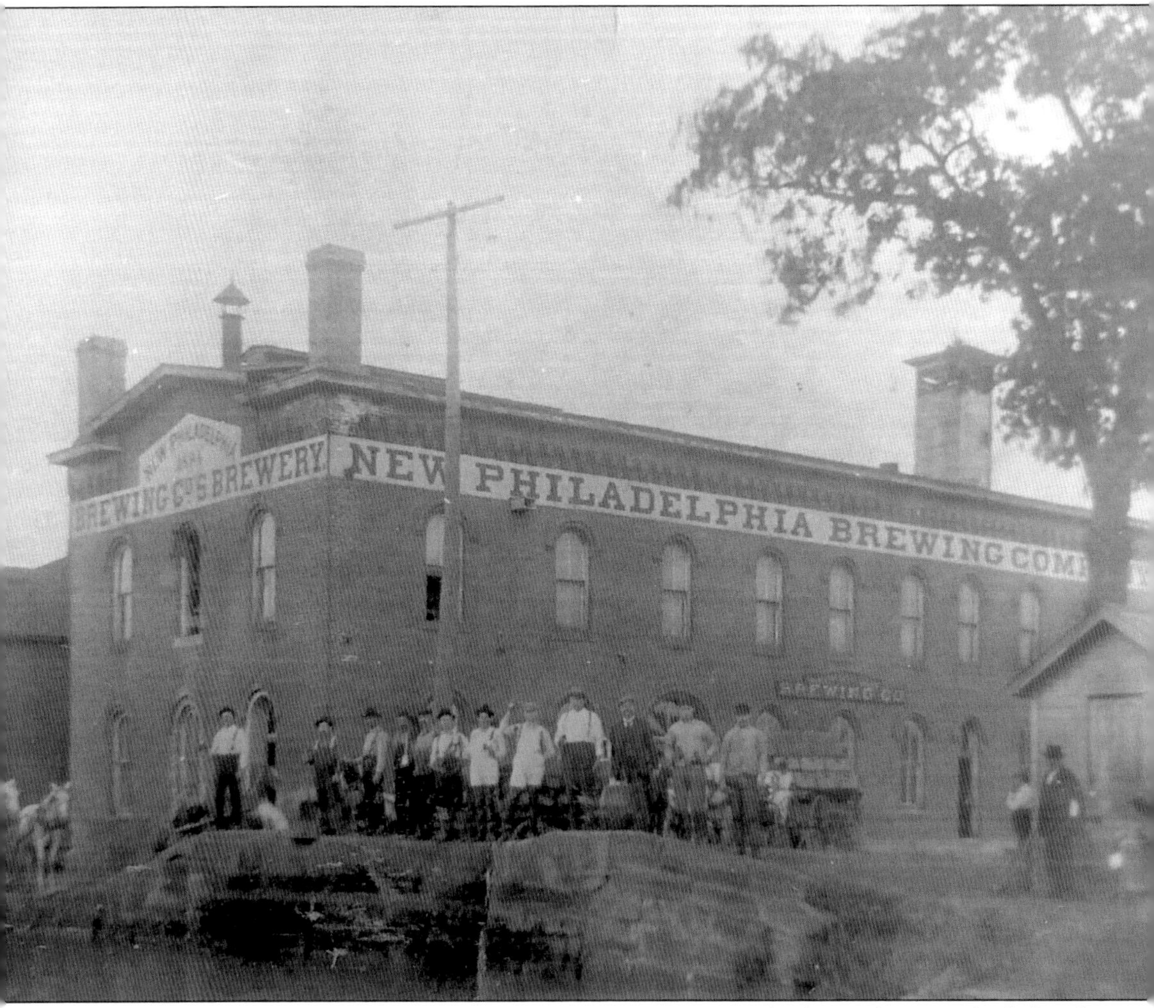

NEW PHILADELPHIA BREWING COMPANY FOUNDED 1884. The large plant was built beside the Ohio Erie Canal near where Commercial Avenue intersects with South Broadway Street today. It began operation in 1884, by the Seibold Brothers. This productive industry continued through the Eighteenth Amendment in 1919, which was to be repealed by the Twenty-first Amendment in 1933. They even made beer shampoo in order to keep the plant operating during these times. They were famous for the Lockport Lager. The Seibold family invested their income in many other business opportunities in the City of New Philadelphia, Ohio.

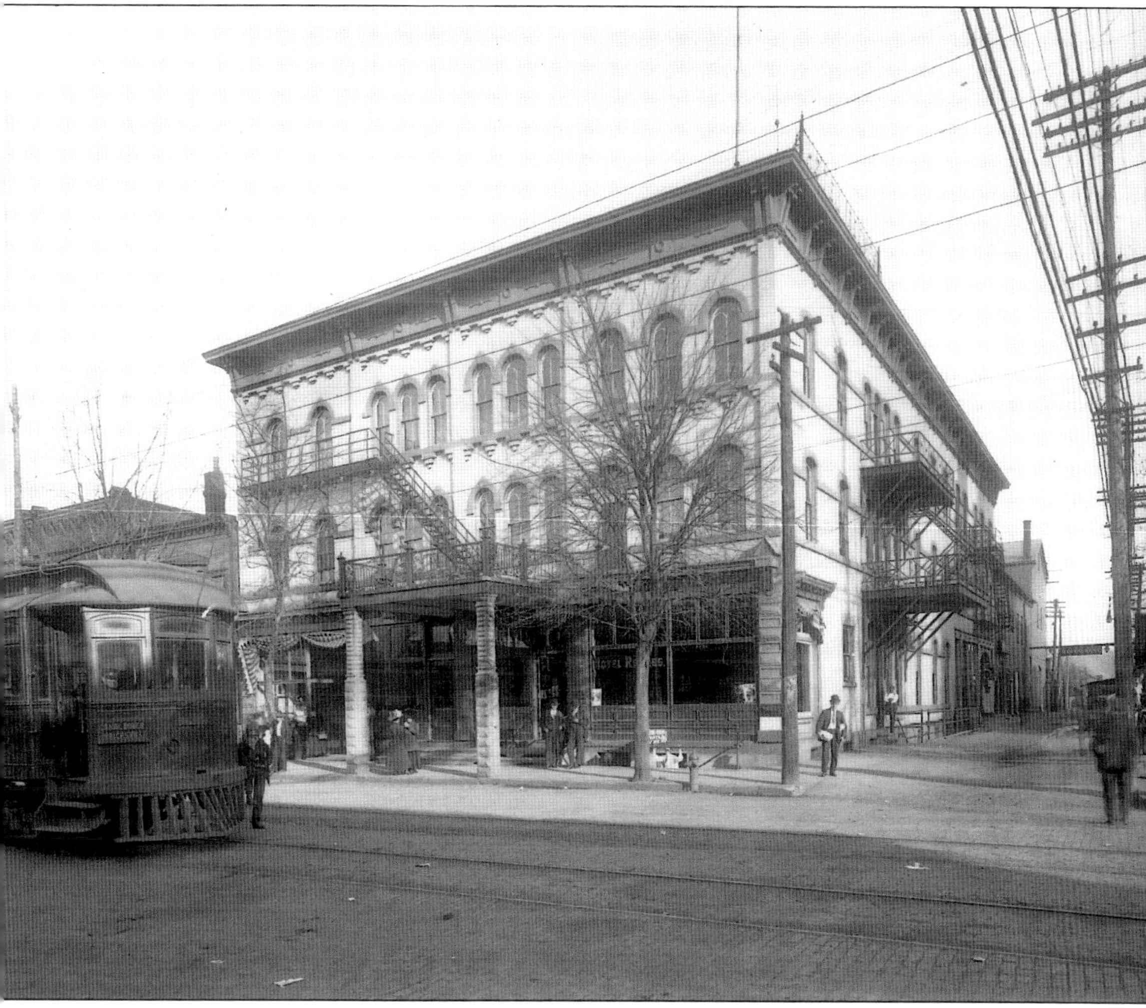

REEVES HOTEL IN DOWNTOWN NEW PHILADELPHIA, OHIO. Ernest Schmidt constructed the first hotel on the North Broadway site, immediately past the courthouse, in 1881. By 1884, this hotel was known as the Sherman House. Shortly thereafter, the Wallick family purchased the house and then sold it to Jeremiah Reeves in 1905. The Reeves family extensively remodeled and enlarged the facility and reopened it as the Hotel Reeves. The hotel remained under the Reeves's control until it was closed, and the building was dismantled in May of 1969.

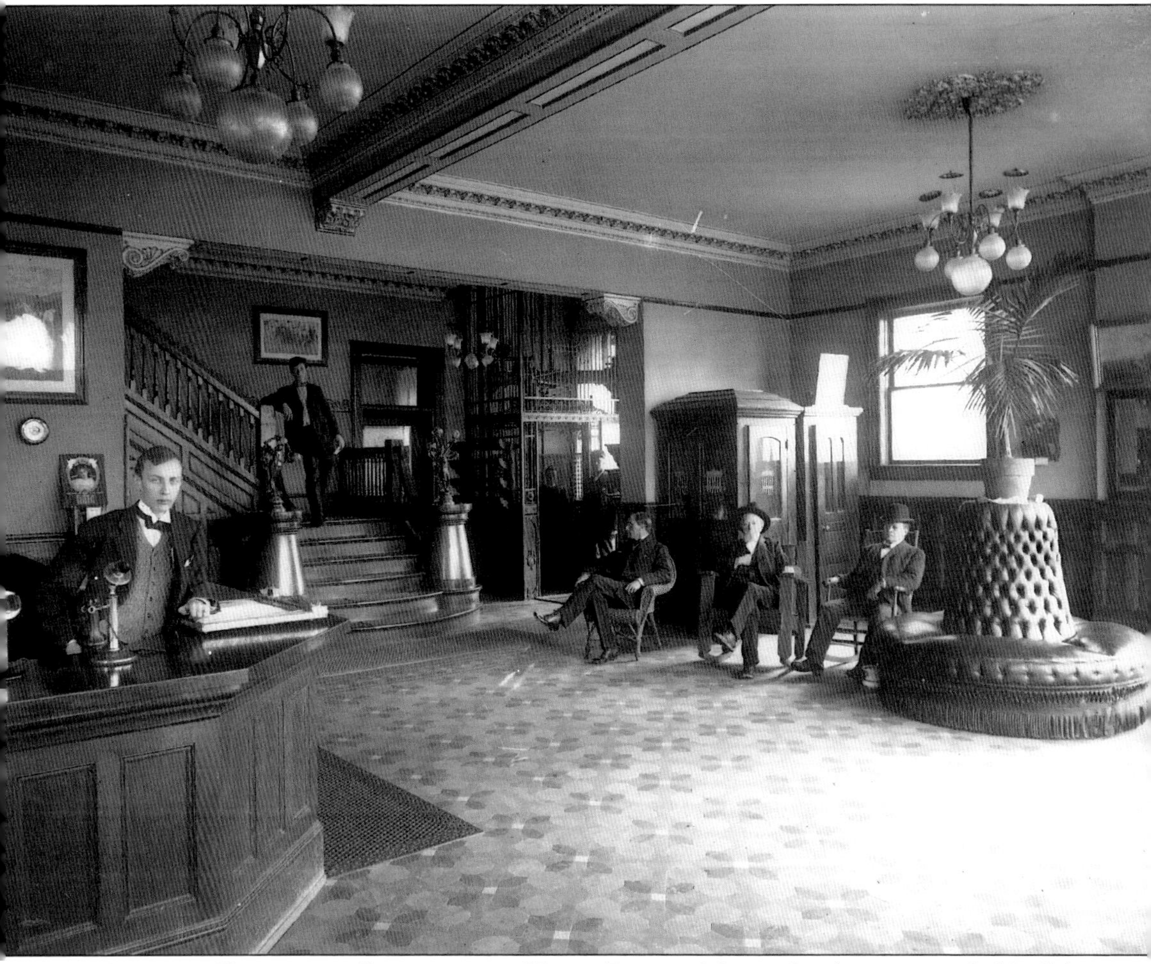

Interior View of the Lobby of the Hotel Reeves. Many a fine banquet was held off this spacious lobby. Into the early 1960s, this lobby remained virtually unchanged from this 1920 picture. Many civic groups held their weekly meetings in the dining room. The young ladies who turned "Sweet Sixteen" had their coming out parties in this structure. Don McNeil of the famous Don McNeil Breakfast Hour, a national radio morning show broadcast from Chicago, came here and held his morning breakfast show from the balcony in the late 1940s. He even considered a run for the presidency and came to New Philadelphia where it was reported he would make this momentous announcement. He came, but then he decided not to run. The Hotel Reeves, a fine grand dame, met the fate of progress in May 1969. Today a bank and a parking lot grace the space of this once important landmark in Tuscarawas County history.

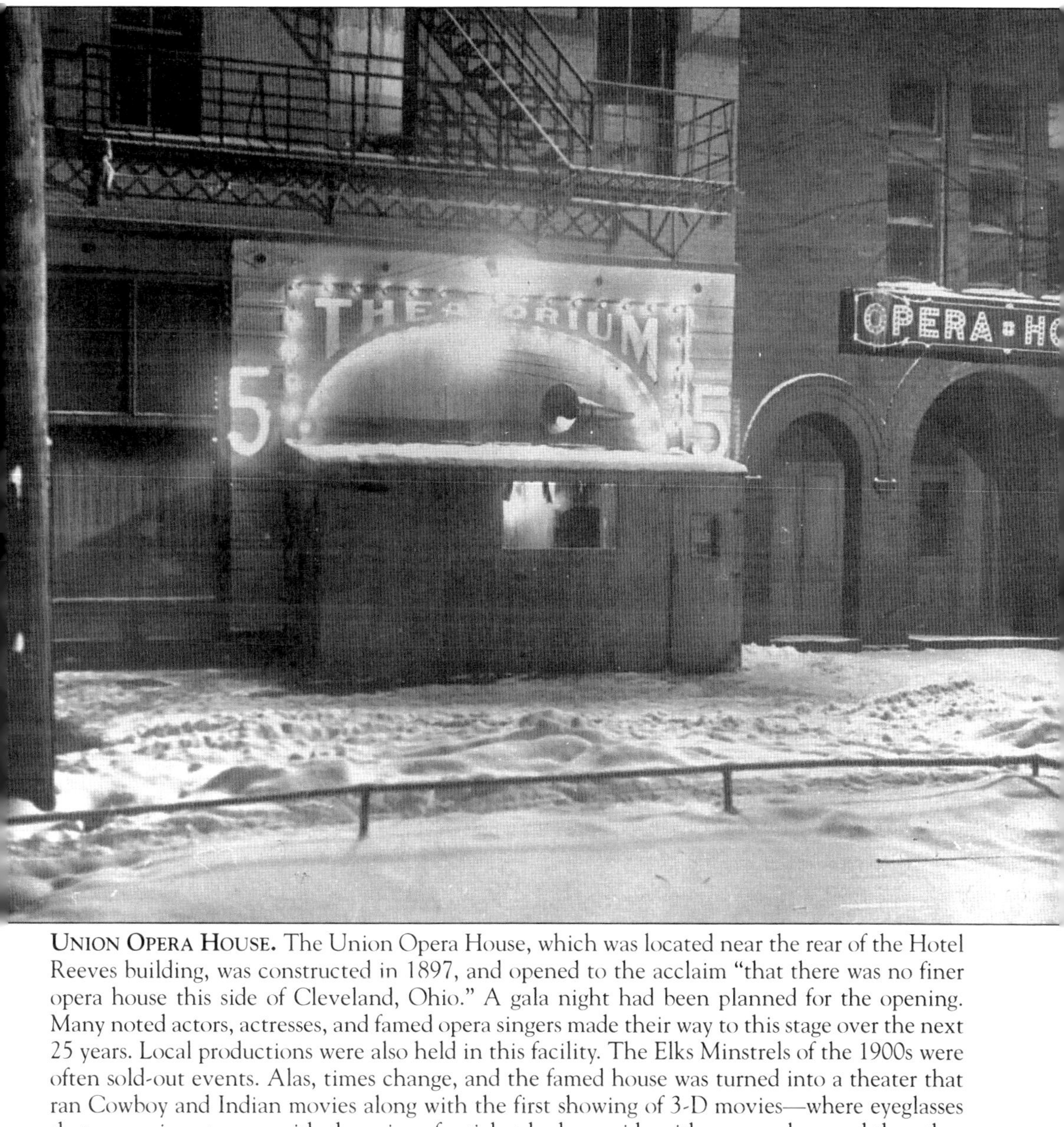

Union Opera House. The Union Opera House, which was located near the rear of the Hotel Reeves building, was constructed in 1897, and opened to the acclaim "that there was no finer opera house this side of Cleveland, Ohio." A gala night had been planned for the opening. Many noted actors, actresses, and famed opera singers made their way to this stage over the next 25 years. Local productions were also held in this facility. The Elks Minstrels of the 1900s were often sold-out events. Alas, times change, and the famed house was turned into a theater that ran Cowboy and Indian movies along with the first showing of 3-D movies—where eyeglasses that were given to you with the price of a ticket had one side with a green lens and the other side with a red lens. Nothing seemed to work, and the theater eventually met its fate when the wrecking ball began its work in 1957.

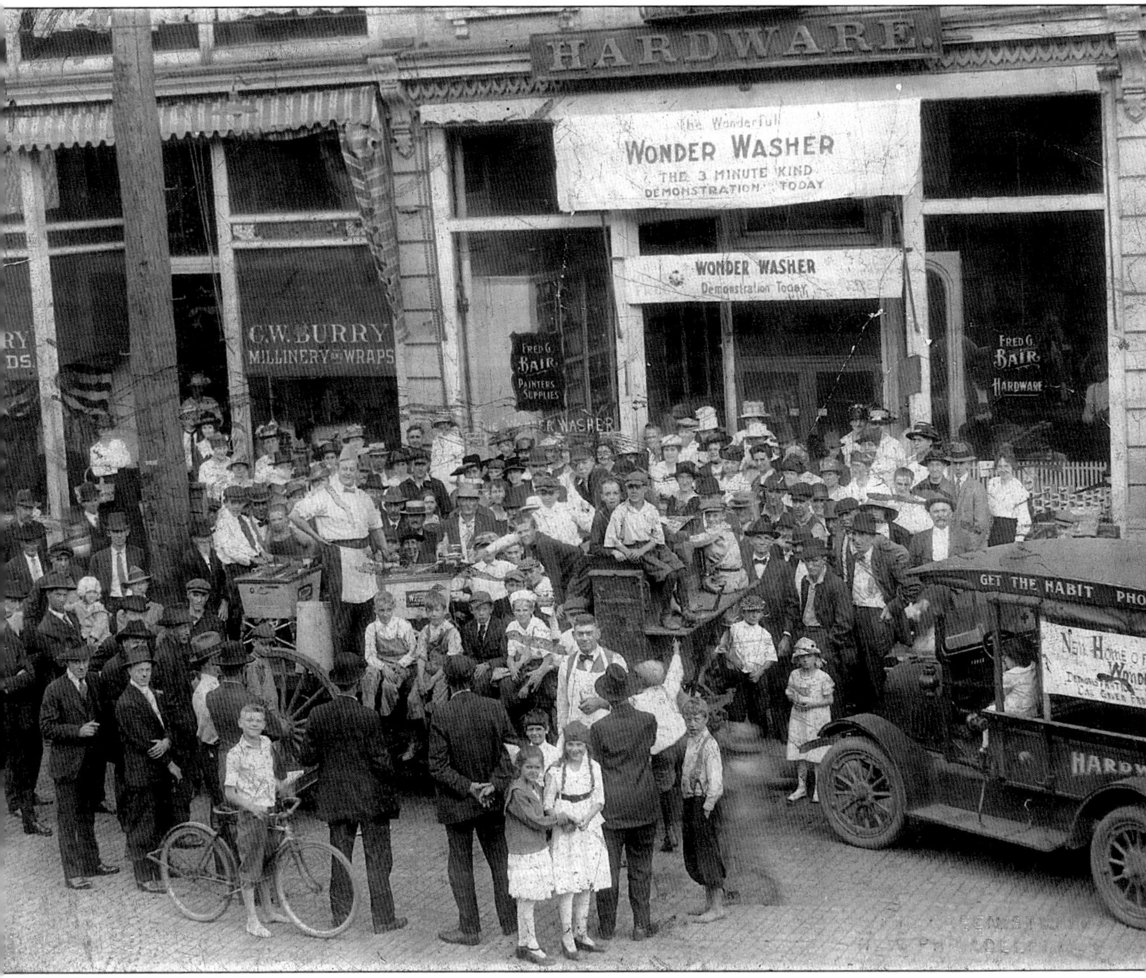

HARDWARE SALE ON SOUTH BROADWAY. The Wonder Washer salesman was in town and gathered many interested folk about him to see his newest contraption. Do any of you remember the Wonder Washer? Ladies, gentlemen, and kids dressed to the nines—and some barefoot—got right into the picture. The photographer captured the scene from across the street in an upstairs room. Fred G. Bair owned the hardware store, and he was taking on this new model.

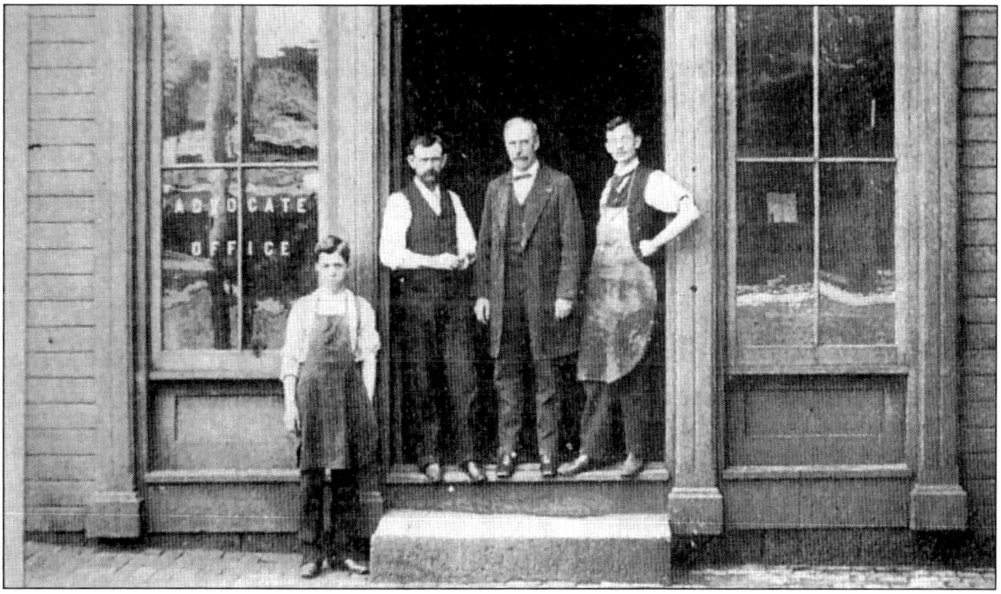

TUSCARAWAS *ADVOCATE* NEWSPAPER. James Patrick started this weekly newspaper in 1834. The boy (Printers Devil) pictured was George Marsh. In 1846, Patrick sold the newspaper to his son Andrew. Joseph L. McIlvaine purchased the paper in 1865 and continued to publish it for nearly 50 years. He is in the center of thc picture. In 1911, he sold the paper to his son Charles McIlvaine. In 1930, it became the *Daily Reporter* published in Dover, Ohio. The picture was taken at the offices at 122 West High Street in New Philadelphia.

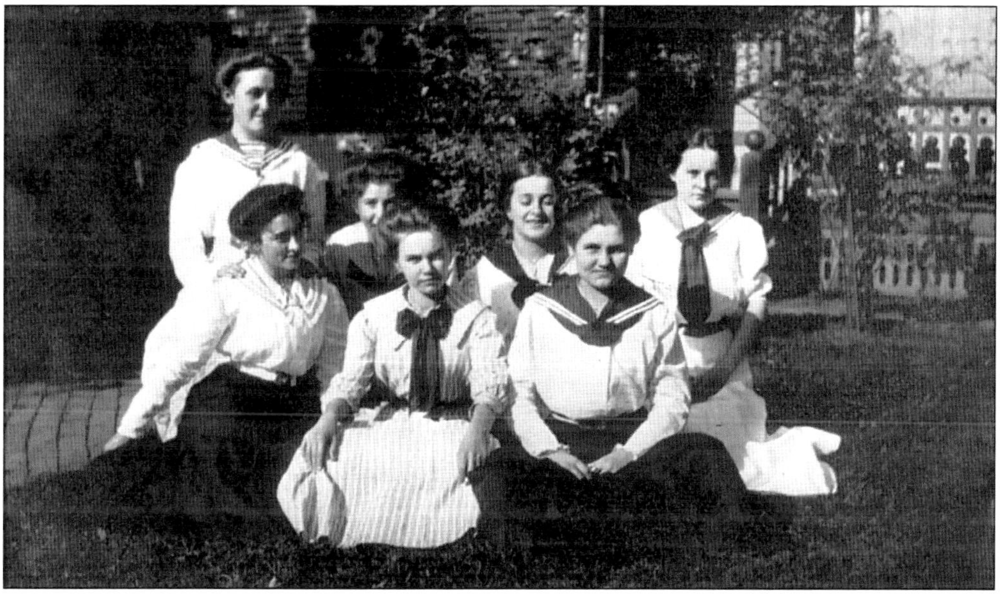

EARLY TELEPHONE OPERATORS NEW PHILADELPHIA, OHIO. In the 1890s, the newspaper ran ads for the telephone company. Phone service slowly caught on, and long distance was offered around 1895. This picture, of which only two ladies have been identified, includes Ethel Stonebrook (first row, right) and Mrs. Grimm in the middle, who were of the first telephone operators. Today we clamor for the sound of a real voice when requesting assistance with the telephone.

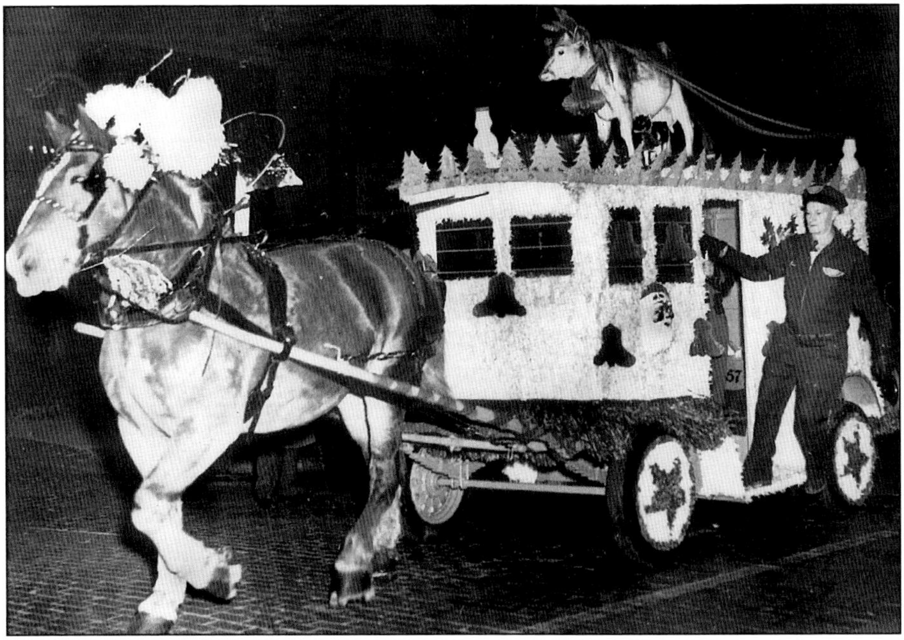

GOSHEN DAIRY DELIVERY. "Tomorrow will be here today." Those words were the phrase that William Bichsel Sr. lived by and passed on to his sons and grandsons. In 1920, William Sr., along with four others, began the Goshen Dairy Company in New Philadelphia, Ohio. In 1921, he became the sole owner. This picture is a symbol of the Goshen Dairy Company, which brings back many pleasant memories of the days of home delivery. It was taken during the 1951 Christmas Parade in New Philadelphia. The driver was George Beans.

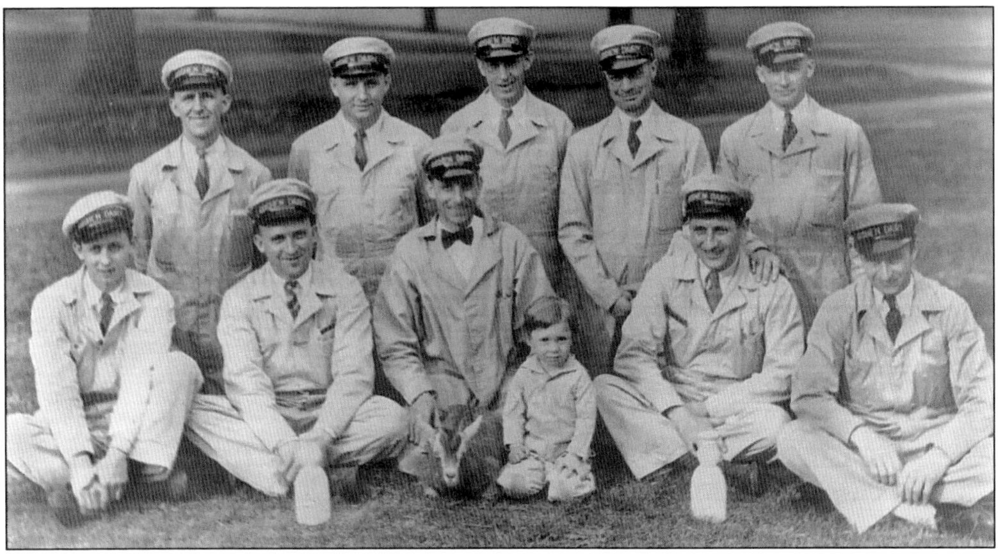

GOSHEN DAIRY SALESMEN. This picture was taken of the principal salesmen for the Goshen Dairy Company in the late 1920s. In the middle is William Sr., and the young boy is William Jr. Note the bottles which are collector items today. The company is still in operation maintained by Jerry Bichsel, a son of William Sr., the president of the company. The only deliveries today are made to large supermarkets, company stores, and the schools in eastern Ohio and northern West Virginia.

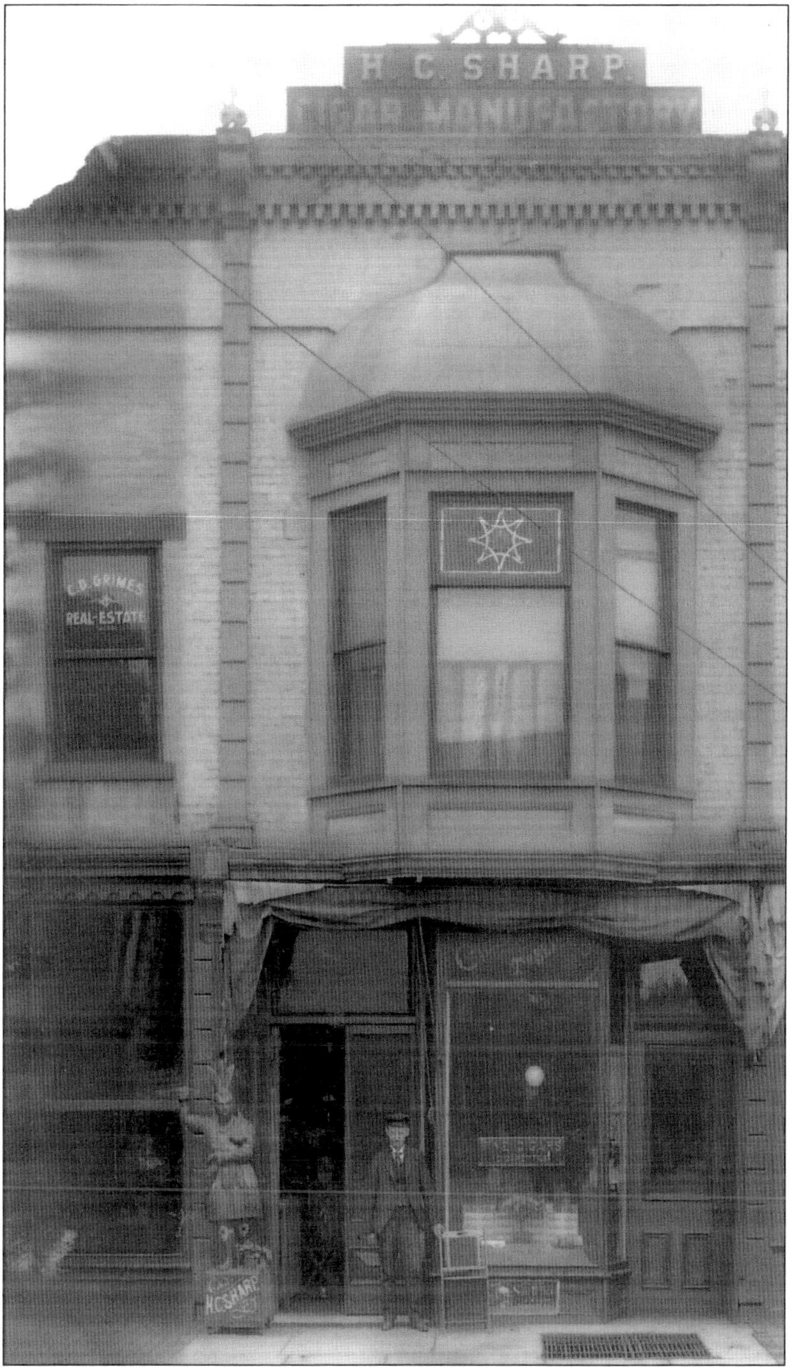

SHARP CIGAR MANUFACTURING CO. The late nineteenth and early twentieth century was a time when it was fashionable for the men to retreat to the parlor after a good meal with friends and smoke a good cigar while engaging in the conversation of the day. In downtown New Philadelphia, as well as in Uhrichsville, enterprising businessmen began companies that rolled their own cigars. H.C. Sharp was just such a businessman. He even built his own building and rented out space for other offices, as can be seen in the C.D. Grimes Real Estate office.

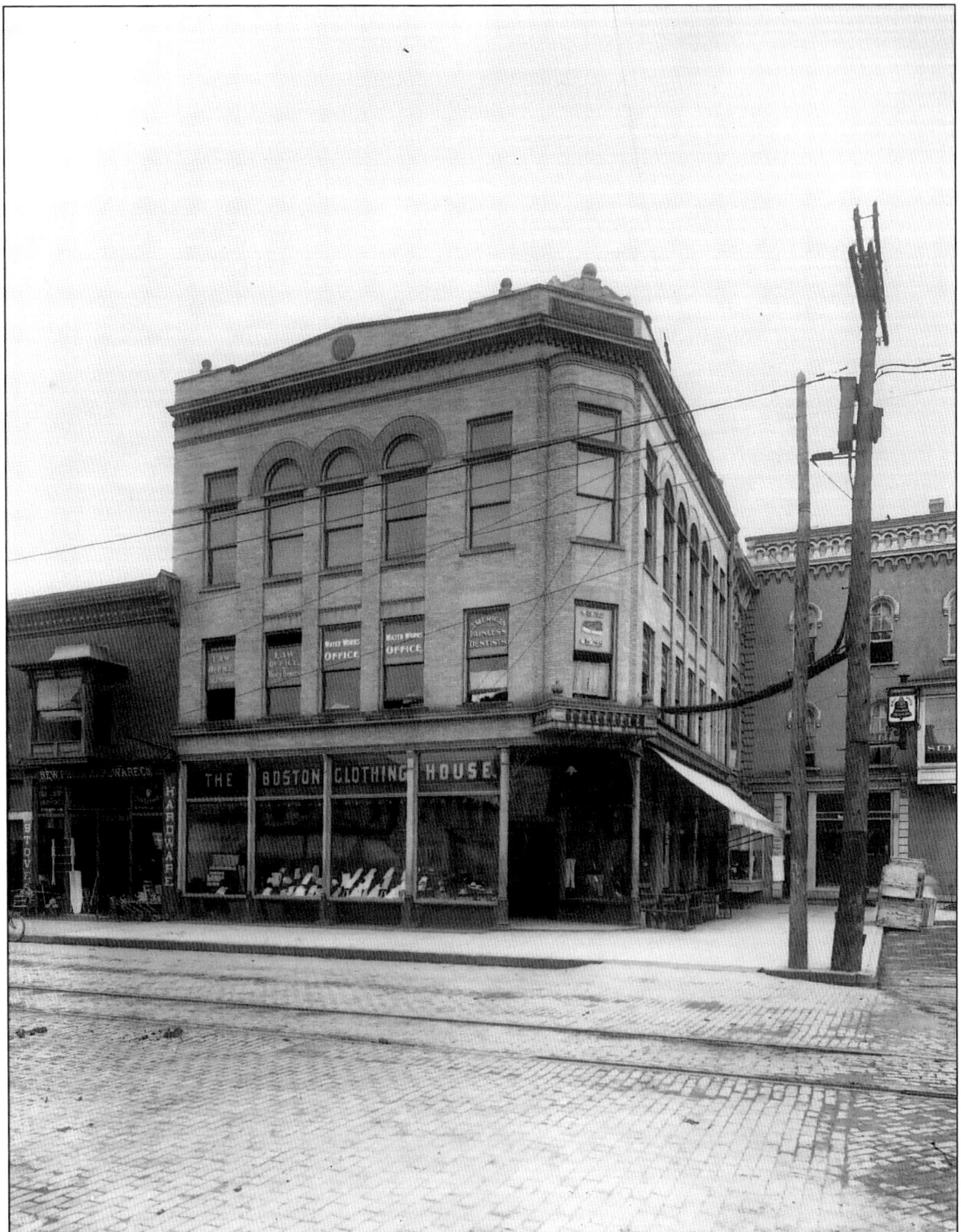

Boston Clothing Store. The Boston Clothing Store was a well-known business located on the southeast corner of the square in New Philadelphia from the 1880s through the 1960s. Today it houses the House of Stones, a jewelry store. This familiar building not only catered to the men of the county, but the second floor was leased to lawyers and dentists, and at one time the third floor was the home of the New Philadelphia B.P.O.E. 510 lodge before they constructed their own building a few doors to the east in 1928. The Alexander Brothers built this structure in 1900. On top of this building was a large lighted "Welcome to New Philadelphia" sign.

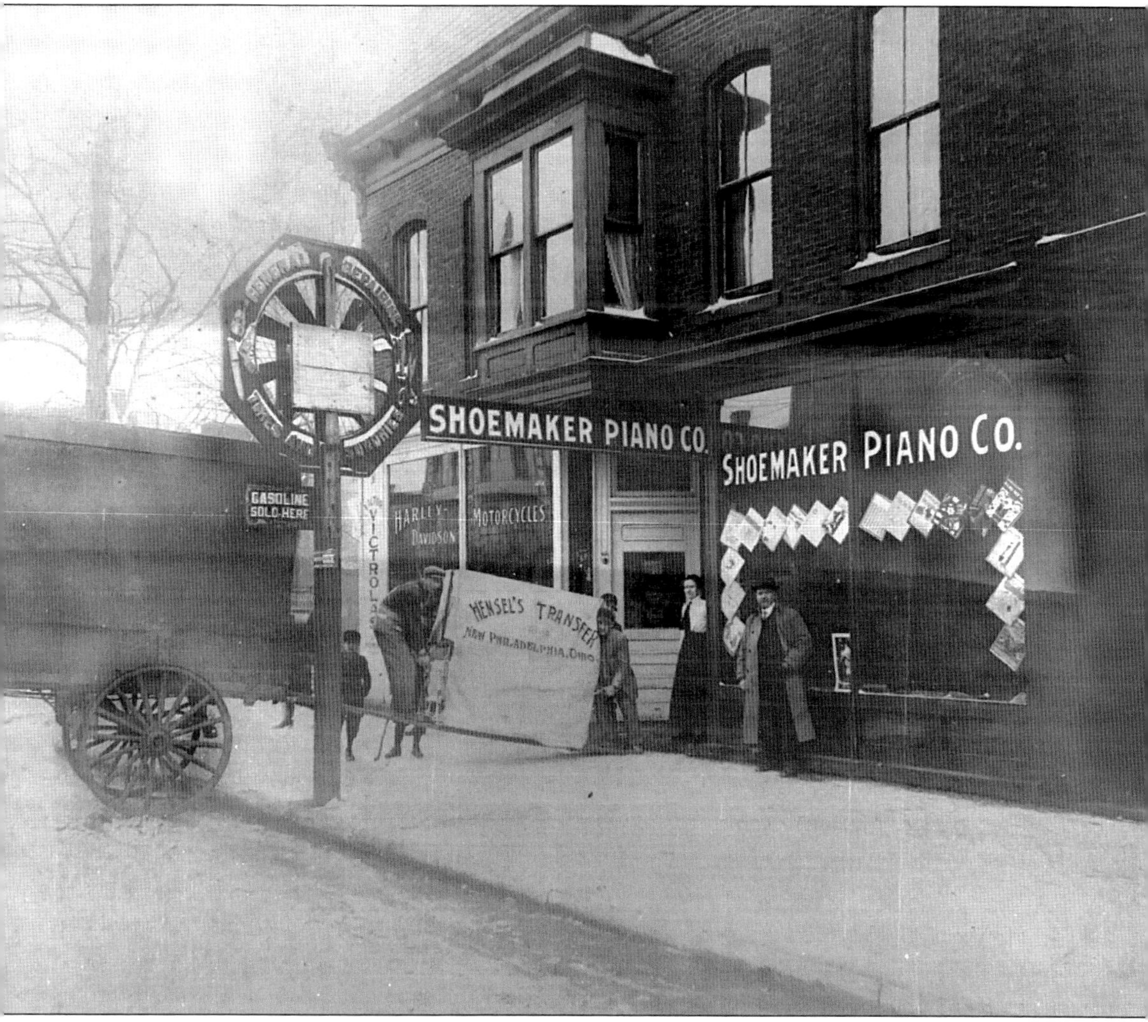

SHOEMAKER PIANO COMPANY. The Shoemaker Piano Company was located on West High Avenue in New Philadelphia. The Tuscarawas *Advocate* ran weekly ads from this company advertising upright pianos. Music was an important part of family life at the turn of the twentieth century. There was no radio or television, so the family retired to the parlor and gathered about the piano to entertain themselves for the evening. A few of these pianos are still in the possession of families today. The Shoemaker Piano Company shared their building with a Harley Davidson Motorcycle business, which is visible on the window behind the workers for the Hensel Transfer Company of New Philadelphia, Ohio.

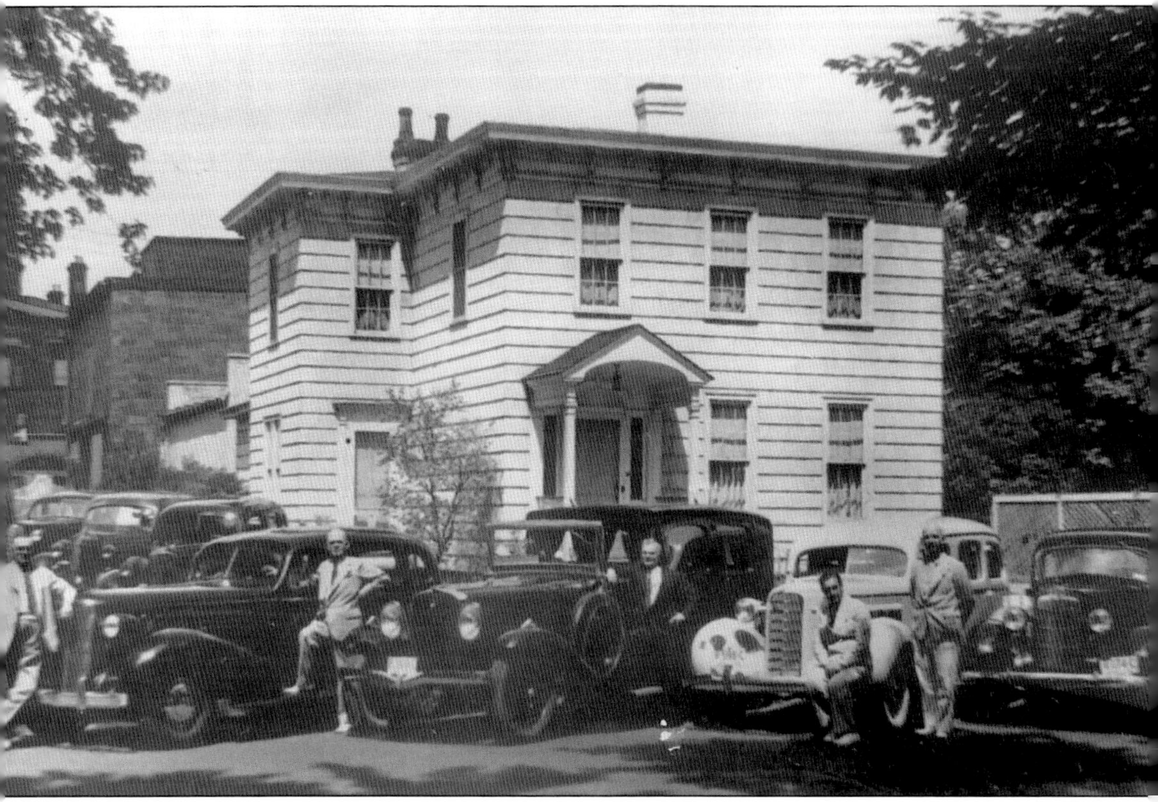

LINN HERT GEIB FUNERAL HOME. In this age of consolidation, it is indeed rare to find a company that is still in operation after over 150 years. The Linn Hert Geib Funeral Home, as pictured here in 1936, is just such a company. In 1846, Joseph McElroy immigrated to the county. He was a cabinetmaker and undertaker. In 1887, James Linn moved to the county and joined the company, purchasing half of the company in 1890. McElroy died in 1892, and Mr. Linn purchased his interest. In 1902, he took on a partner—Jacob A. Geib. In 1903, they moved from their South Broadway location to 2nd and East High Streets, the location of this picture. In 1916, it was incorporated with James Linn as president, Jacob Geib as vice president, and Alfred E. Hert as secretary treasurer. Jacob died in 1952, and his son Carl, who had joined the business in 1920, took over the business. Carl retired in 1970, and his son Richard D. Geib Sr. became president. Today Richard D. Geib Jr., the third generation of the family to be associated with the firm, is the president.

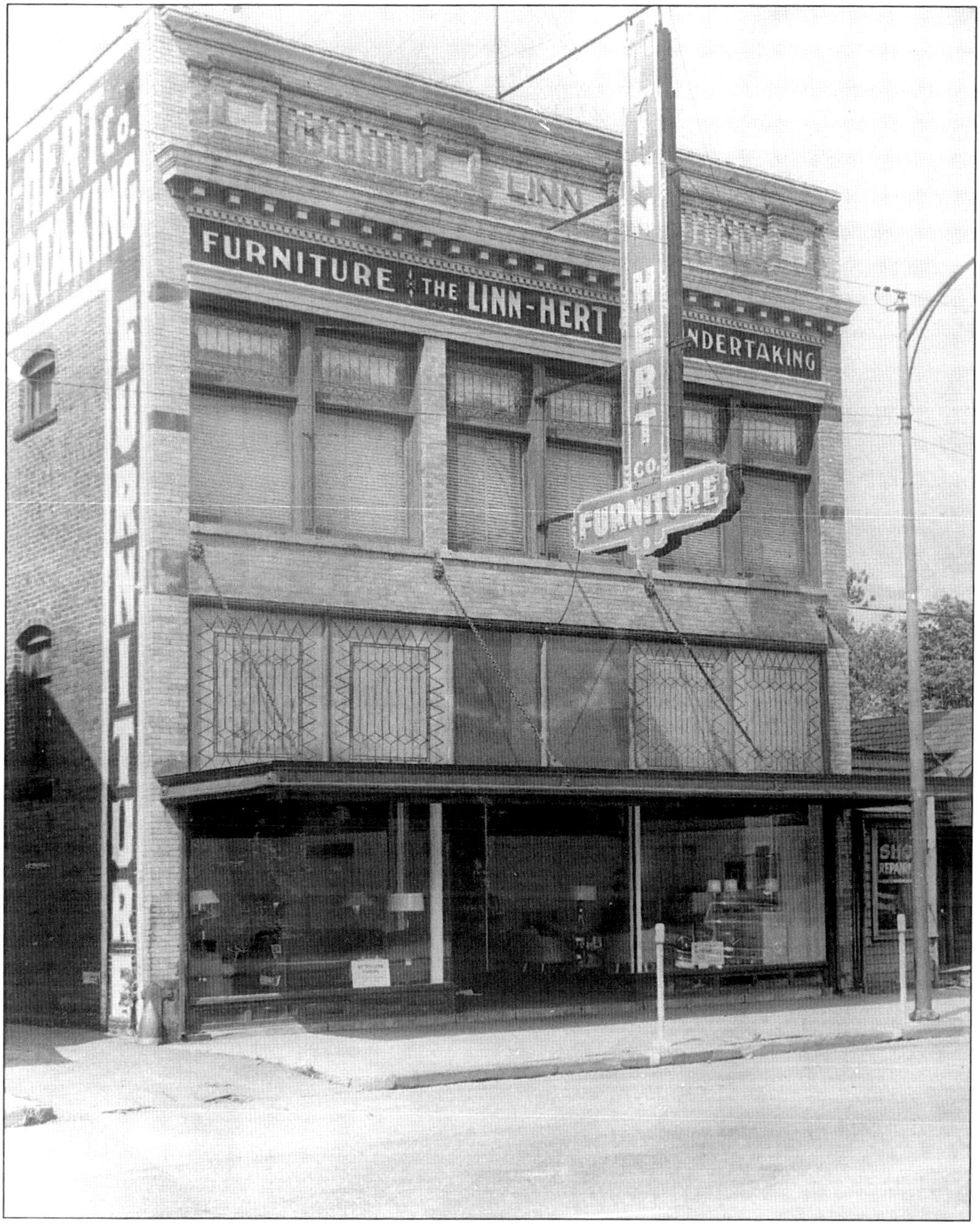

LINN HERT FURNITURE COMPANY. James Linn, mentioned in the previous story, had joined the funeral business with Joseph McElroy in 1887. Being an astute businessman, he placed a portion of his wealth in a building, and along with his later partner, Alfred E. Hert, began a furniture store. Most undertakers at the turn of the twentieth century built their own caskets and were excellent woodworkers. Therefore, having a small furniture business alongside the funeral business helped to provide income between funerals. This building was located at the site of the current Geib Community Building. After a disastrous fire in the 1970s, Addie Williams continued his furniture business in this location a few doors up the street. The building was torn down in the 1980s to make room for the expanded funeral business of the Linn Hert Geib Funeral and Crematory Company.

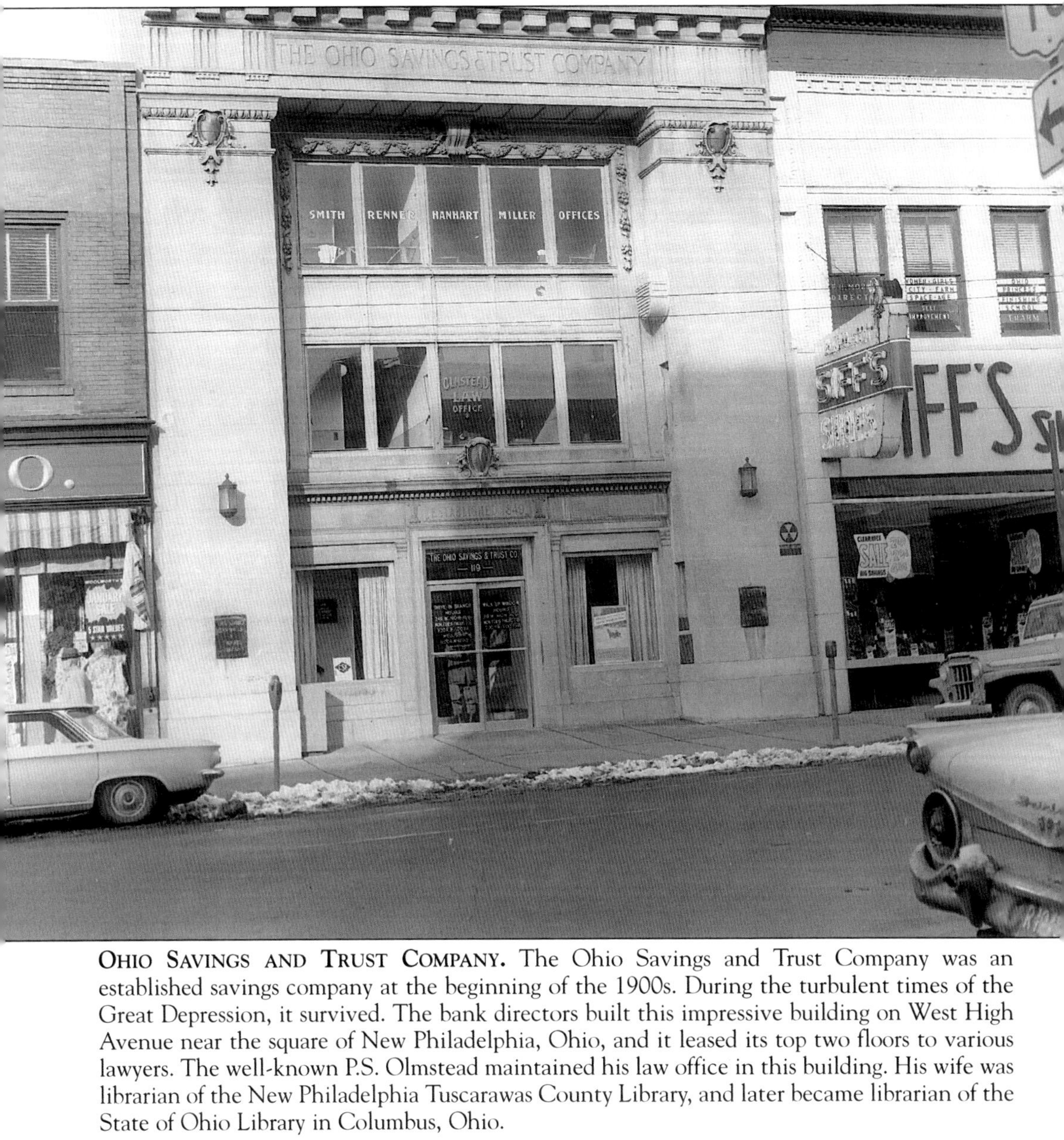

OHIO SAVINGS AND TRUST COMPANY. The Ohio Savings and Trust Company was an established savings company at the beginning of the 1900s. During the turbulent times of the Great Depression, it survived. The bank directors built this impressive building on West High Avenue near the square of New Philadelphia, Ohio, and it leased its top two floors to various lawyers. The well-known P.S. Olmstead maintained his law office in this building. His wife was librarian of the New Philadelphia Tuscarawas County Library, and later became librarian of the State of Ohio Library in Columbus, Ohio.

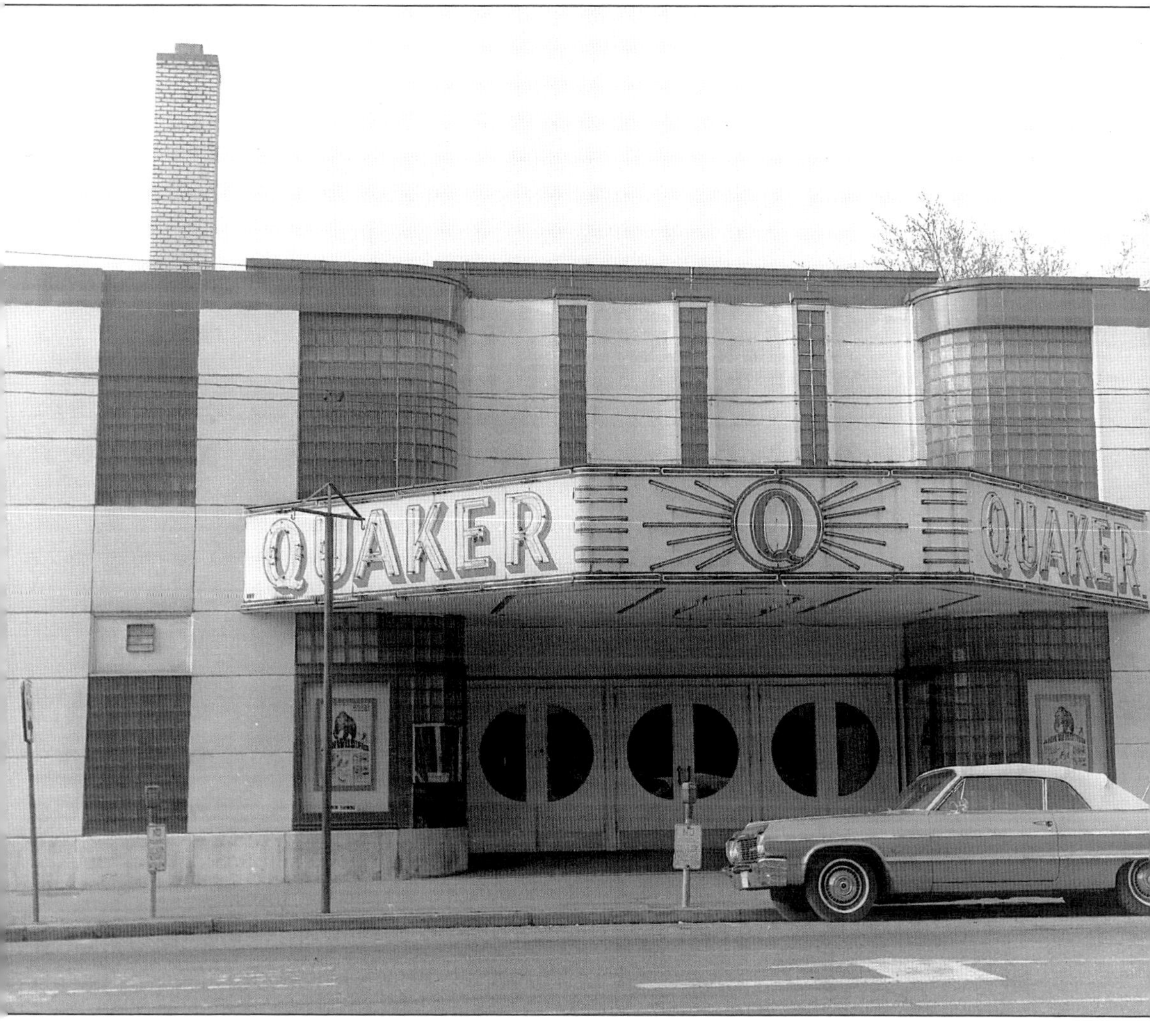

QUAKER THEATER. Rumblings of war were the feature stories in the papers of Tuscarawas County when it was announced that New Philadelphia would have a new motion picture emporium. The town's nickname, Quakers, taken from the founders of Pennsylvania and their namesake City of Philadelphia, was incorporated as the name for this theater, which opened in 1940. Saturday afternoon matinees, snake dances which wound down the aisles on the eve before the big game of the year, special promotions such as drawings for a new bike...ah, the memories of this place where one could go and forget one's troubles for a few hours. When the mega-theater complexes came onto the scene in the 1980s, the Quaker Theater came upon hard times and closed for a short period. Today, the theater has reopened due to the efforts of the enterprising young people who are associated with the Main Street Restoration program.

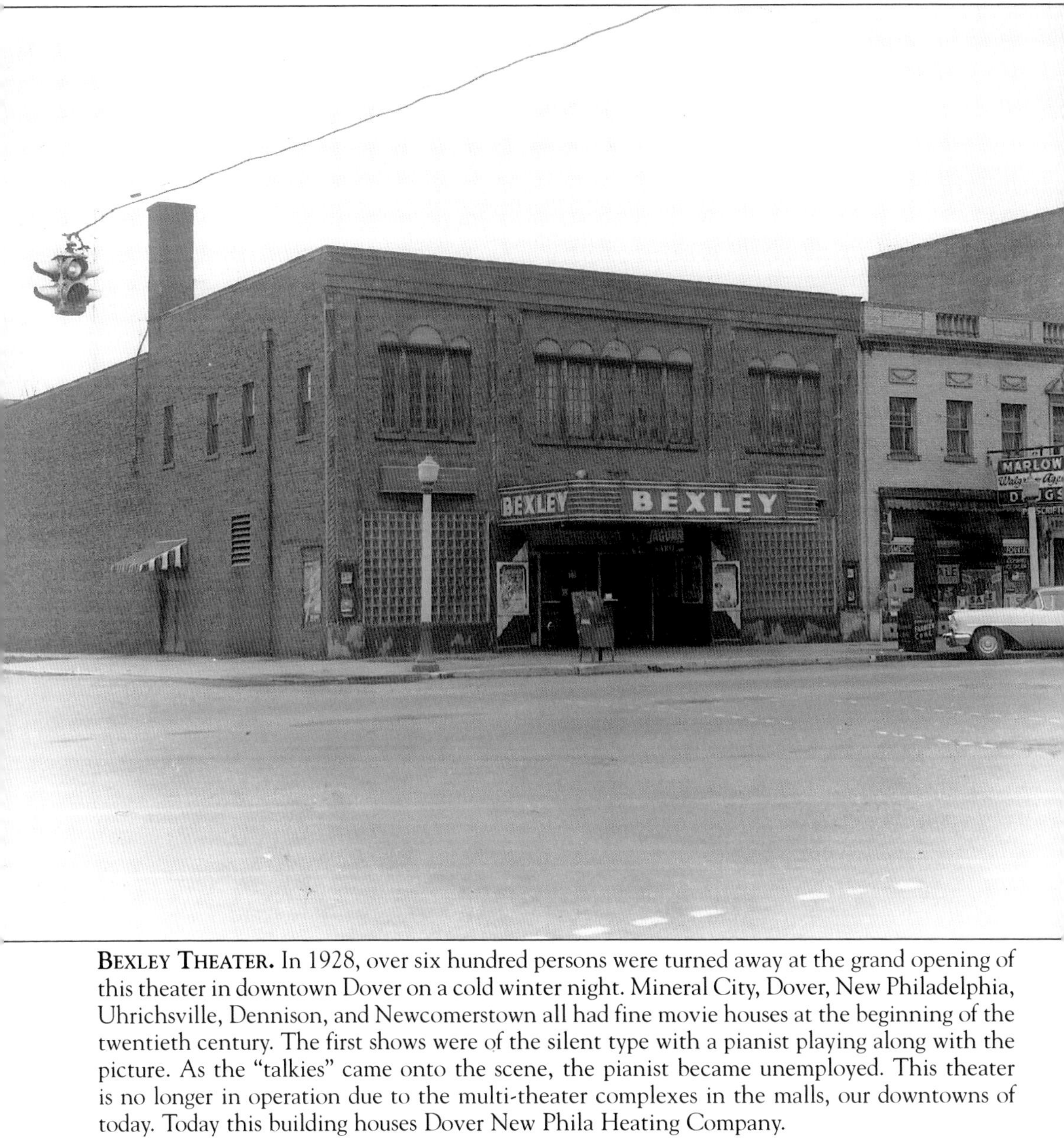

BEXLEY THEATER. In 1928, over six hundred persons were turned away at the grand opening of this theater in downtown Dover on a cold winter night. Mineral City, Dover, New Philadelphia, Uhrichsville, Dennison, and Newcomerstown all had fine movie houses at the beginning of the twentieth century. The first shows were of the silent type with a pianist playing along with the picture. As the "talkies" came onto the scene, the pianist became unemployed. This theater is no longer in operation due to the multi-theater complexes in the malls, our downtowns of today. Today this building houses Dover New Phila Heating Company.

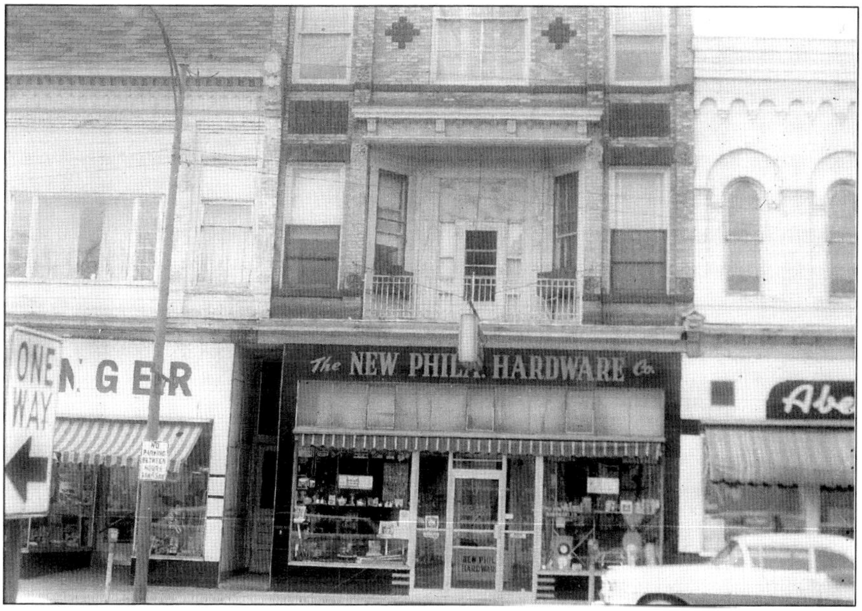

NEW PHILADELPHIA HARDWARE. We include this picture to document the passing of the times. Where once the villages and towns of the county had several small hardware stores and neighborhood groceries, today the mega stores have almost replaced the smaller businessman in these types of service. The upper two floors were rented out as apartments or for offices. Today Miller Clothing Company uses the building.

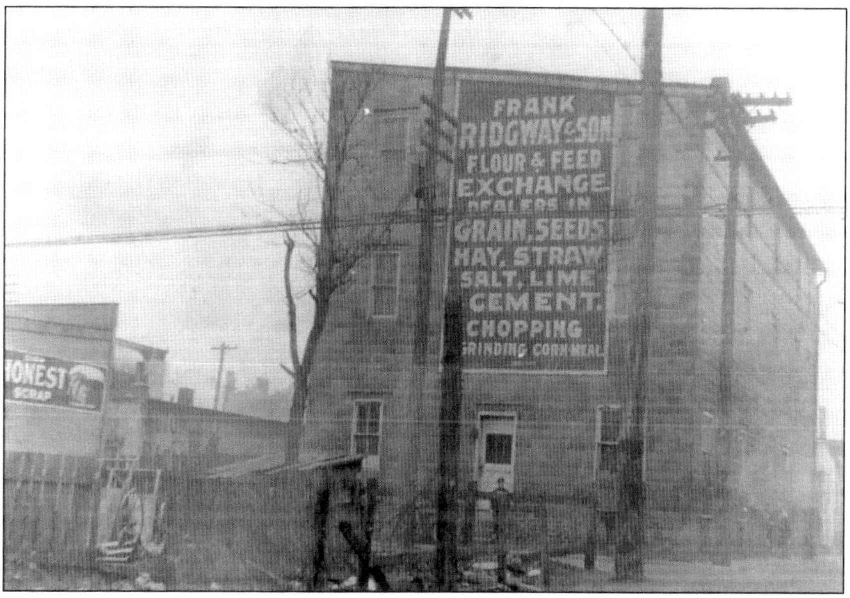

FRANK RIDGWAY & SON. A large and imposing building on the southwest section of downtown New Philadelphia was the Ridgway & Son Flour and Feed Exchange. A disastrous fire in 1910 nearly destroyed this concern, but the owners rebuilt and continued to provide service to local farmers into the 1960s. As one may gather from their prominent advertising, the company was a dealer in grain, seeds, hay, straw, salt, lime, cement, and provided services for the chopping and grinding of cornmeal.

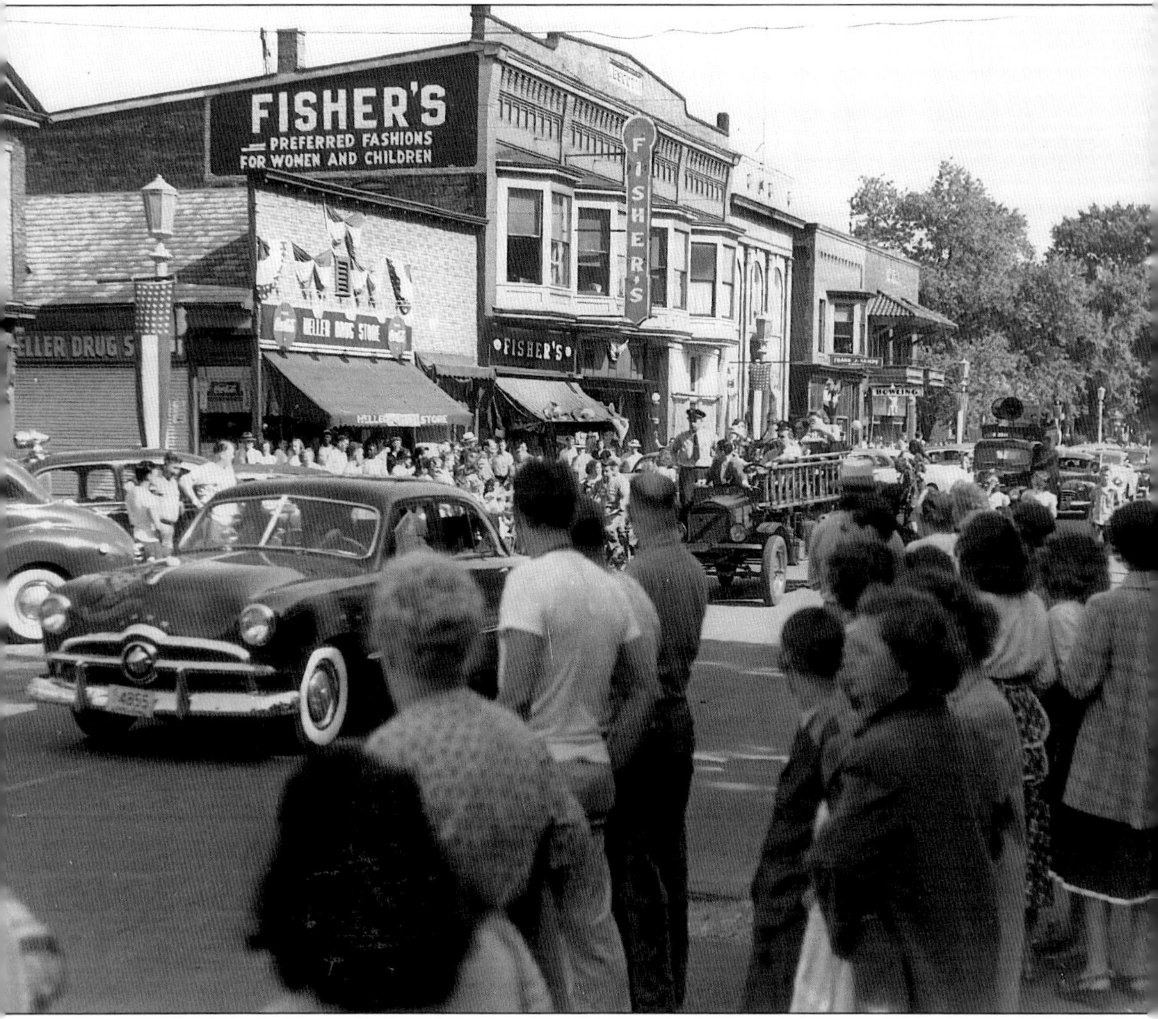

NEW PHILADELPHIA PARADE 1949. Each summer, parades were a big attraction to draw people to an event. This remarkable photograph is included to demonstrate the changes that have occurred within the cityscape of North Broadway in New Philadelphia, Ohio. Taken across the street, beside the Tuscarawas County Courthouse, the photographer recorded the last time the fire engine in the middle of the picture belonged to the City of New Philadelphia. The engine was sold later that year and is currently located in a private collection in northern Ohio. The grandparents of former attorney general of Ohio, Lee Fisher, owned the Fisher store. Fifty-one years later, there is not one business still in operation shown in this picture.

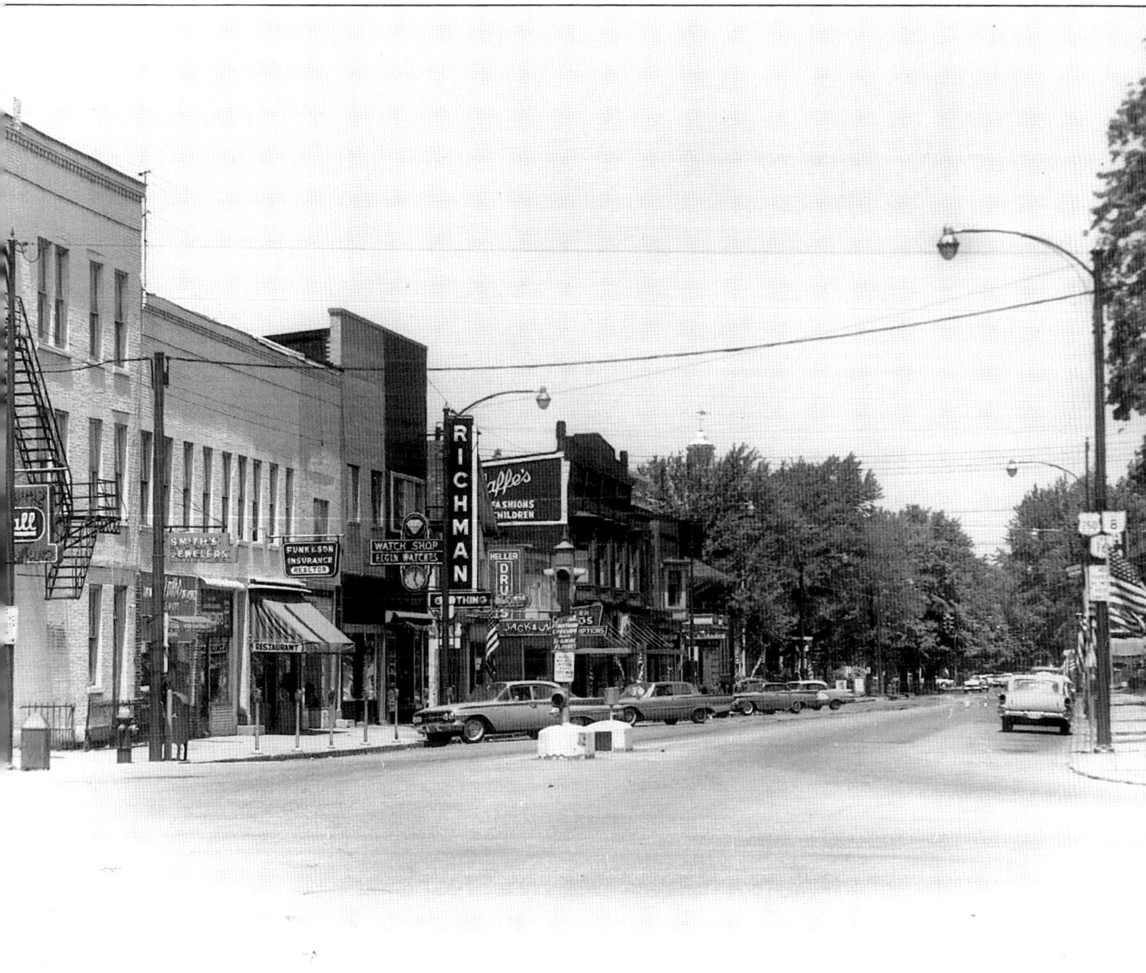

NORTH BROADWAY NEW PHILADELPHIA 1960S. This picture, taken a little closer to the square in New Philadelphia very early in the 1960s, shows a few of the changes that had already taken place in the ownership of a few of the buildings—Jaffe's Clothing Store took over for the Fisher's. Notice the flashing warning lights in the center of North Broadway and the change in the streetlights from the previous picture. How many remember the Leggett Restaurant between Smith Jewelers and the Watch Shop?

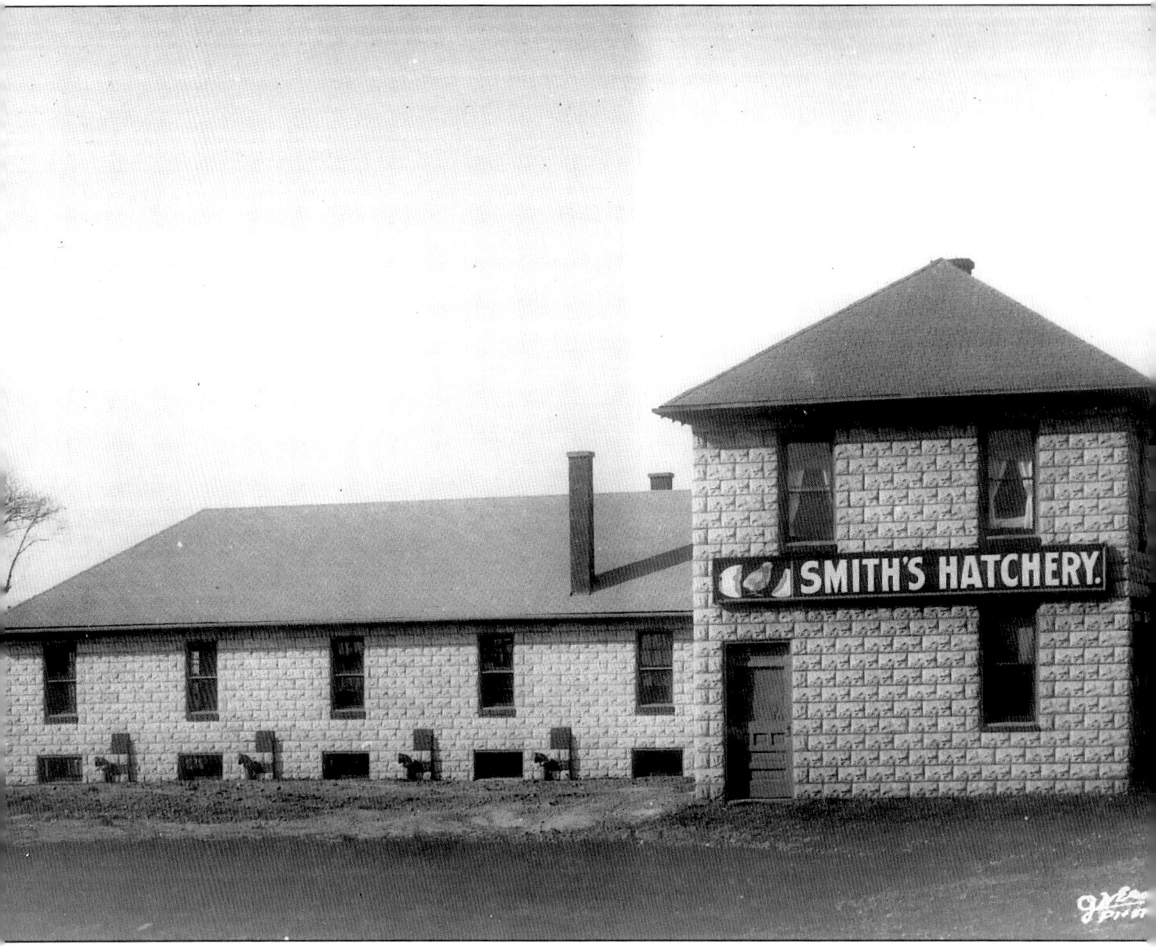

SMITH HATCHERY NEW PHILADELPHIA, OHIO. The economy of Tuscarawas County at the turn of the twentieth century revolved around the farming industry. In the middle of the villages and towns, one could always find businesses that catered to the farmer. Also, many families owned their own horses and wagons and needed supplies, thus creating the need for the Ridgeway Company and others like it in each community of Tuscarawas County. Many families also raised their own chickens at home. Smith Hatchery provided the incubation of chicks for farmers and for the townspeople who raised their own chickens. This building was located just off the boulevard where the Tuscarawas County AAA Worldwide Travel Offices are located today.

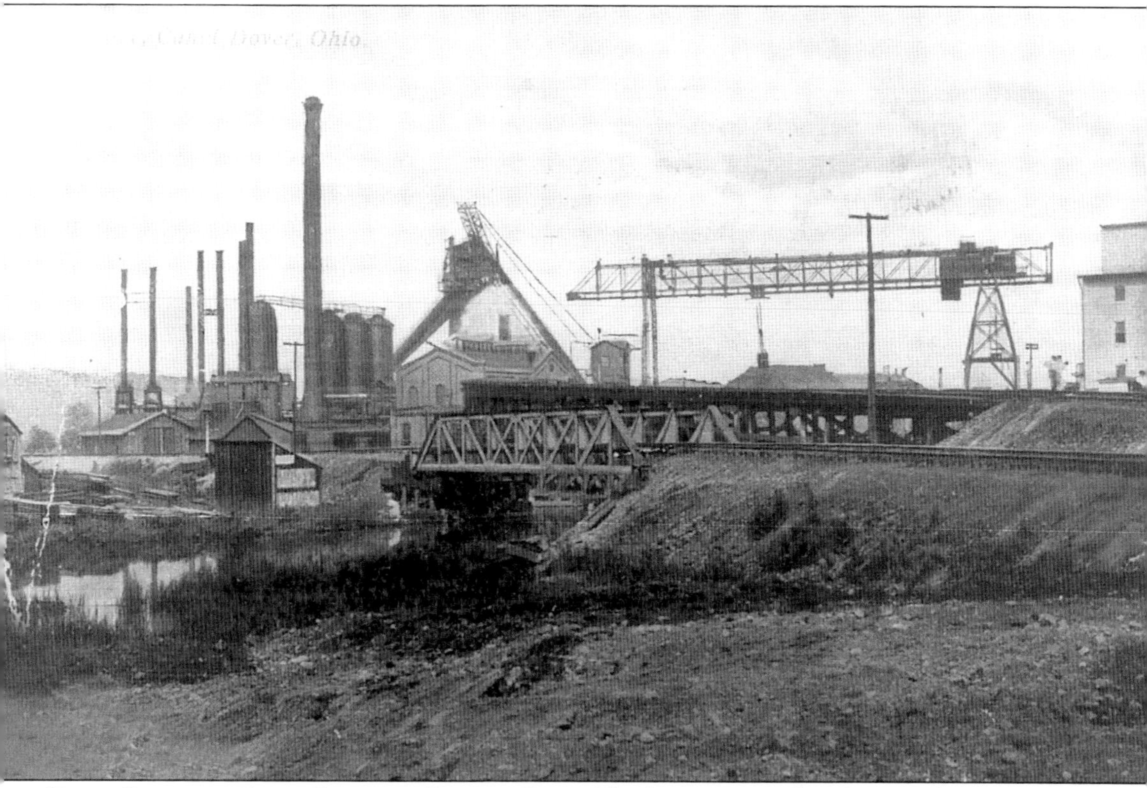

PENN COAL AND IRON COMPANY DOVER, OHIO. The late 1800s and early 1900s began the Industrial Revolution for Tuscarawas County with its rich supply of raw materials such as coal, iron ore, and clay. With a ready supply of coal and iron ore, companies such as Penn Coal and Iron Company were formed in the valley. Located between Third Street and Factory Street (now Tuscarawas Avenue), the company processed coal and iron for some of the following steel manufacturing companies: Reeves Manufacturing and the American Sheet and Tin Plate Company.

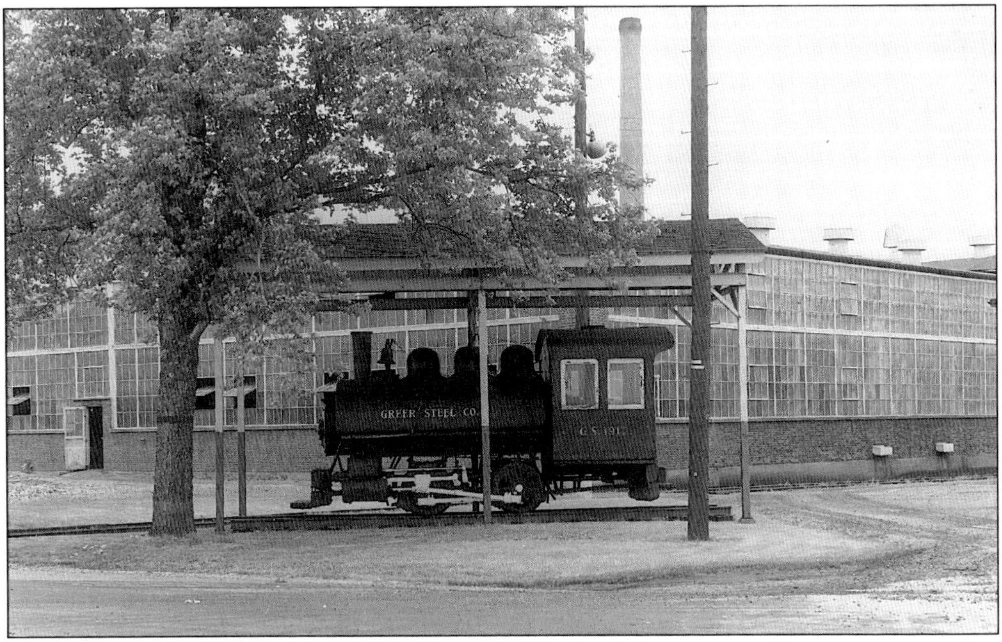

GREER STEEL COMPANY DOVER, OHIO. The Greer Steel Company, still in operation today, opened beside the Reeves Manufacturing Company in 1916. Its major product was cold-rolled steel. H.C. Greer of Morgantown, West Virginia, was a son-in-law of Jeremiah E. Reeves, the owner of the Reeves Steel and Manufacturing Company.

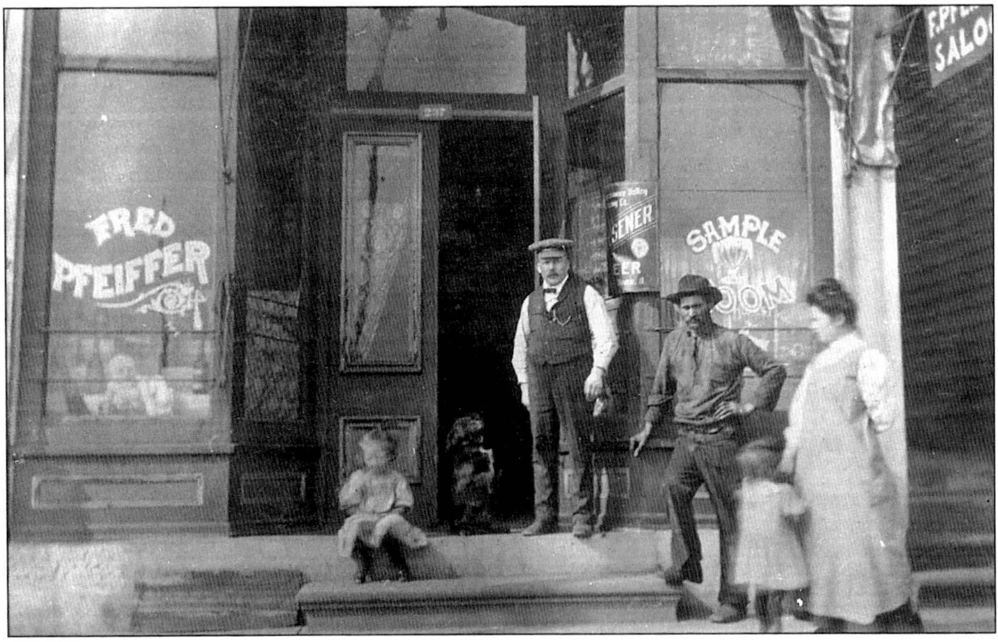

PFEIFER SALOON DOVER, OHIO. During the late 1800s through the period of Prohibition, small saloons served as the gathering places in which to clear the coal, dust, and ash from one's throat after a hard day's work in the mills. The Fred Pfeiffer Saloon in Dover was just one of many small saloons that dotted the cityscapes of the towns and villages of Tuscarawas County. With two breweries in Dover and one in New Philadelphia, the supply was certainly close at hand.

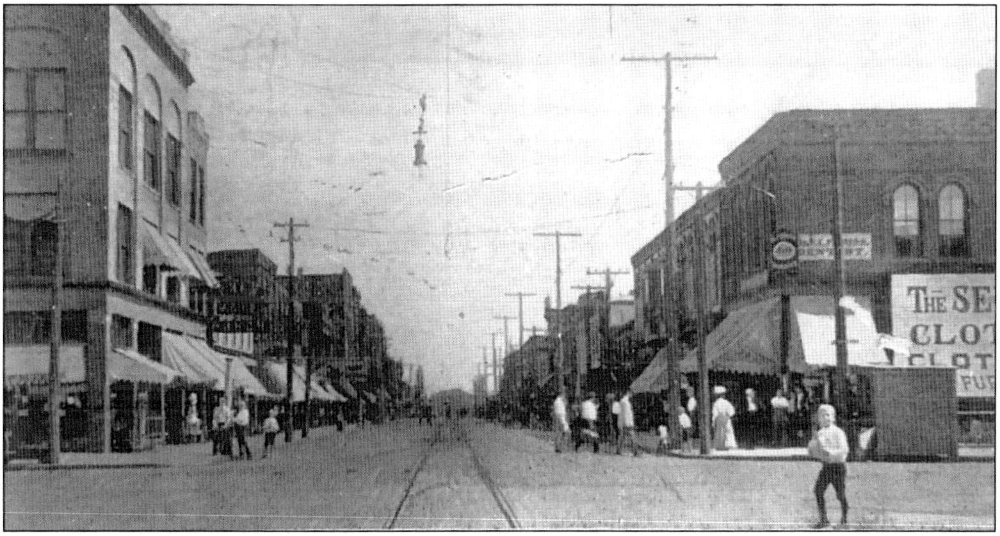

FACTORY STREET LOOKING EAST, CANAL DOVER, OHIO, 1907. This scene captured on many of the popular postcards of the time depicts the very busy factory street in downtown Canal Dover. In 1912, the town's name was changed to Dover. The Senhauser Clothing Company maintained stores in Canal Dover, New Philadelphia, Steubenville, and Zanesville, Ohio, at one time. The building today houses a bicycle shop. Factory Street is currently known as Tuscarawas Avenue.

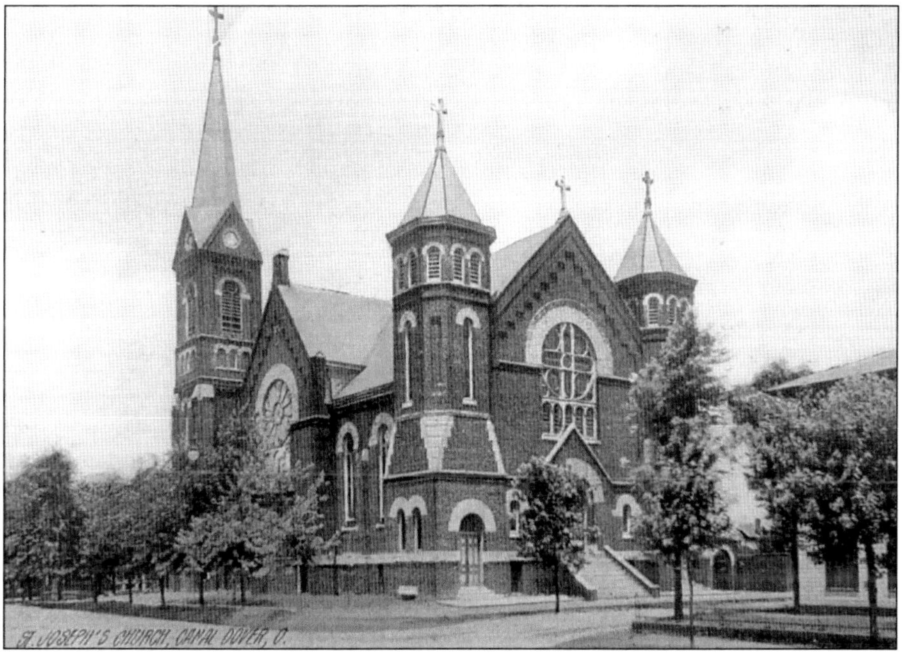

ST. JOSEPH CATHOLIC CHURCH CANAL DOVER, OHIO. The early German immigrants of the Roman Catholic faith established St. Joseph's Church on Factory Street between Sixth and Seventh Streets in Canal Dover, Ohio. The parishioners built this fine structure, which served the faithful until the early 1960s when it was discovered to have many dangerous structural problems. The church was removed, and a new, modern church was built which still serves the parish today.

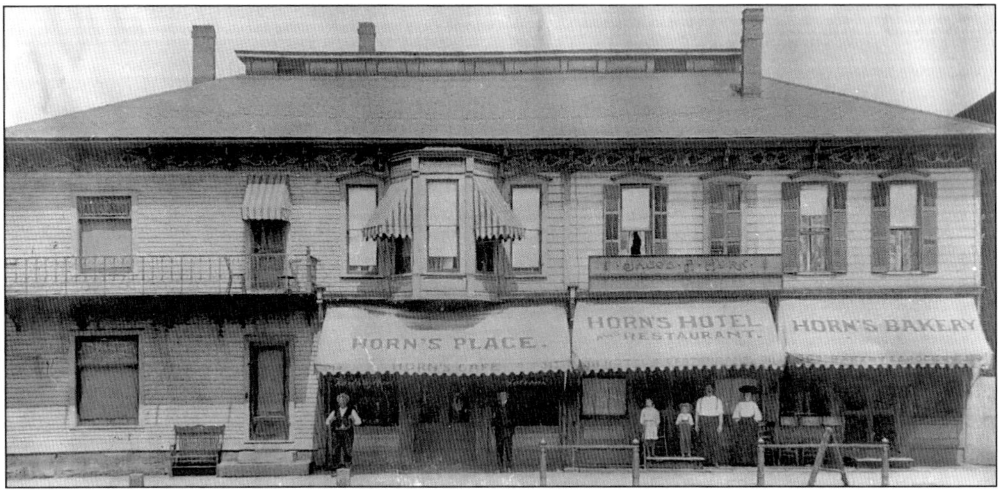

HORN BLOCK CANAL DOVER, OHIO. Jacob A. Horn, born September 1, 1849, was the son of immigrants from Bavaria and became a very prominent businessman of Canal Dover. He began to learn the malting trade, which led to a successful business career. He was one of the four owners of the Big Four Opera House, a fine establishment built in 1890. He owned the block pictured above—two farms, a coal mine, and speculated town lots in Canal Dover.

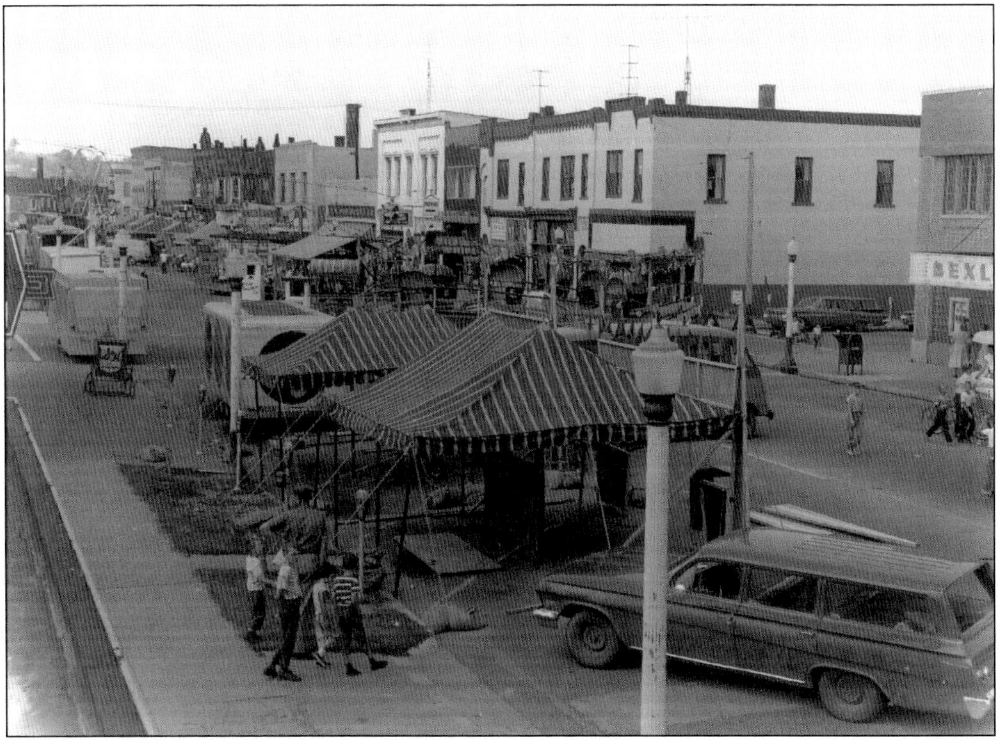

DOVER STREET SCENE 1960S. The towns and villages held street fairs each summer. Today Canal Dover Festival celebrates those days the last weekend in May. This photograph provides a scene of the cityscape of downtown Dover on West Third Street sometime in the 1960s.

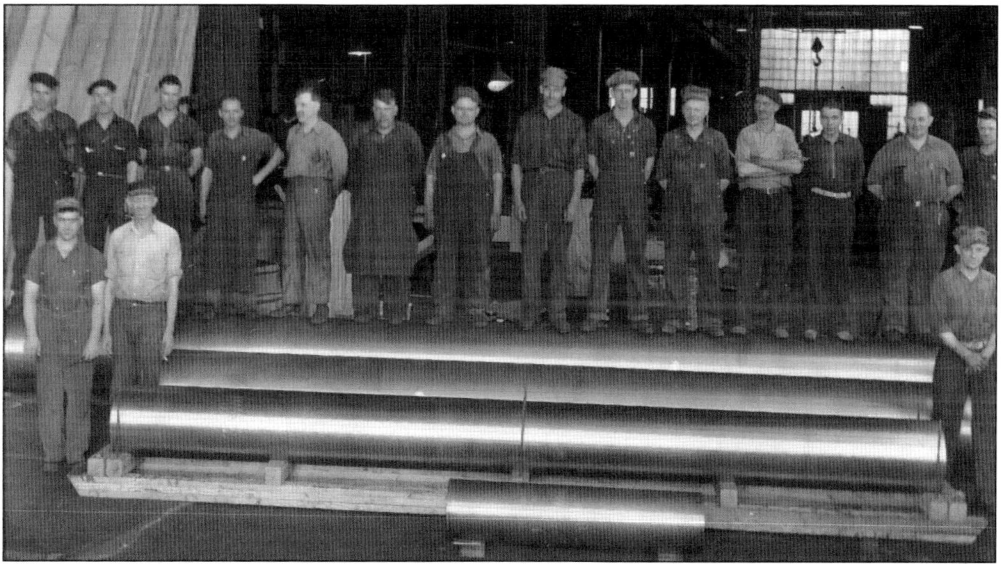

SHENANGO—PENN MOLD COMPANY DOVER, OHIO, LATE 1940S. The Shenango—Penn Mold Company was located at the site of the former Dover Boiler Works on West Third Street in Dover, Ohio. This photograph of a group of the workers was taken in the late 1940s or early 1950s. The company produced fine metals and alloys at its plant. During World War II, it was one of only three companies in Tuscarawas County to receive the Army Navy E Award for exemplary production in aiding the country in its war effort.

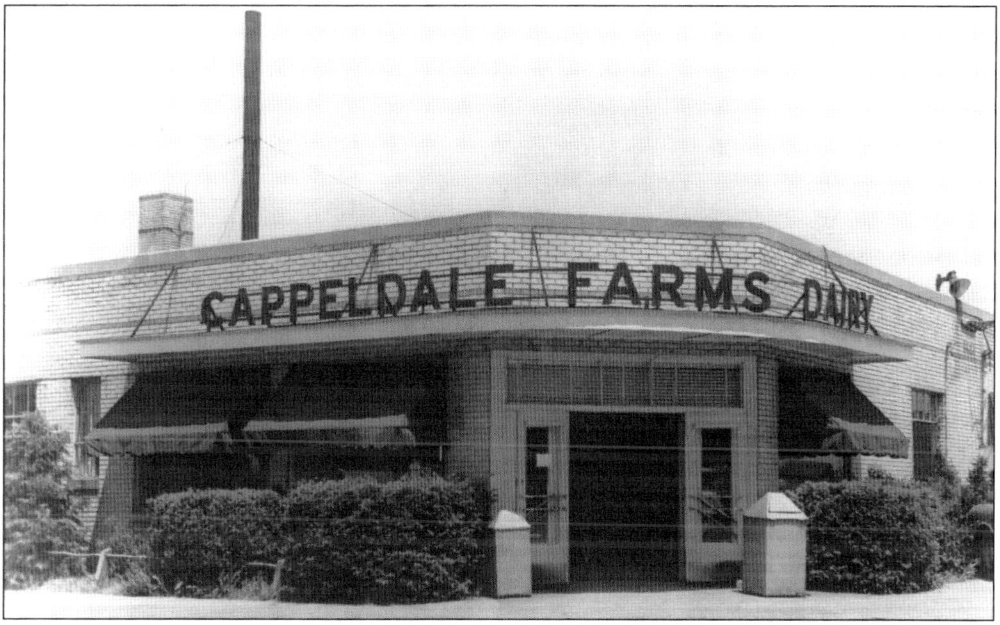

CAPPELDALE FARMS DAIRY DOVER, OHIO. This company, like its competitor in New Philadelphia, the Goshen Dairy Company, produced milk, butter, and ice cream for many customers in Dover and the surrounding area. The store pictured here was built on Crater Avenue, and they had an additional store on the southwest corner of East Fourth and Race Streets. Cappeldale Dairy is no longer in operation, but the building still stands in front of the Dover High School Stadium.

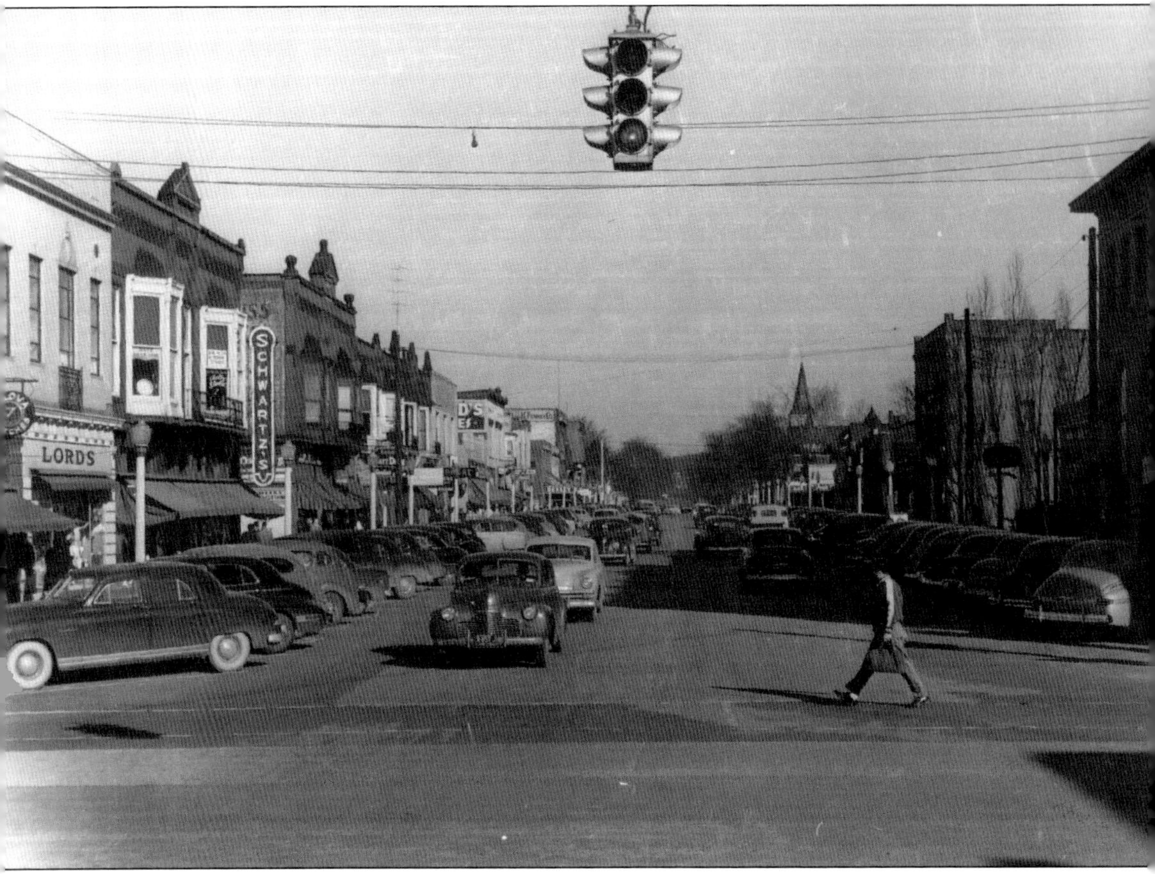

STREET SCENE DOVER, OHIO. This street scene captured in Dover, Ohio, at the intersection of West Tuscarawas Avenue and West Third Street illustrates how the downtown has changed over the years. This photograph taken in the 1950s presents the viewer with many of the businesses that are no longer a part of the downtown. Most of these businesses are not even located in the New Towne Mall—one more reminder of how much things change and yet the cityscape remains the same.

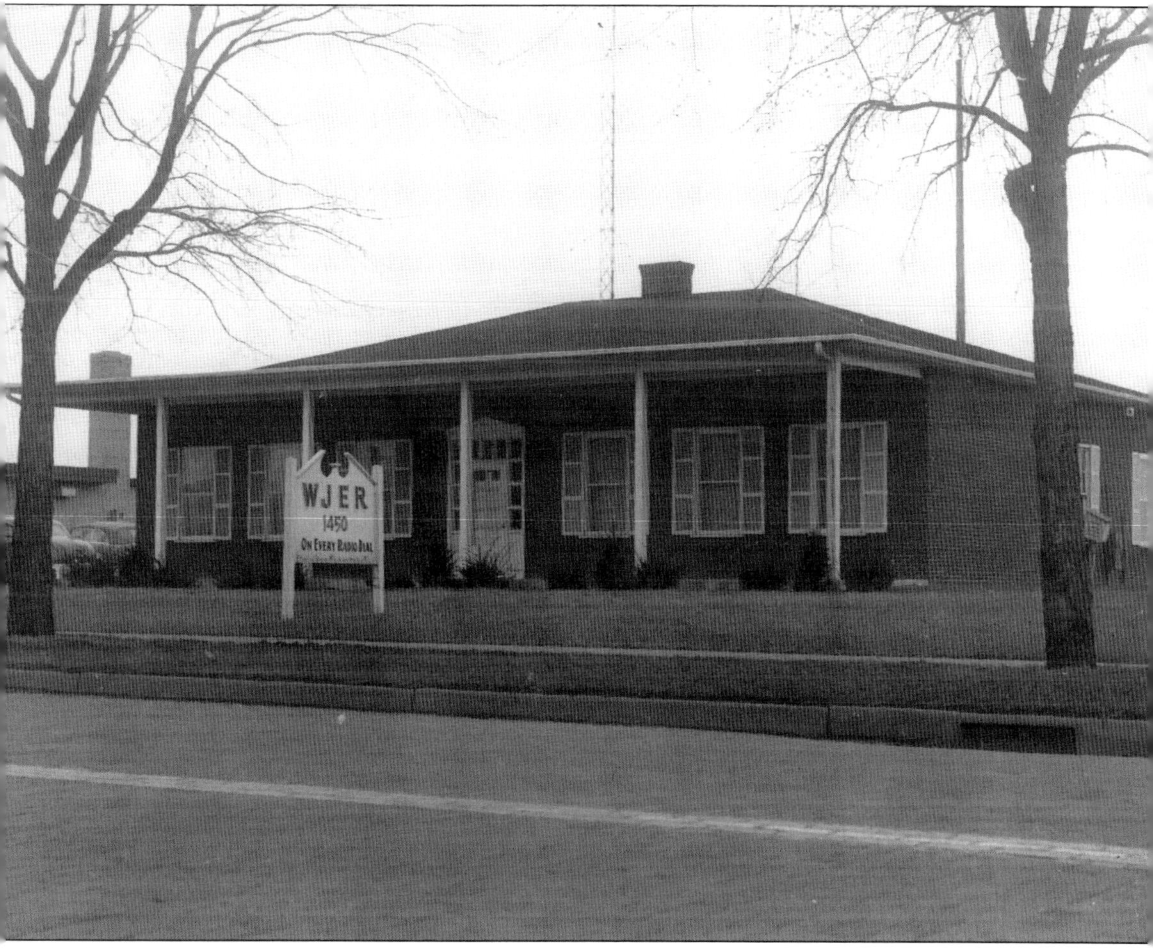

WJER RADIO STATION EARLY 1950S DOVER, OHIO. On the morning of February 22, 1950, the residents of Tuscarawas County turned on their radios to hear the latest in the news. Unlike many previous mornings, they now turned their dials to WJER 1450 AM to hear the latest in the news and happenings in Tuscarawas County. Before they had had to tune in Canton, Zanesville, Pittsburgh, or Cleveland. However, on this day WJER Radio began its operations for the citizens of the valley. The JER stands for Jeremiah E. Reeves, a most prominent businessman and citizen of Tuscarawas County. Today the radio station broadcasts not only on the AM band, but also on FM, has a morning cable television show, and broadcasts over the Internet. The building is located across from Union Hospital on the boulevard in Dover, Ohio.

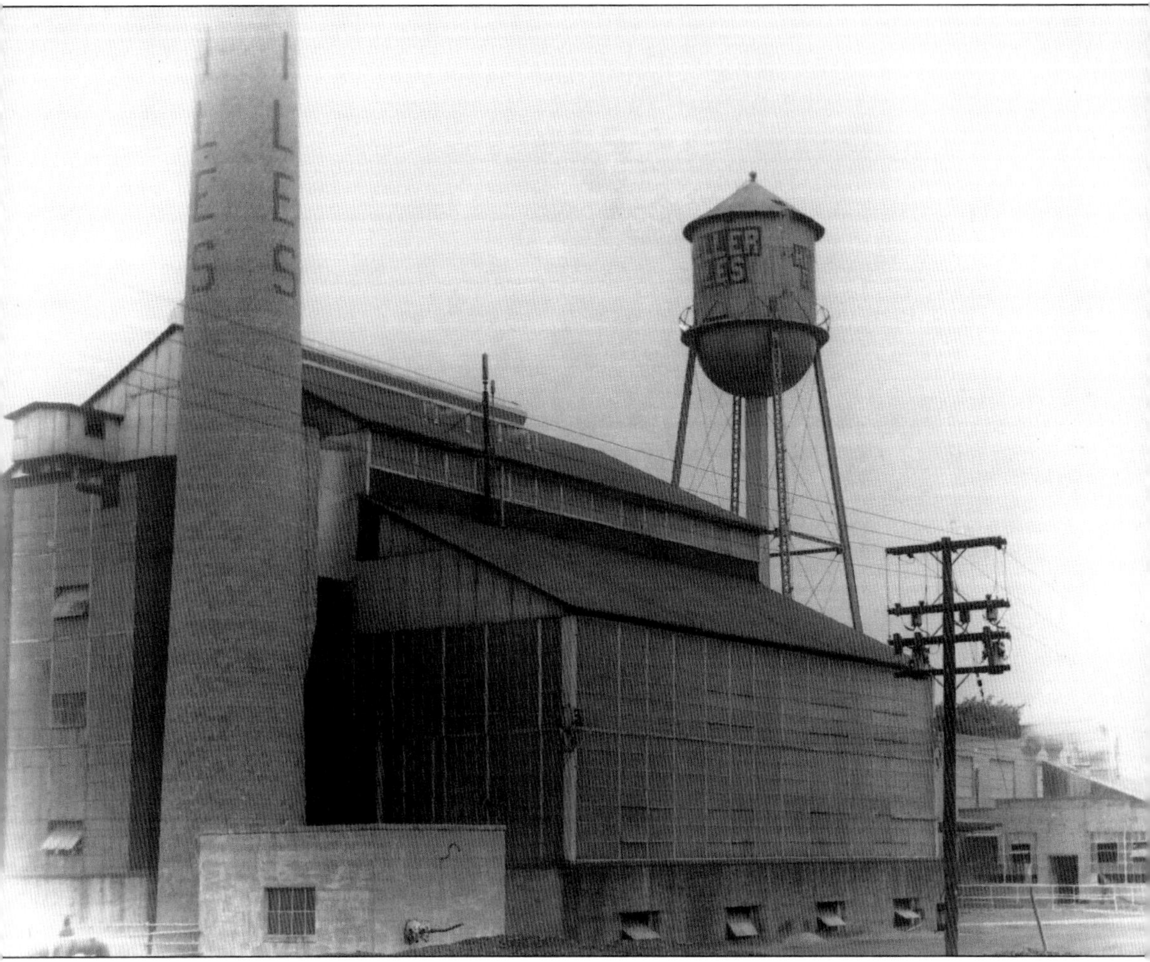

HELLER FILES IN NEWCOMERSTOWN, OHIO. The Heller Files Company of Newcomerstown was one of the three companies in Tuscarawas County to achieve the Army Navy E Award for outstanding production toward the country's war effort in World War II. The company provided many jobs for the citizens of this southern community in Tuscarawas County. Quality files were produced for many years by this firm. In the 1930s, they sponsored a local baseball team coached by none other than Cy Young.

Four

SCENES OF TOWNS AND VILLAGES OF TUSCARAWAS COUNTY

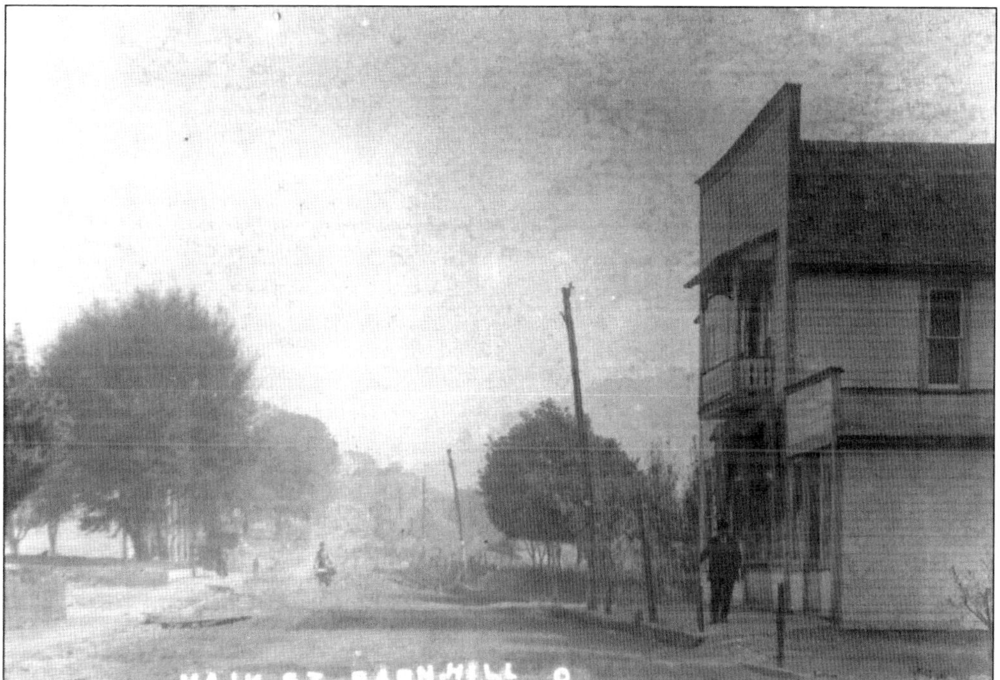

BARNHILL, OHIO. Barnhill, Ohio, named after a prominent judge of Tuscarawas County who had resided in Barnhill, was formerly called Pike's Run. The community prospered from 1880s through the early 1900s as a result of the rich coal fields which lay around the community.

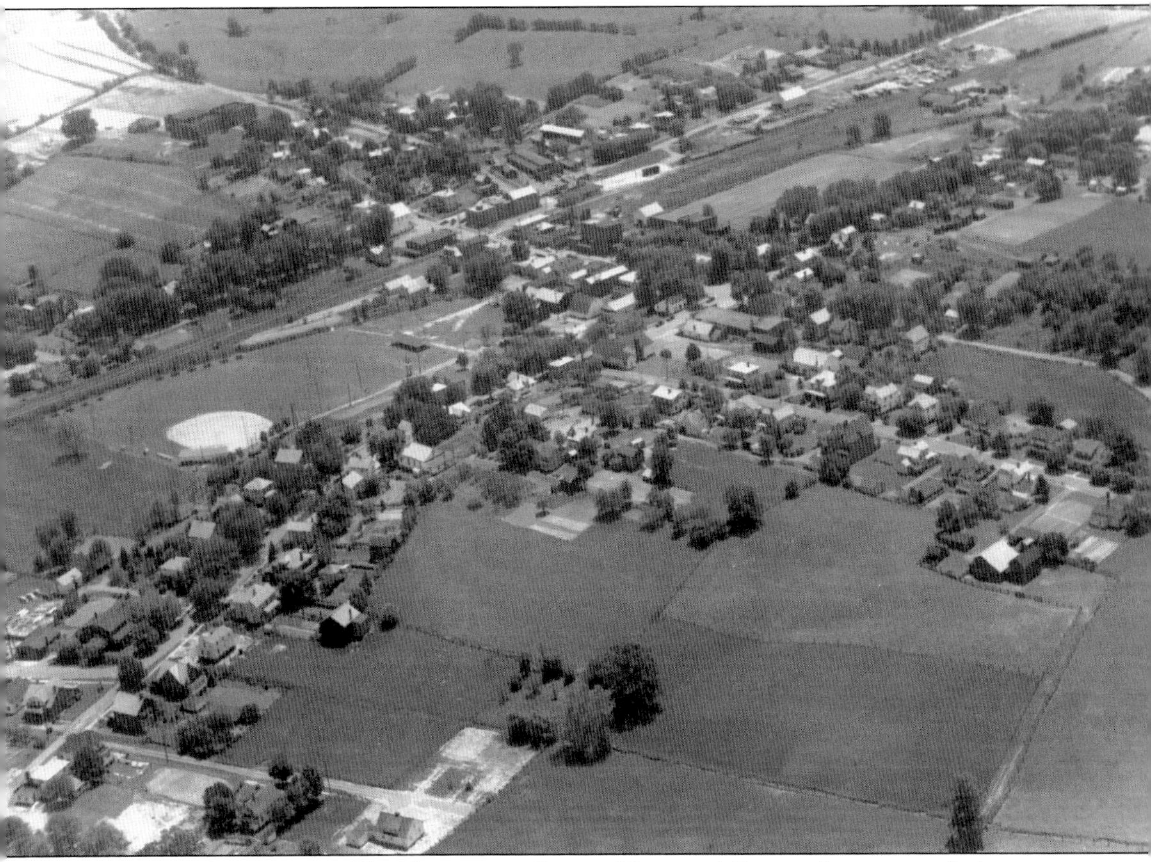

BALTIC, OHIO, 1950. The Tuscarawas County Historical Society has graciously been given over three thousand negatives by the *Times Reporter* which covered the period from the 1950s through the 1970s. Several of the negatives were photographs taken in the summer of 1950 of the towns and villages in Tuscarawas County. This aerial photograph is the Village of Baltic, which lies in the midwestern corner of Tuscarawas County near the Coshocton County line. Baltic was situated on the first official road authorized by the Ohio State Legislature in 1828, which was called the Port Washington Road. Another famous path crosses that road and is known as the Bouquet Trail of 1764, where Col. Bouquet led an army of 1,500 men from Fort Pitt to near present-day Coshocton to retrieve approximately two hundred white captives of the Native Americans who had been taken from their homes in Pennsylvania.

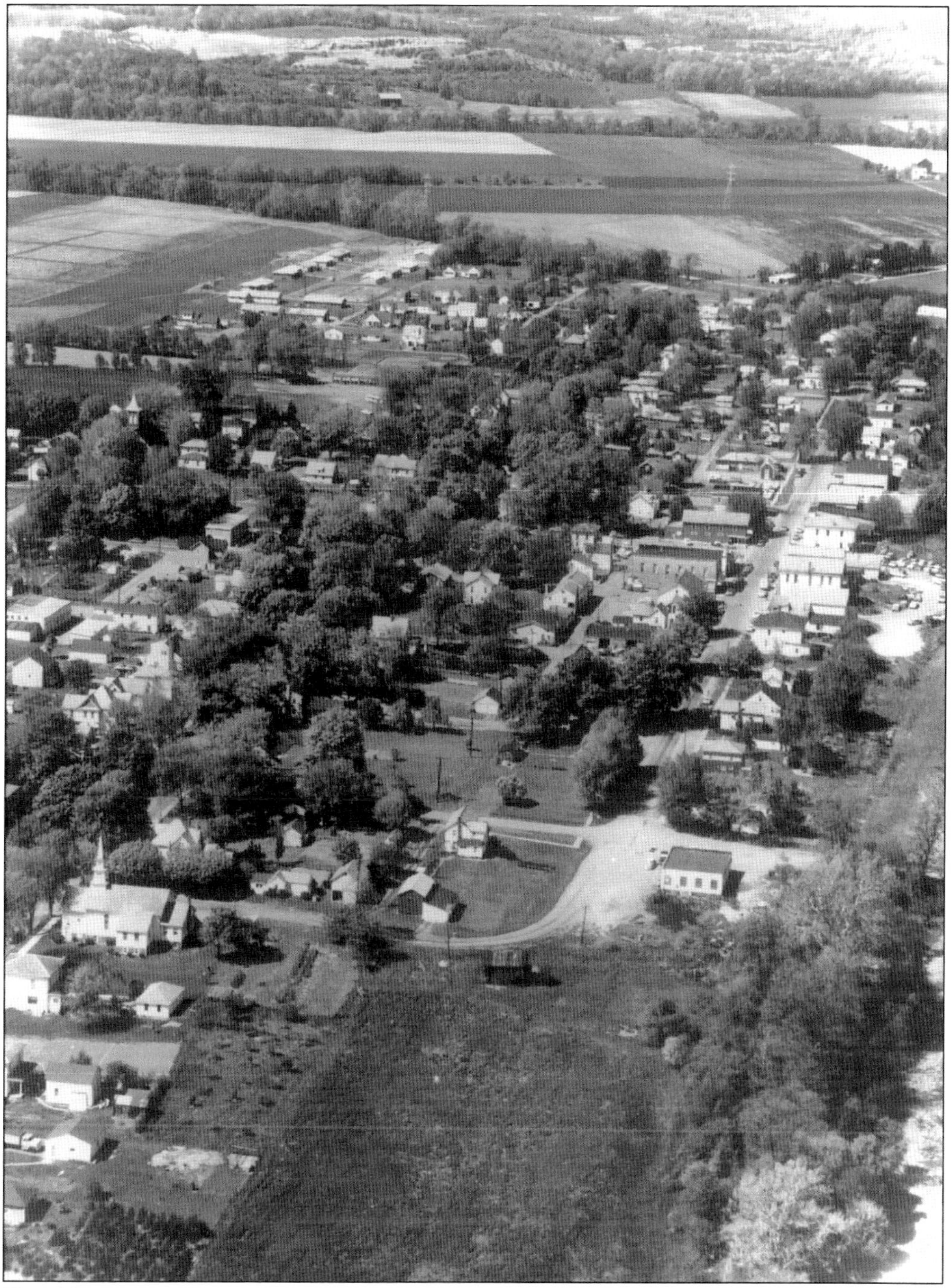

THE VILLAGE OF BOLIVAR LOOKING NORTH 1963. This aerial photograph shows the town of Bolivar, Ohio, looking to the north. Along the right side of the picture, remnants of the Ohio Erie Canal are visible. In the upper right hand portion of the photograph, southern Stark County, where the site of the cabin of Christian Frederick Post and John Heckewelder was built in 1761, is visible. The Town of Bolivar was laid out in 1825 and was named after "the George Washington of South America," Simon Bolivar. The town boomed during the canal period.

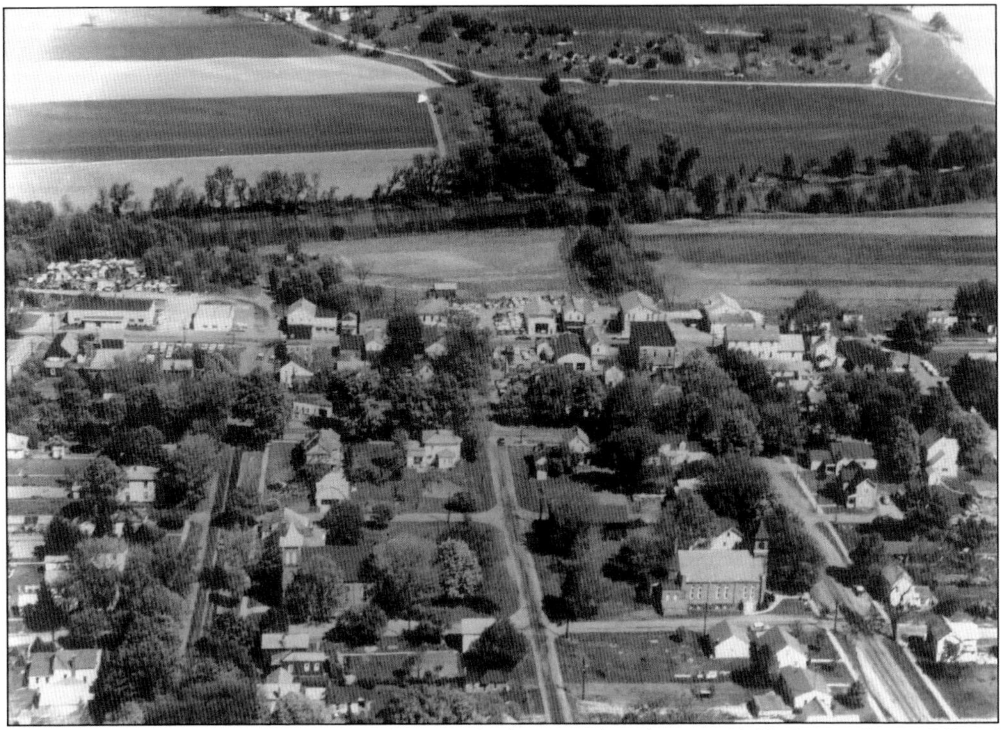

BOLIVAR, OHIO, LOOKING EAST. This aerial photograph taken in 1963 shows the middle of Bolivar, Ohio, looking east. The grove of trees in the middle of the picture is demonstrative of the end of the Sandy Beaver Canal which joined the Ohio River with the Ohio Erie Canal. Interstate 77 is not represented in this picture, for the super highway was not completed through this section of Ohio until the late 1960s.

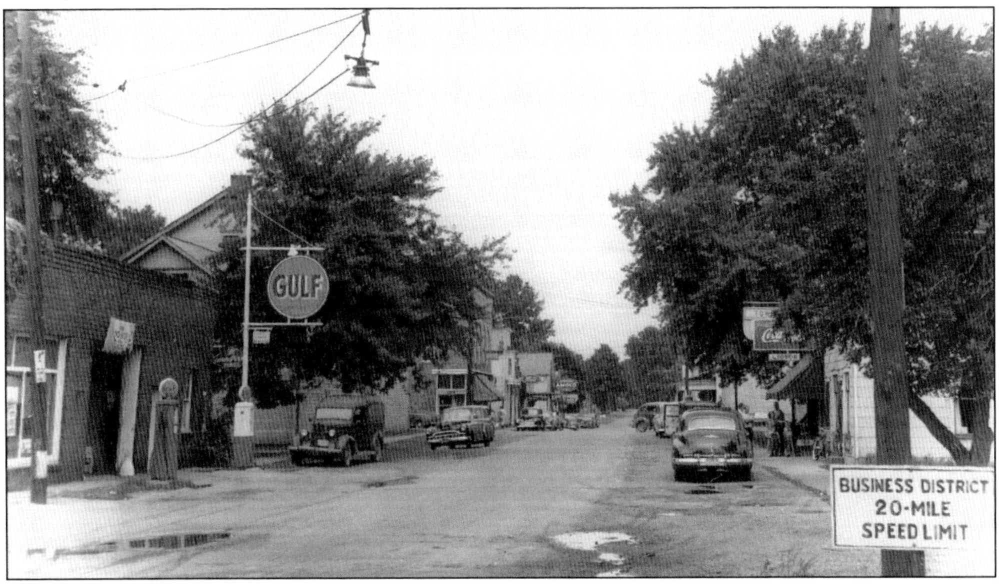

STREET SCENE OF BOLIVAR, OHIO, IN THE 1940S. This photograph depicts a street scene of downtown Bolivar during the late 1940s. This was the main street which fronted the Ohio Erie Canal, and the buildings in this picture were regularly used during the canal period.

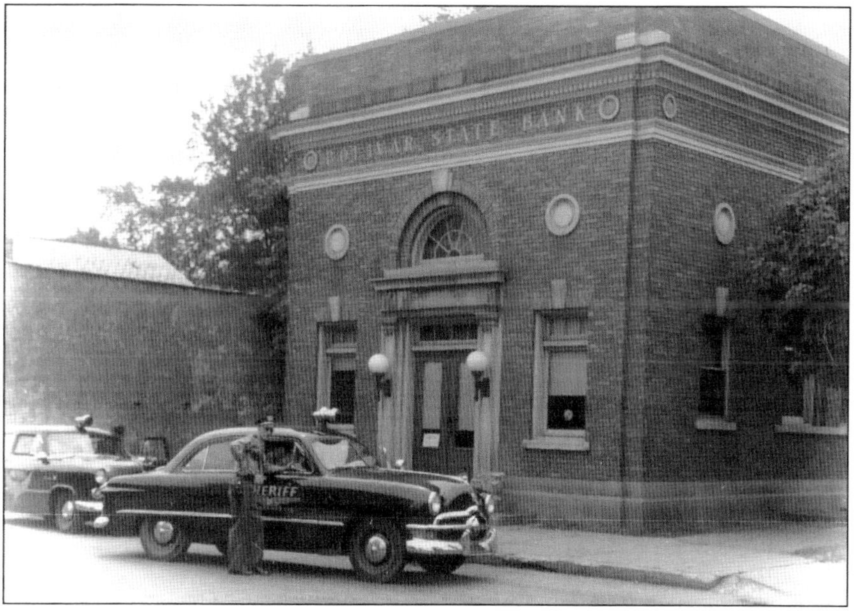

BOLIVAR STATE BANK BOLIVAR, OHIO, EARLY 1950S. A few businessmen of the community established the Bolivar State Bank in the very early 1900s. The Reeves Banking and Trust Company of Dover, Ohio, purchased the bank, which was later bought out by the Huntington Bank of Columbus, Ohio. It is unknown why the highway patrol car and Tuscarawas County Sheriff's car are included in this image.

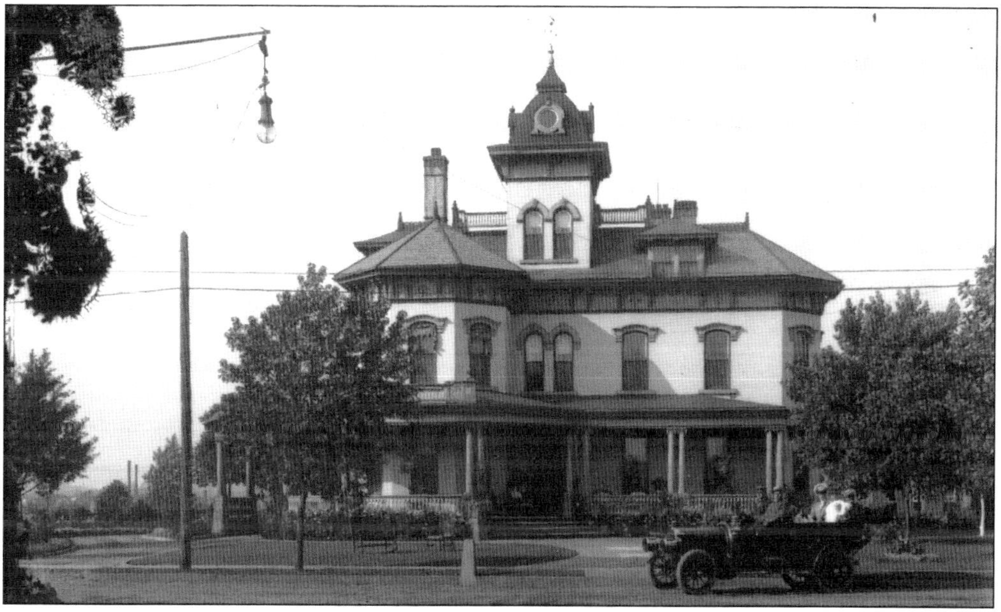

REEVES HOME DOVER, OHIO, EARLY 1900S. The stately Reeves Home on East Iron Avenue, Dover, Ohio, has been lovingly preserved and maintained by the Dover Historical Society. The home reflects the status and prominence of this family, who provided so much for Dover and Tuscarawas County citizens. They have provided jobs for thousands in Tuscarawas County for nearly one hundred years. In addition, their trust fund has provided much-needed capital for the many organizations, schools, and government entities.

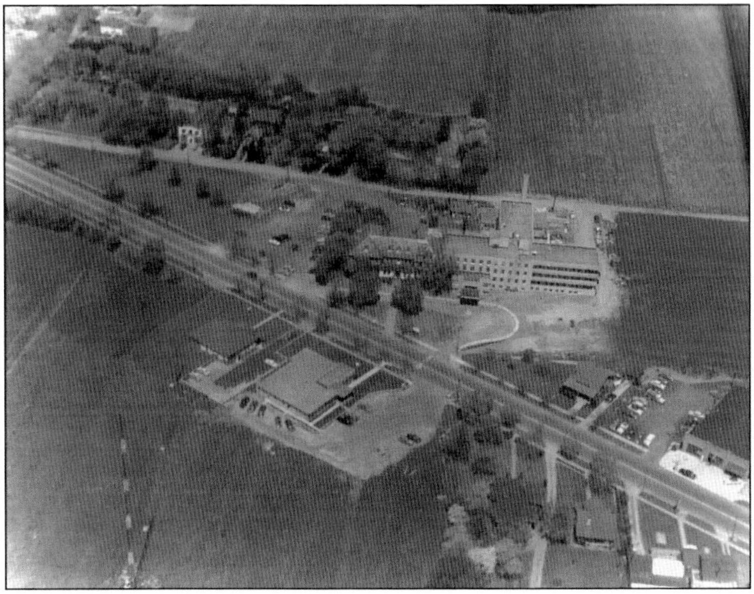

UNION HOSPITAL DOVER, OHIO. The older portion of Union Hospital, the smaller structure in the middle of the picture surrounded by trees, was begun in 1908. This remarkable photograph depicts the building in the late 1950s. Today the open fields in this picture are filled with buildings and businesses that have expanded the outreach of the health community. Tuscarawas County also has a hospital which serves the Dennison Uhrichsville area known as the Twin City Hospital.

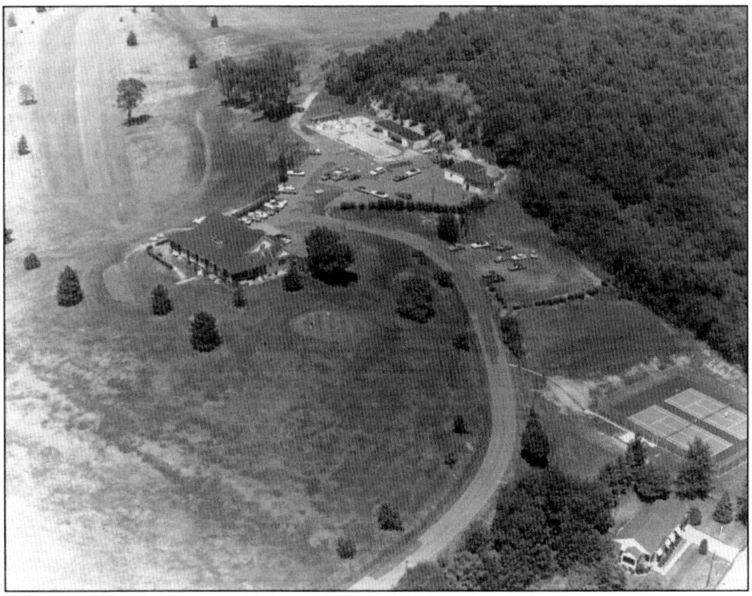

UNION COUNTRY CLUB DOVER, OHIO, 1960. The Union Country Club, established in 1909, had a disastrous fire in 1916. It then moved to this structure on the hills between Dover and New Philadelphia, Ohio, where they established a fine 18-hole golf course and added a swimming pool and tennis courts over the years. This picture shows the old country club, for this facility is now the new golf course. A modern club, including a swim and tennis site was constructed nearer to Union Hospital.

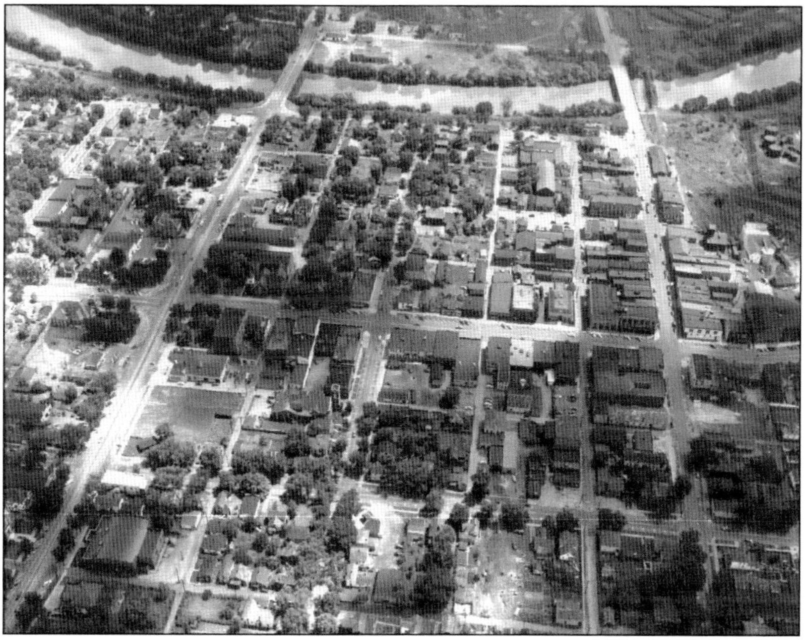

DOWNTOWN DOVER, OHIO, 1962. This photograph of Downtown Dover illustrates the many changes that have occurred over the past 38 years. In the lower left-hand corner is the famous Dover Memorial Hall, where on many a cold February night thousands of rabid basketball fans would come to support their communities in the famous Tuscarawas County B Tournaments.

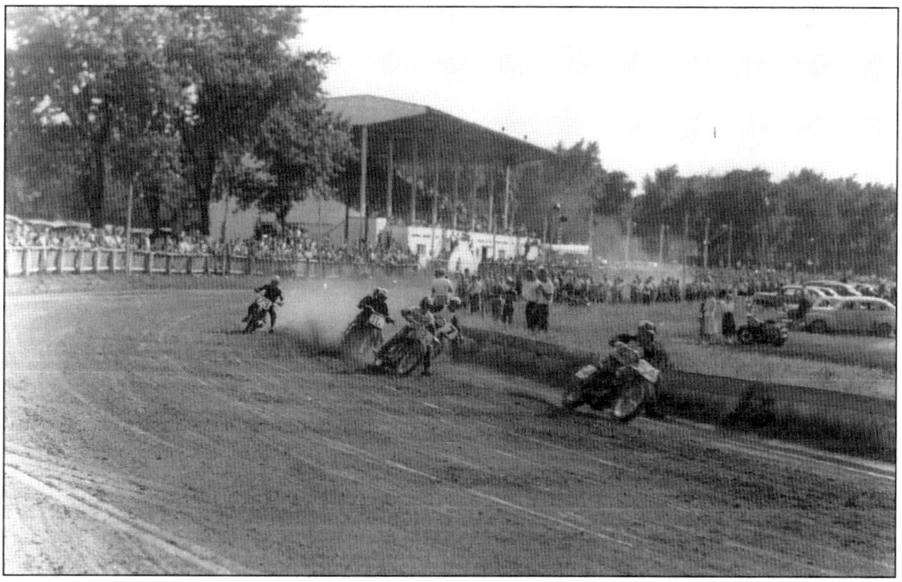

TUSCARAWS COUNTY FAIRGROUNDS 1950S. The Tuscarawas County Fair began in the year 1850. This area was turned into Camp Meigs during the Civil War in order to train members of the 51st OVI and other regiments for their responsibilities in assisting the Union forces during that tragic event in American history. The first few Dover-New Philadelphia football games were held on Thanksgiving Day at the fairgrounds, and during the 1930s, the Cleveland Indians came to the fairgrounds. From the 1940s through the 1960s, motorcycle racing was held on the dirt track at the fairgrounds.

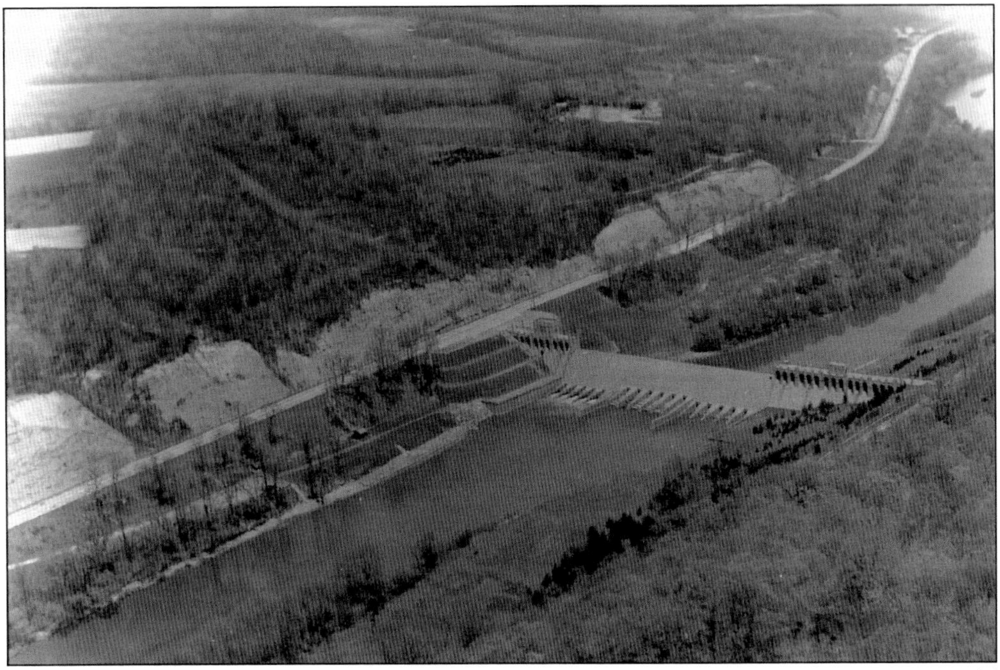

DOVER DAM. During a heavy rain, the creeks, streams, and rivers of Tuscarawas County would overflow their banks and flood the surrounding countryside. There were many floods of major proportions up to the flood of 1913. In the 1930s, it was decided to build a series of dams to establish flood storage areas in eastern Ohio. This resulted in the creation of Bolivar Dam, Atwood Dam, and Dover Dam in Tuscarawas County. The Bolivar and Dover Dams are storage dams to pool runoff water from severe storms. Dover Dam, pictured here, is one of the most scenic dams in the county.

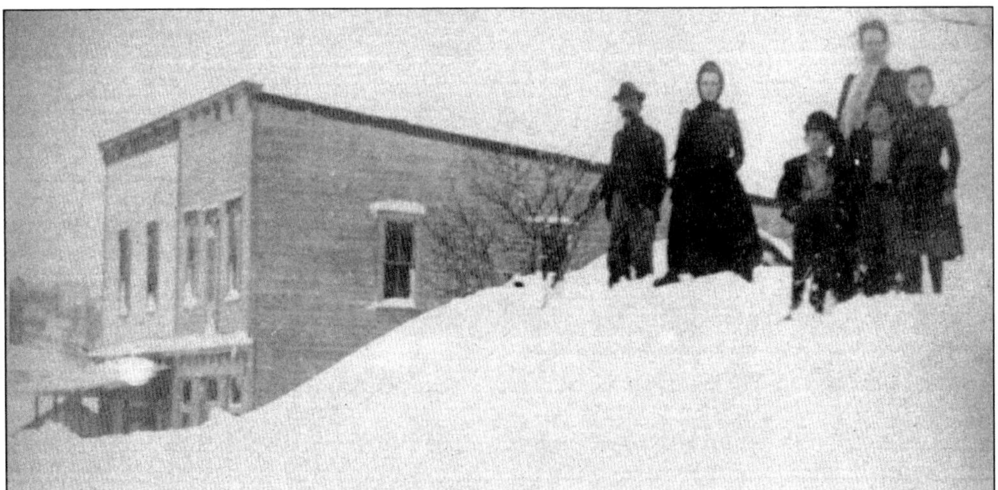

SNOWSTORM GILMORE, OHIO. Located in southeastern Tuscarawas County is the small community of Gilmore. On a cold winter day in 1901, the residents of this community awoke to the aftermath of this huge snowstorm which lasted for four days in April. The residents are not standing on a small hill, but rather on a large drift which formed from the snow and winds associated with one of the largest snowfalls (in some places 2–4 feet) in Tuscarawas County.

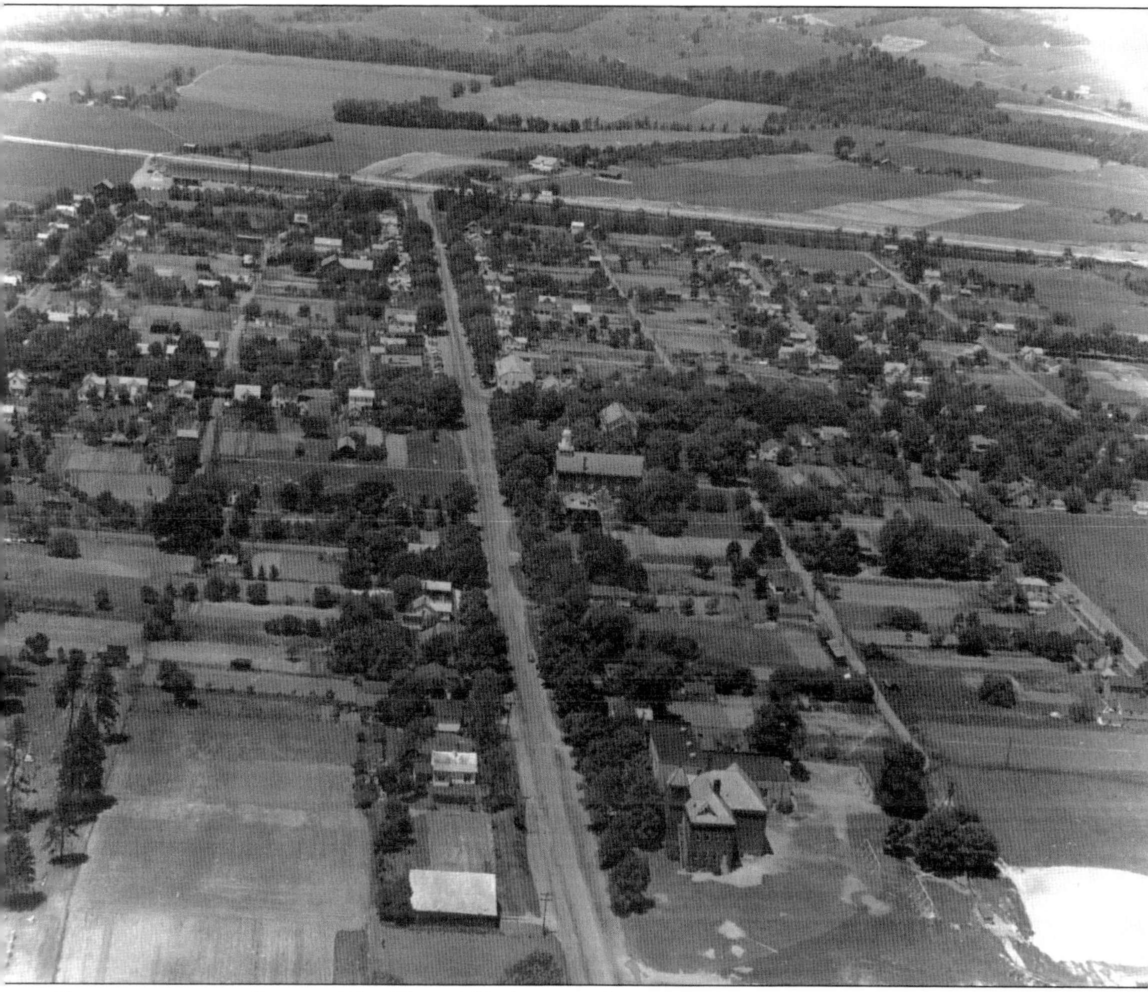

GNADENHUTTEN, OHIO, 1950. This 1950 photograph is of the historic town of Gnadenhutten, Ohio. It provides us with an excellent example of why John Heckewelder, David Zeisberger, and the Delaware Indians settled in this region, which included long, open fields in which to plant 300 acres of corn. The Tuscarawas River is shown along the tree line at the top of the picture. The Indian Village lay to the left of this picture.

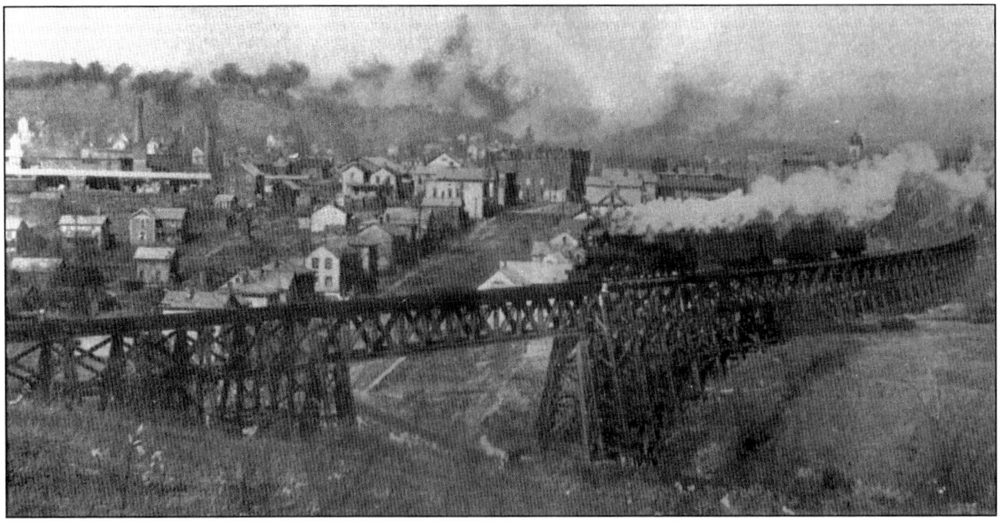

MINERAL CITY, OHIO, 1907. The Village of Mineral City was once a very busy and bustling center of economic activity in the county. Situated near coal fields and clay deposits, the town soon became a thriving community with many businesses and factories. Every few minutes, a train would pass through the village filled with coal or passengers. They even published their own newspaper, which was called the *Mineral Pointer*.

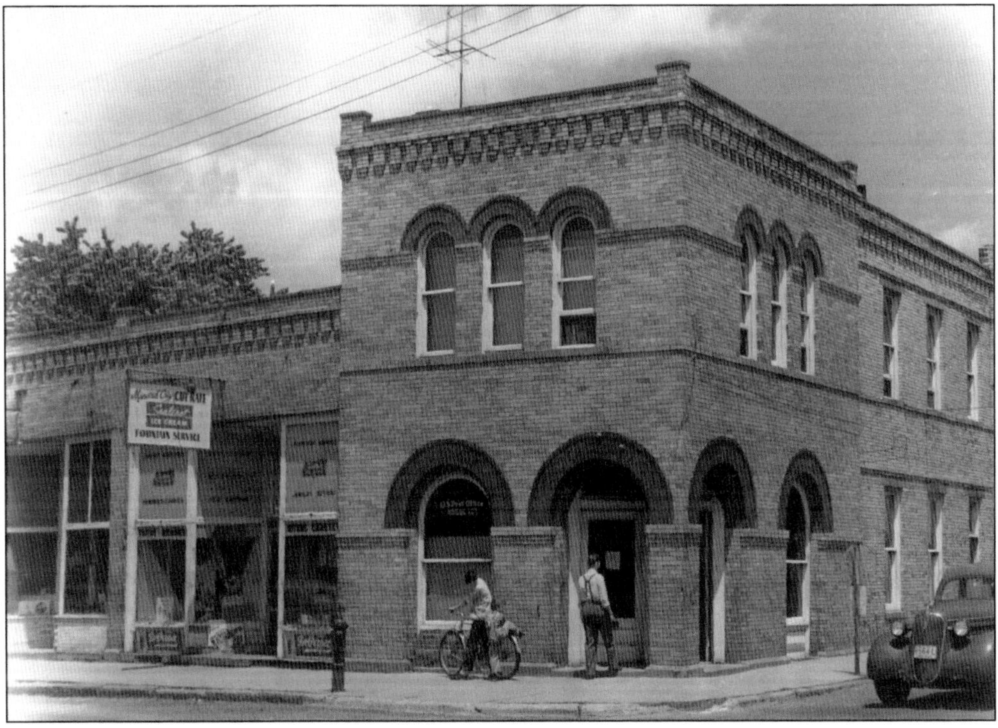

MINERAL CITY, OHIO, LATE 1940s. This photograph was taken of one of the buildings which had been constructed during the heyday of the town. The photographer was standing alongside State Route 8—now 800—when he snapped this picture of the Mineral City Post Office. The building still stands, but the post office was moved into more modern facilities further up the street in the 1970s.

CY YOUNG IN HIS FAVORITE CHAIR EARLY 1950S. The most famous name in baseball, Cy Young, was born in Tuscarawas County, Ohio, in 1867. After a successful career in which he established records that still stand, he was inducted into the first class of the National Baseball Hall of Fame in Cooperstown, New York, in 1939. Cy returned to his home after his illustrious career and picked up the vocation he loved most, tilling the soil of his native county. Cy Young passed away on November 4, 1955, and is buried on a hillside not far from his birthplace in the small community of Peoli.

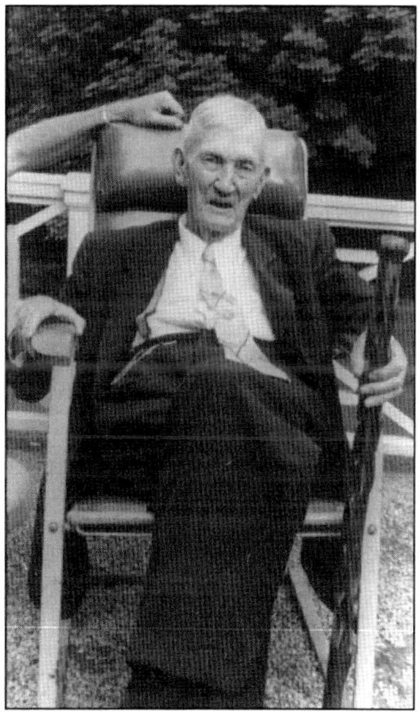

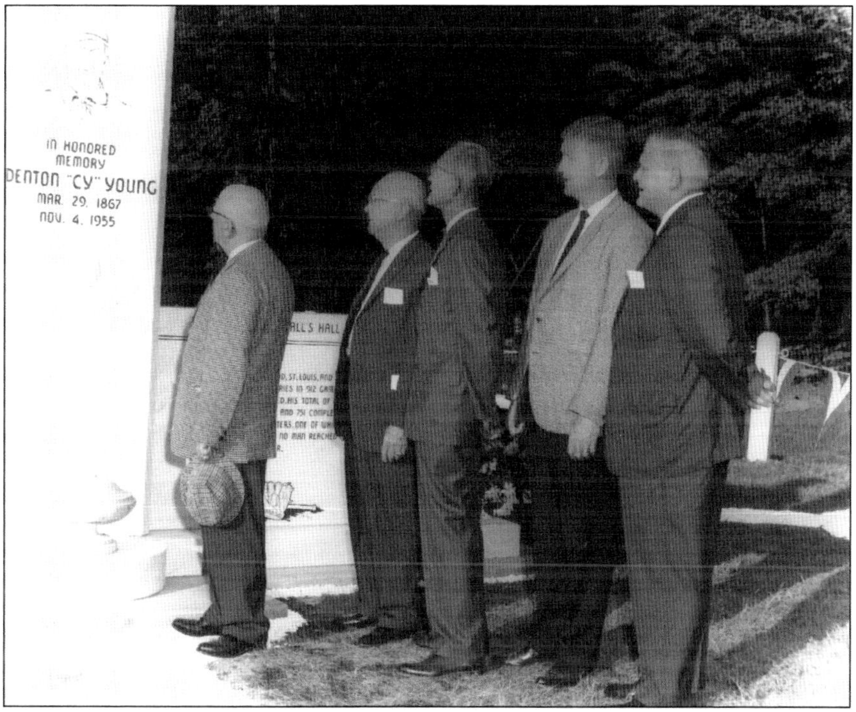

CY YOUNG MEMORIAL NEWCOMERSTOWN, OHIO, 1967. On the centennial of Denton True Young's birth, the citizens of Newcomerstown created this memorial which stands in Cy Young Memorial Park. On the day of the dedication, many of the greats of baseball and other celebrities returned to pay their respect to one of baseball's legends. In this picture observing the memorial are (second from the right) noted Cleveland Indian pitcher and longtime radio sportscaster Herb Score, and (on the far right) Newcomerstown graduate, Wayne Woodrow "Woody" Hayes, the revered coach for three decades of the Ohio State Buckeyes.

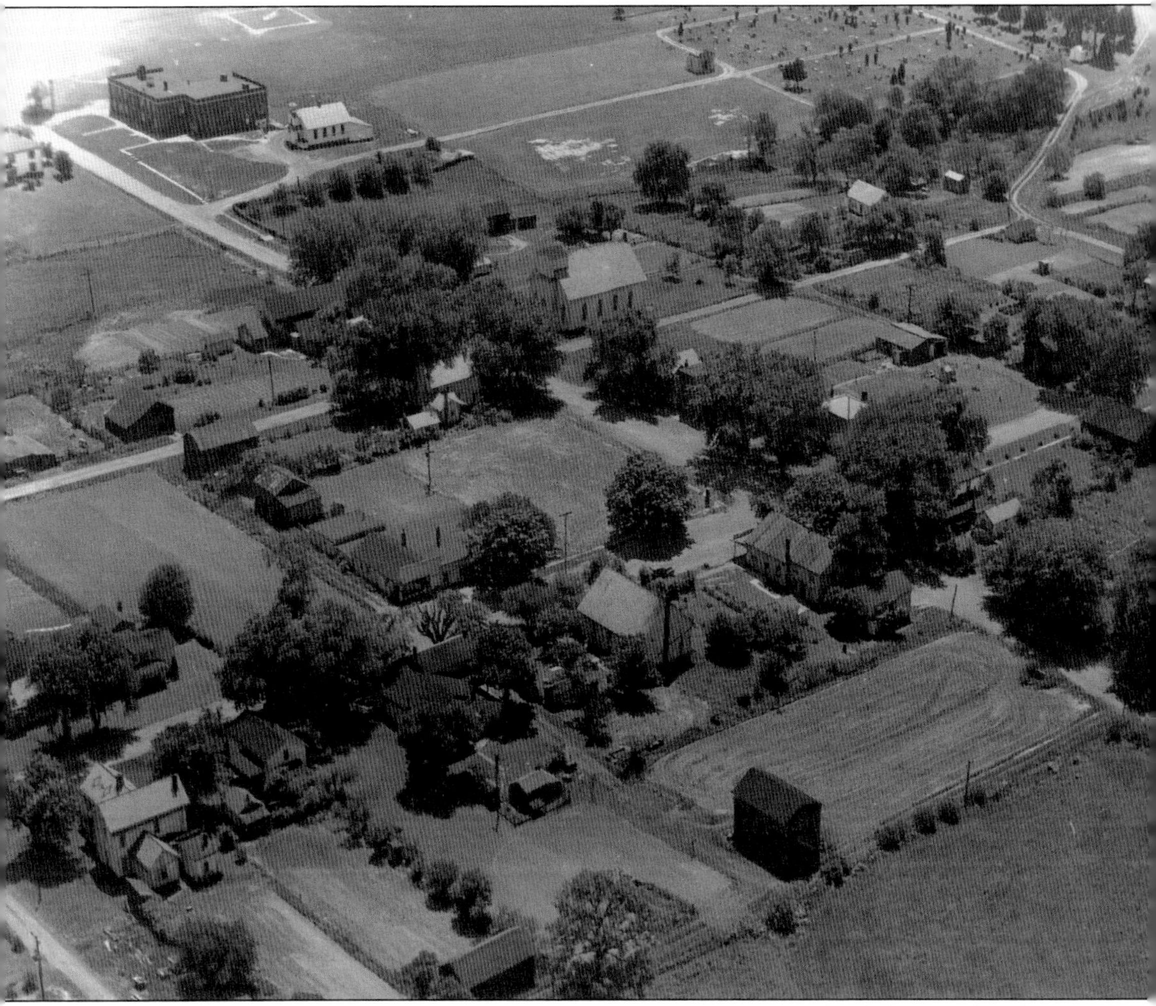

NEW CUMBERLAND, OHIO, 1950. The Village of New Cumberland lies at the furthest northeast point in Tuscarawas County. Philip Sutter established the town in the year 1826. Its first post office was built in 1831 with David McConnell, a merchant, serving as the postmaster. The Grist Mill built in 1820 by George Stoody—later known as the Stoneman Mill—was razed in the mid-1930s due to the construction of the Atwood Dam. The town was incorporated in 1949 with Joseph Kerr as the first mayor. However, as the town's population decreased, it later became unincorporated. The schoolhouse which sits in the upper left-hand corner of the picture is now a grade school for children in grades K–4. The author has many fond memories of the community—its parents and children—for he served as head teacher at the building in the mid-1960s.

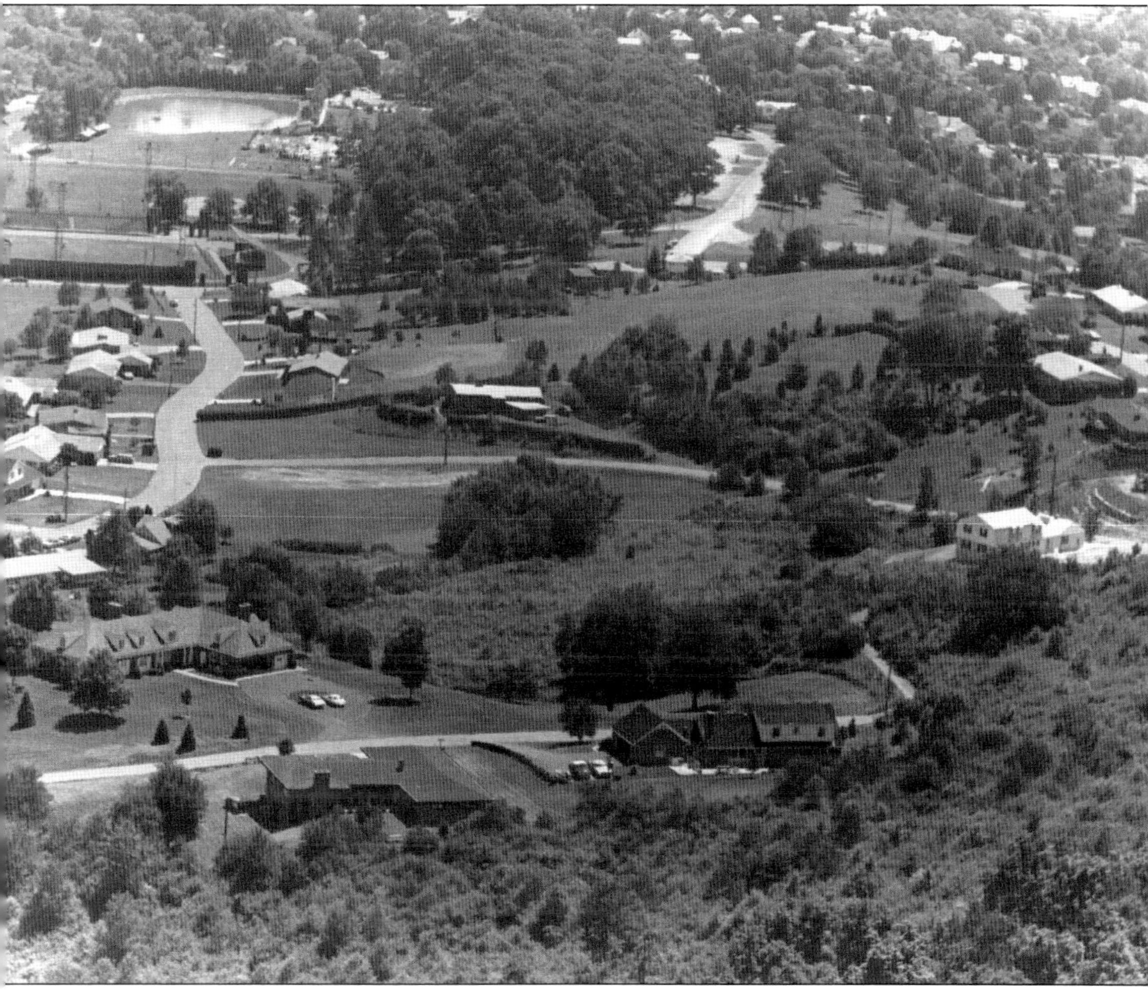

LAGOON AND TUSCORA PARK IN NEW PHILADELPHIA, OHIO. In 1907, this region at the northern end of New Philadelphia was purchased to provide a recreational site for the people of New Philadelphia. That park, which was taken over by the City of New Philadelphia in 1912, has become a living jewel for the citizens of not only New Philadelphia but also for those who live in eastern Ohio. The stadium, which can be seen in the upper left-hand corner of the picture, was the place where three Ohio Hall of Fame coaches plied their art—Johnny Brickels, Woody Hayes, and Bill Kidd. The park's many amusements were rejuvenated by the formation of RTY, Inc., a non-profit civic organization, which has renovated the historic Spillman Carousel, along with the many other mechanical amusement rides for children and adults.

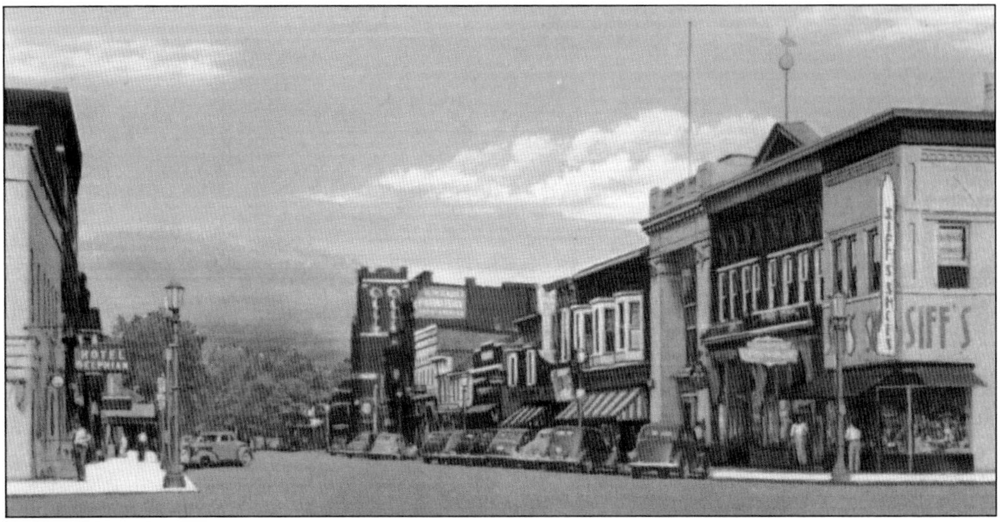

WEST HIGH STREET IN NEW PHILADELPHIA, OHIO. Postcards help to recall many sites and cityscapes that refresh our memories of how things had been. This scene of West High Street from the square looking west, has the famous fish weathervane atop the second building on the right. The story associated with this symbol is interesting and factual. When the men returned from the Civil War, they fired their guns as they began to reach the square. Legend has it that one of the bullets pierced the weathervane fish. It is no longer on the building pictured but is now in a private collection.

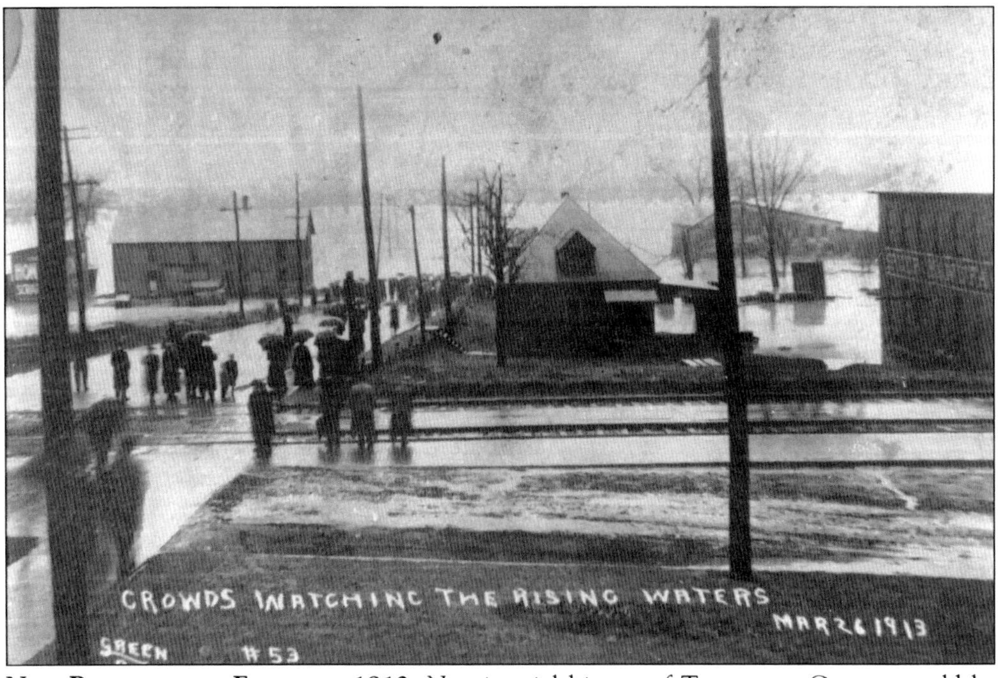

NEW PHILADELPHIA FLOOD OF 1913. No pictorial history of Tuscarawas County would be complete without a few documents on the terrible flood of 1913. The Society possesses a number of flood pictures from the New Philadelphia and Port Washington area. This picture was taken just above the B&O Railroad tracks looking toward what is currently known as the south side in New Philadelphia.

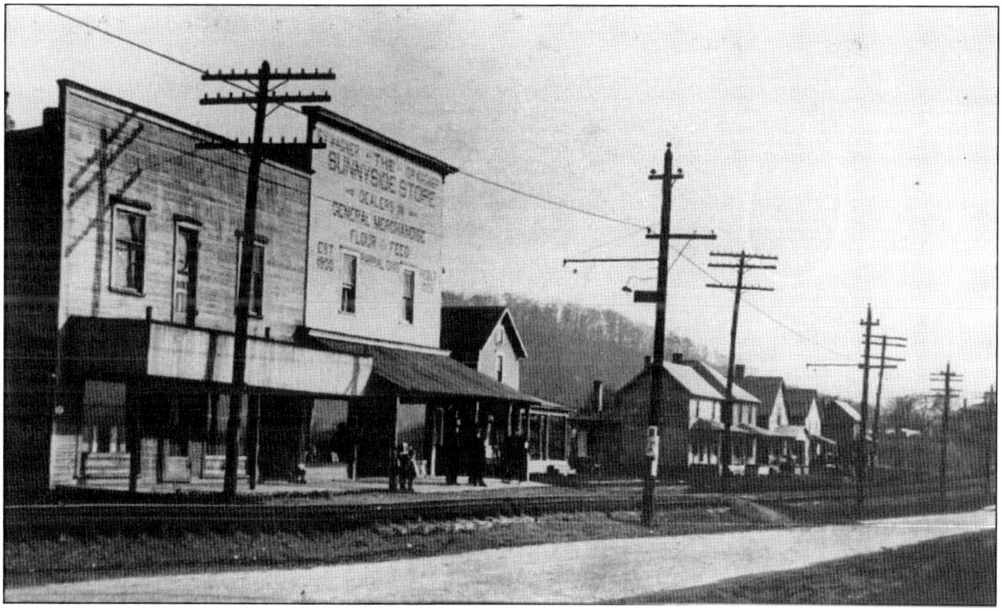

PARRAL IN 1908. The little village of Parral, which is now incorporated into the town of Dover, was on a major highway—US Route 21—and was on the Interurban line which ran from Massillon through the Dover-New Philadelphia area. The area was known as Sunnyside at the turn of the twentieth century. It had one of the best baseball fields in the county and fielded a top-notch team for many years.

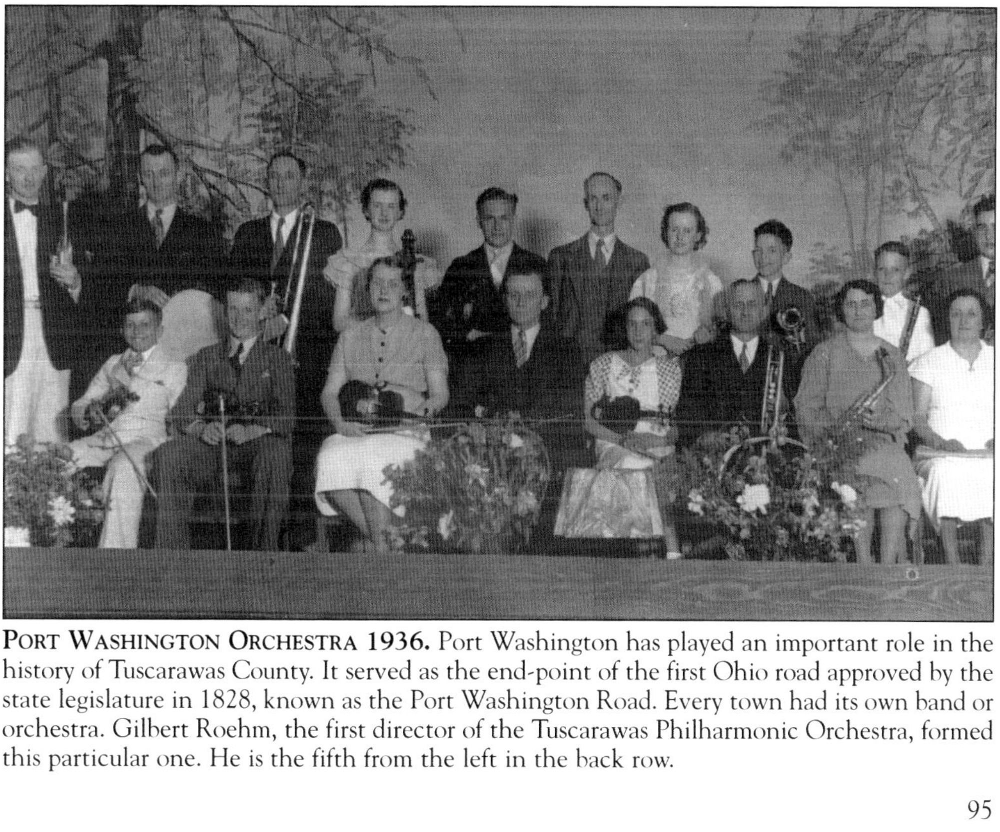

PORT WASHINGTON ORCHESTRA 1936. Port Washington has played an important role in the history of Tuscarawas County. It served as the end-point of the first Ohio road approved by the state legislature in 1828, known as the Port Washington Road. Every town had its own band or orchestra. Gilbert Roehm, the first director of the Tuscarawas Philharmonic Orchestra, formed this particular one. He is the fifth from the left in the back row.

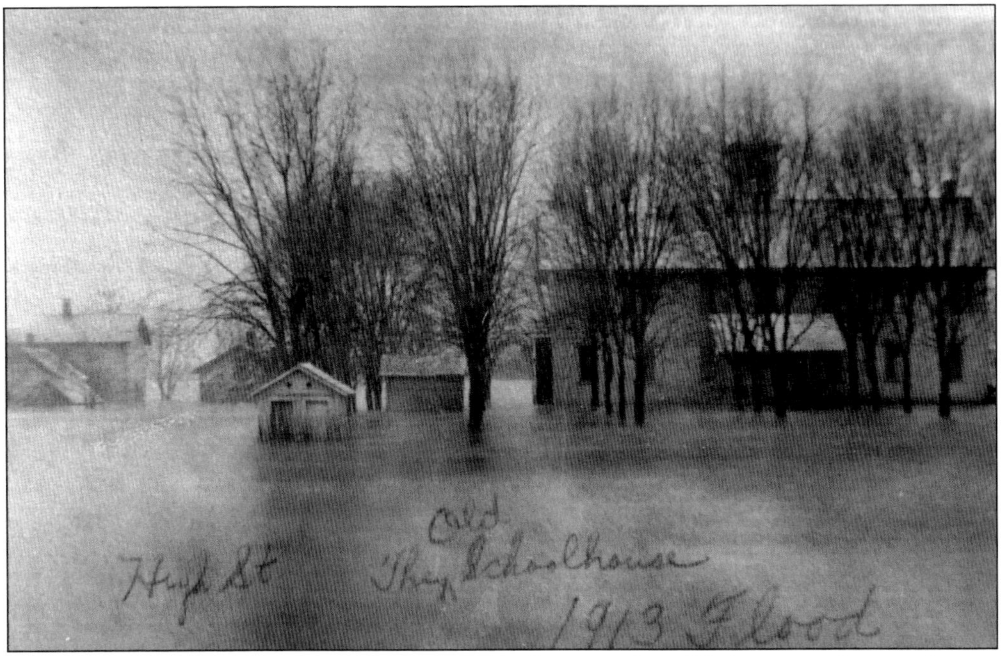

PORT WASHINGTON FLOOD OF 1913. The schoolhouse at Port Washington, along with most of the homes of the town, was caught in the ravages of that disastrous flood.

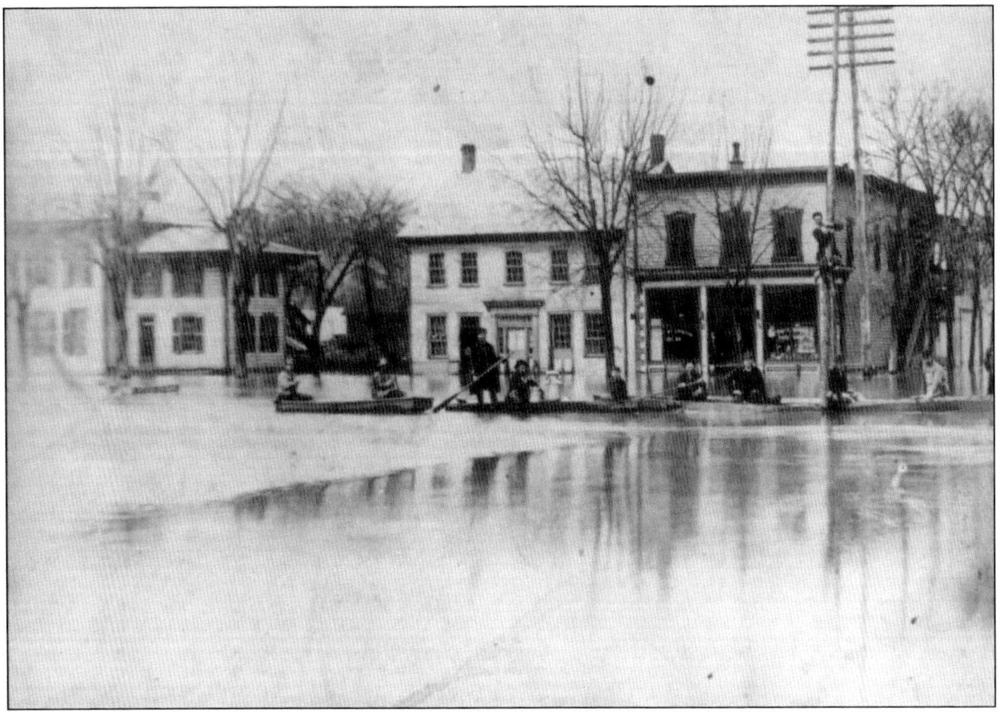

PORT WASHINGTON FLOOD OF 1913—A VIEW OF DOWNTOWN. The photograph of the Kilgore Home on the left captured the serious nature of the flood in Port Washington in the spring of 1913. Notice the young man on the pole in the center near right of the picture. In spite of the destruction caused by the flood, a sense of humor still prevailed.

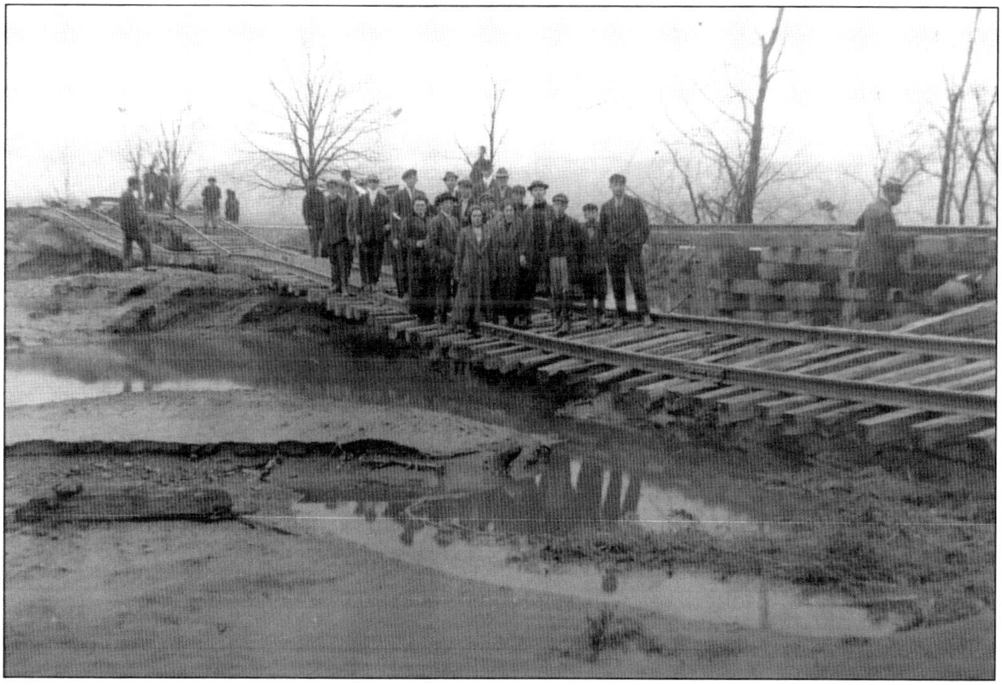

THE MIGHTY FORCE OF THE FLOOD OF 1913. The roads, bridges, and many homes suffered a great deal of damage from this flood. However, no picture better illustrates that destruction more than the twisted railroad lines as seen in this picture of the Pennsylvania rail lines, which run to the east of the Village of Port Washington. Most of our pictures depict the townsfolk gathered for a group picture after the floodwaters receded.

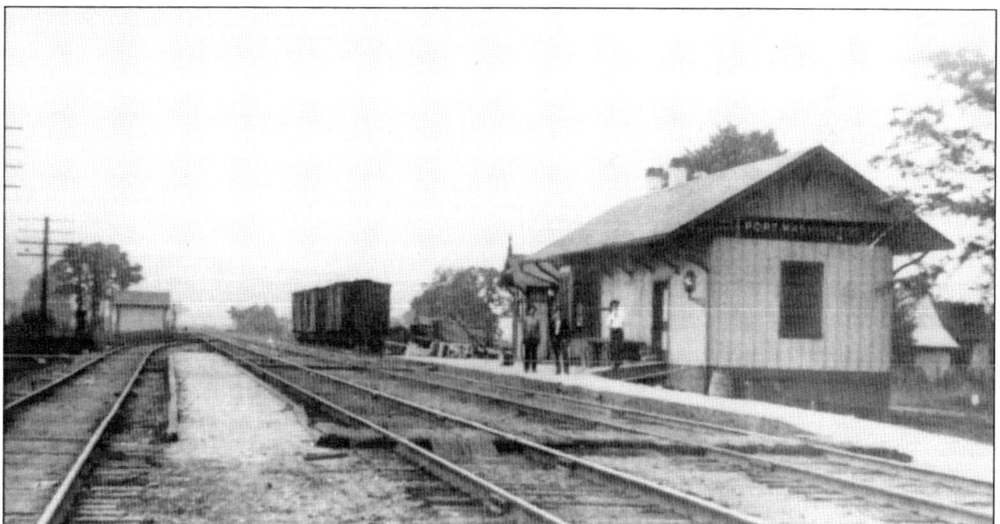

PORT WASHINGTON RAILROAD DEPOT. The resourcefulness of the people will always rise to the occasion. The towns were cleaned, roads and bridges rebuilt, and within months, life was back to normal in the areas that had been so deeply affected by the flood of 1913. This photo shows the depot in Port Washington cleaned and ready for daily traffic. From this town came such notables as the Lamneck family and William Wiant, the famous landscape painter.

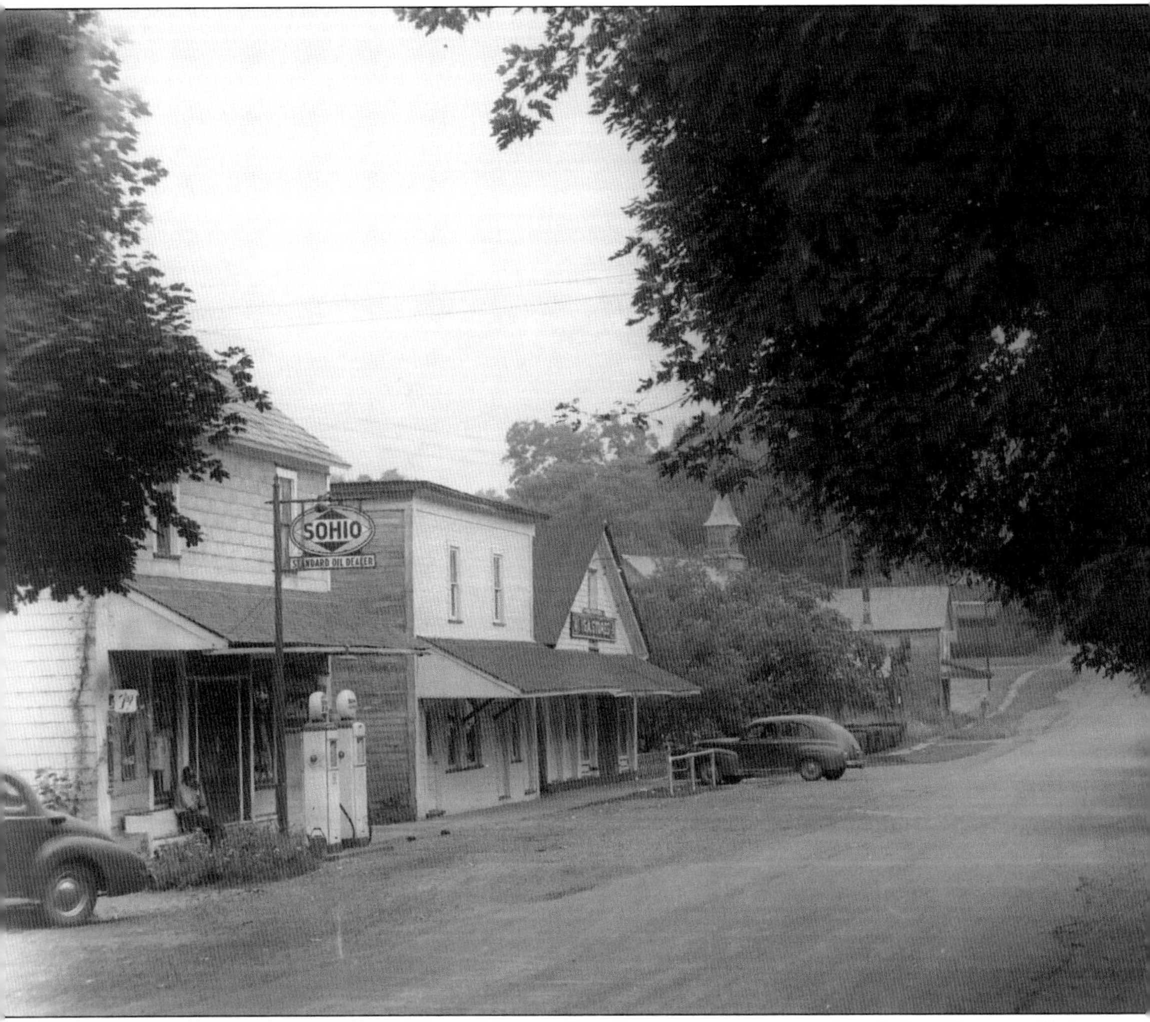

STREET SCENE OF RAGERSVILLE, OHIO. For the most part, people of the German-Swiss nationality settled the town of Ragersville. The area reminded them so much of their homeland. Conrad Rager came to the area in 1830 as one of the first merchants. Jacob Neff, a shoemaker, bought the first lot and erected the first cabin the village. This was a bustling village which had three doctors. One of the doctors was none other than the famous pitcher Alta Weiss, who pitched at the turn of the twentieth century, not with the girl teams but against the very best men's teams throughout the state. The one-room schoolhouse has been faithfully restored by the Ragersville Historical Society and is listed on the National Register of Historic Places. This scene captured in the late 1940s is looking west toward the center of the village.

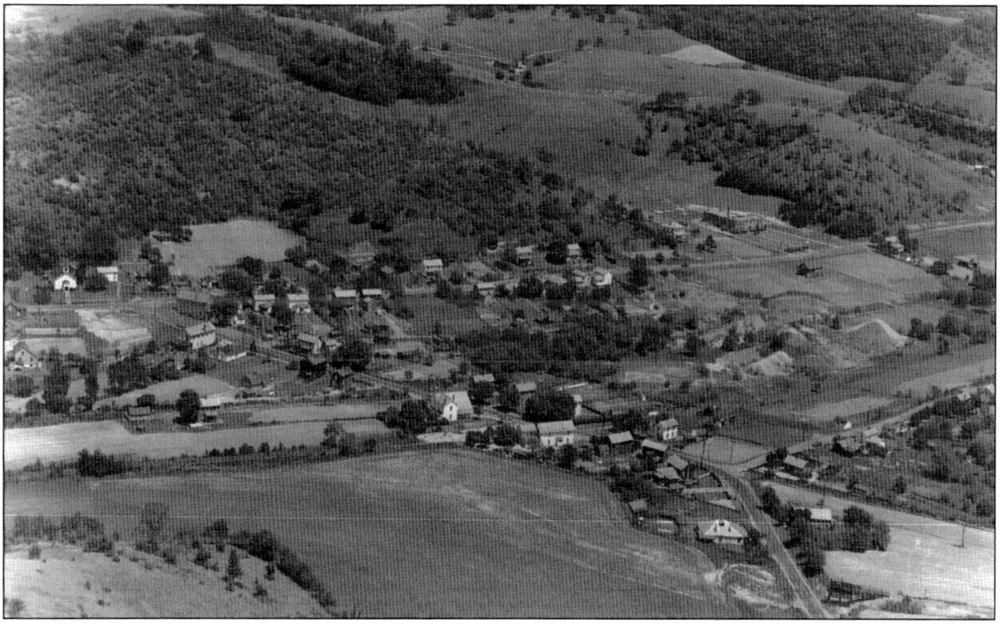

An Aerial View of the Village of Roswell 1950. This excellent view of the Village of Roswell and its surrounding hills filled with coal was taken in 1950. By then most of the deep mines had closed, and the men of the area found work in the factories and mills of nearby New Philadelphia or Dover. The new State Route 39 had not yet been completed when this photo was taken.

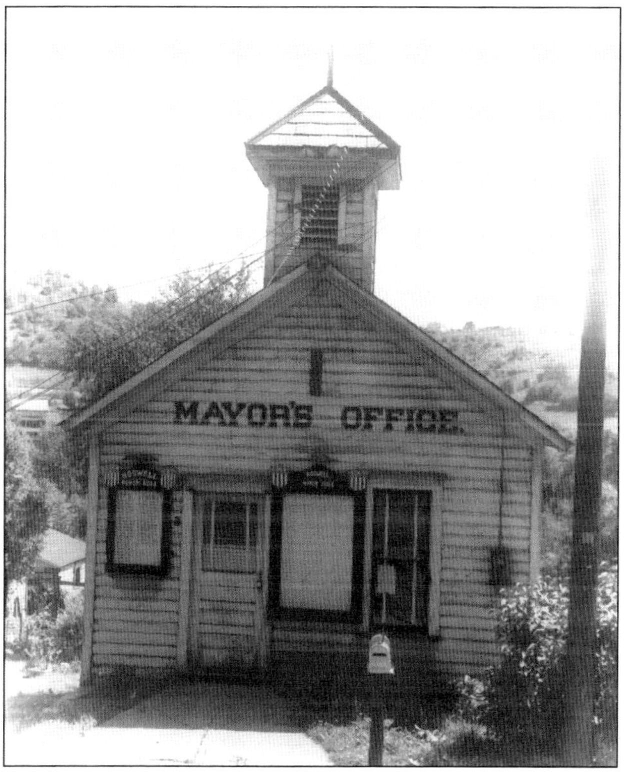

The Mayor Hall in Roswell 1940s. The mayors during this period held Mayor's Court, where the incidents in the village were judged and the punishment appropriate to the misdeed was delivered—usually in a fine. Today there are still city halls in the incorporated villages, but the mayor's court has been centralized into the large municipal courts in New Philadelphia and Uhrichsville.

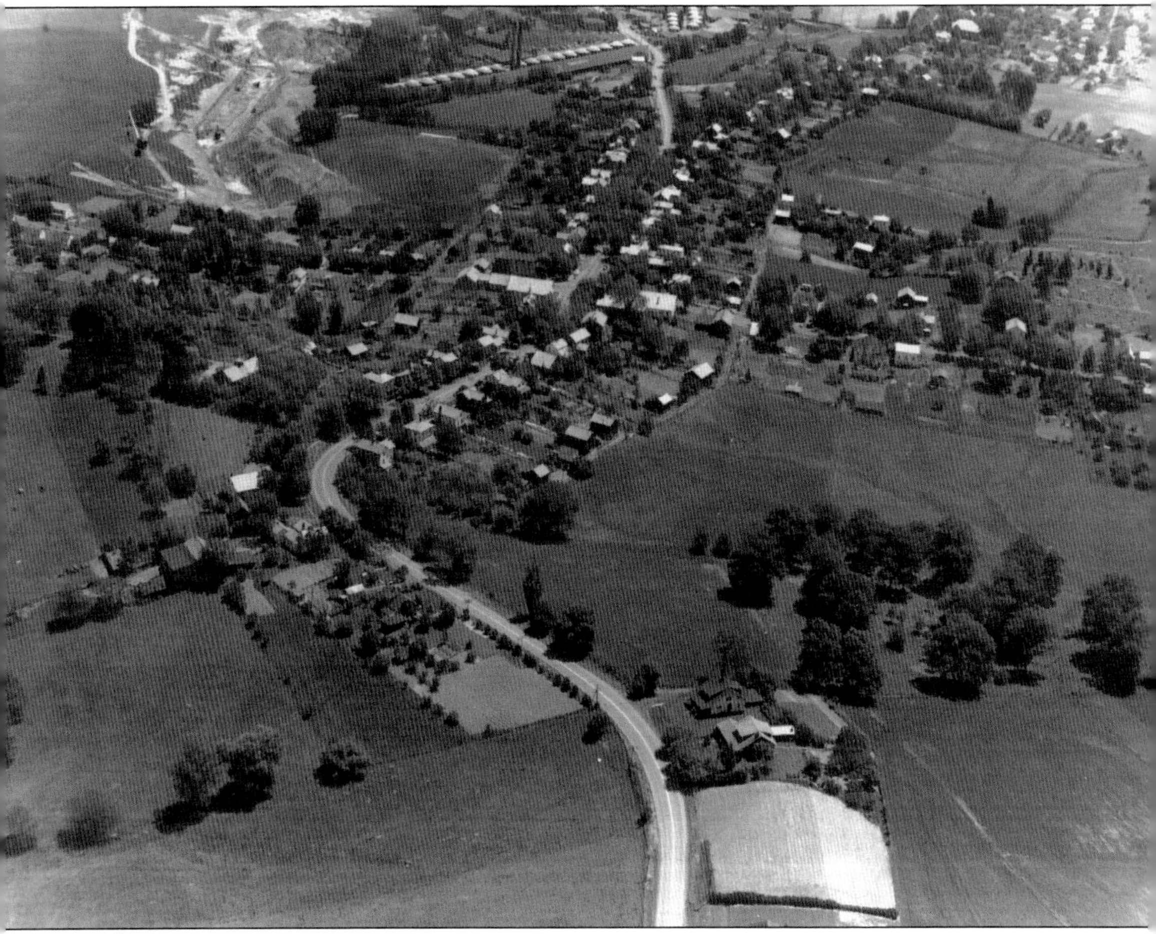

SHANESVILLE, OHIO 1950. The town of Shanesville will never forget the disastrous New Years Eve explosion and fire, which caused many deaths and great suffering in 1881. The town was named after General Abraham Shane, a militia commander, who had resided in Dover, Ohio. When this picture was taken, the population of Shanesville numbered 460. In 1968, the towns of Shanesville and Sugarcreek incorporated as Sugarcreek. This area was known for its rich farmlands, the making of Swiss cheese, and brickmaking. Today it is an internationally-known tourist area.

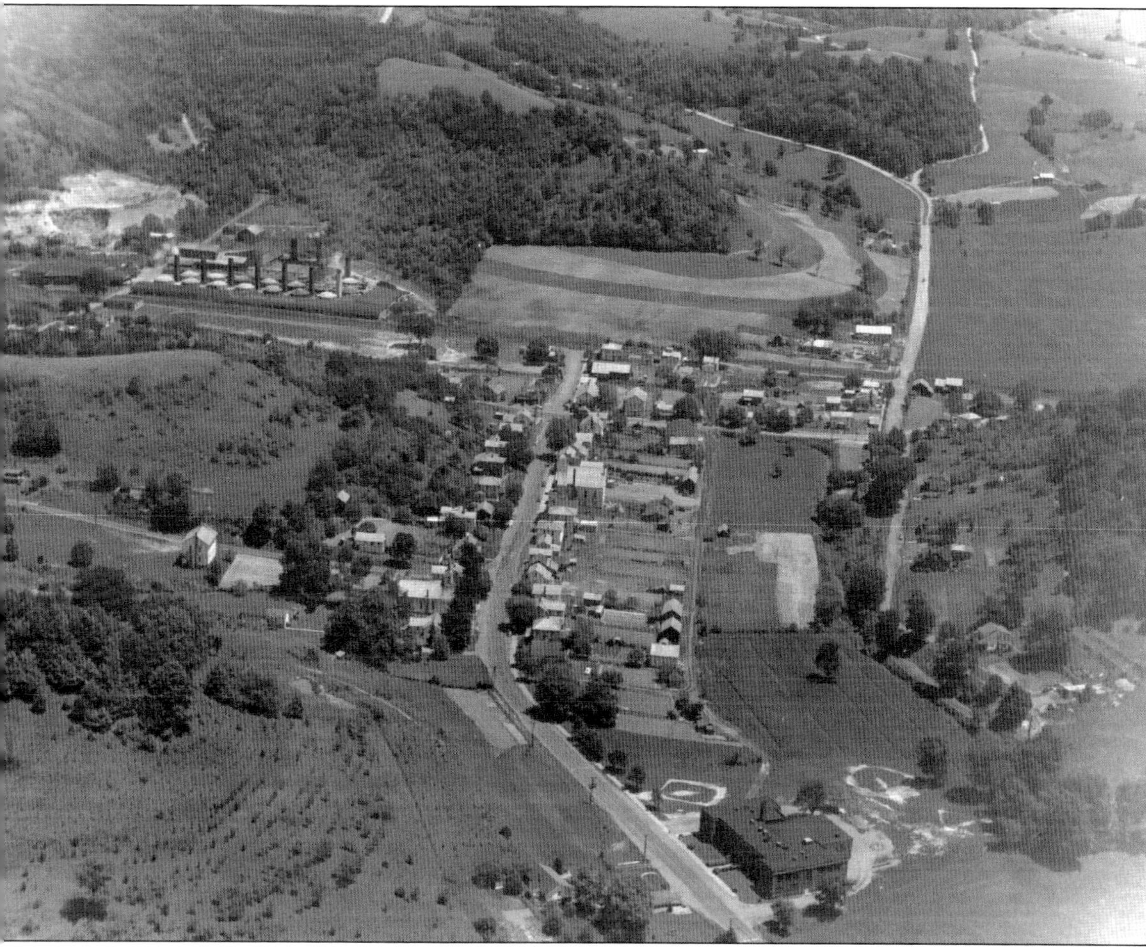

The Village of Stonecreek, Ohio. The Village of Stonecreek was formed in 1848 by Philip Leonhart and was named Phillipsburg. It was later changed to Stonecreek. The town grew as a result of the construction of the Cleveland and Marietta Railroad. The population of the village in 1950 was 225.

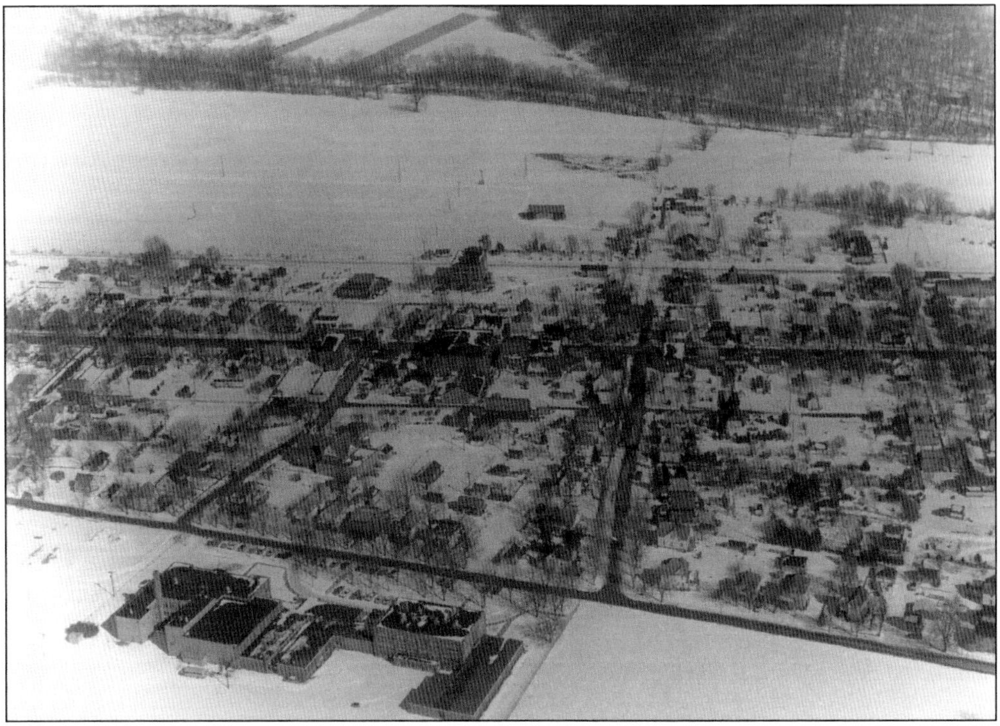

STRASBURG, OHIO, 1950. A man of German descent named Jonathan Folck formed Strasburg in 1825. The town was best known for almost a century as the home of the world's largest department store, the Garvers Brother Company, which was founded by Philip A. Garver in 1866. Strasburg was incorporated in the year 1893, and the population of the village when this photograph was taken in 1950 was 1,365.

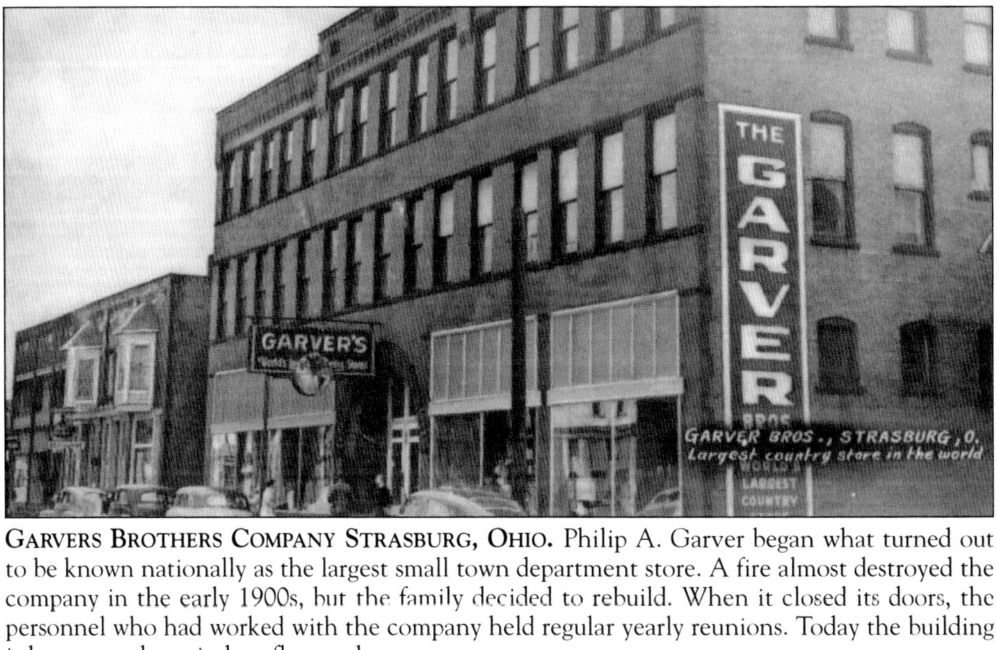

GARVERS BROTHERS COMPANY STRASBURG, OHIO. Philip A. Garver began what turned out to be known nationally as the largest small town department store. A fire almost destroyed the company in the early 1900s, but the family decided to rebuild. When it closed its doors, the personnel who had worked with the company held regular yearly reunions. Today the building is home to a large indoor flea market.

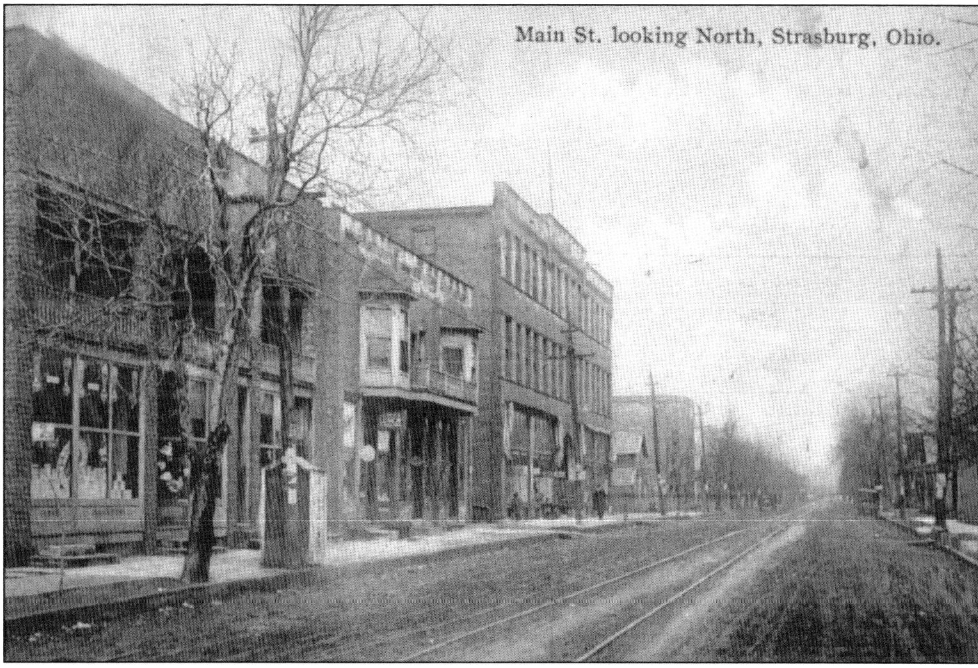

STRASBURG STREET SCENE 1910. Looking north along the unpaved US Route 21, one can see the Interurban rail lines running through the center of the street. The famous Garver Brothers store is the large building on the left.

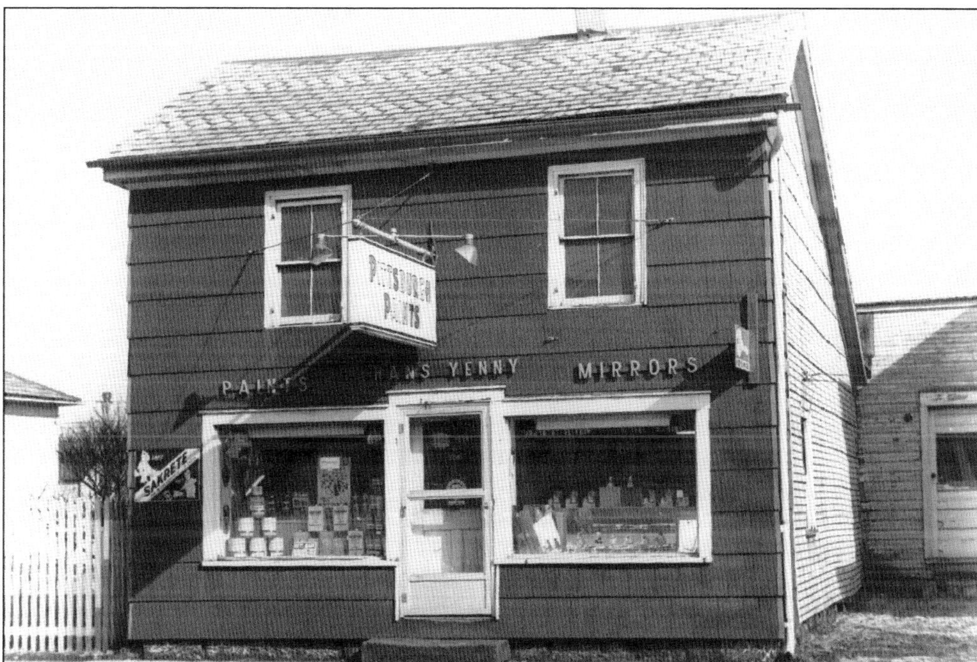

YENNY GLASS COMPANY. This picture is included to show that even in small-town America, the independent business person can still compete in today's marketplace. The business still operates with the replacement of windows, screens, and mirrors as its major line of work.

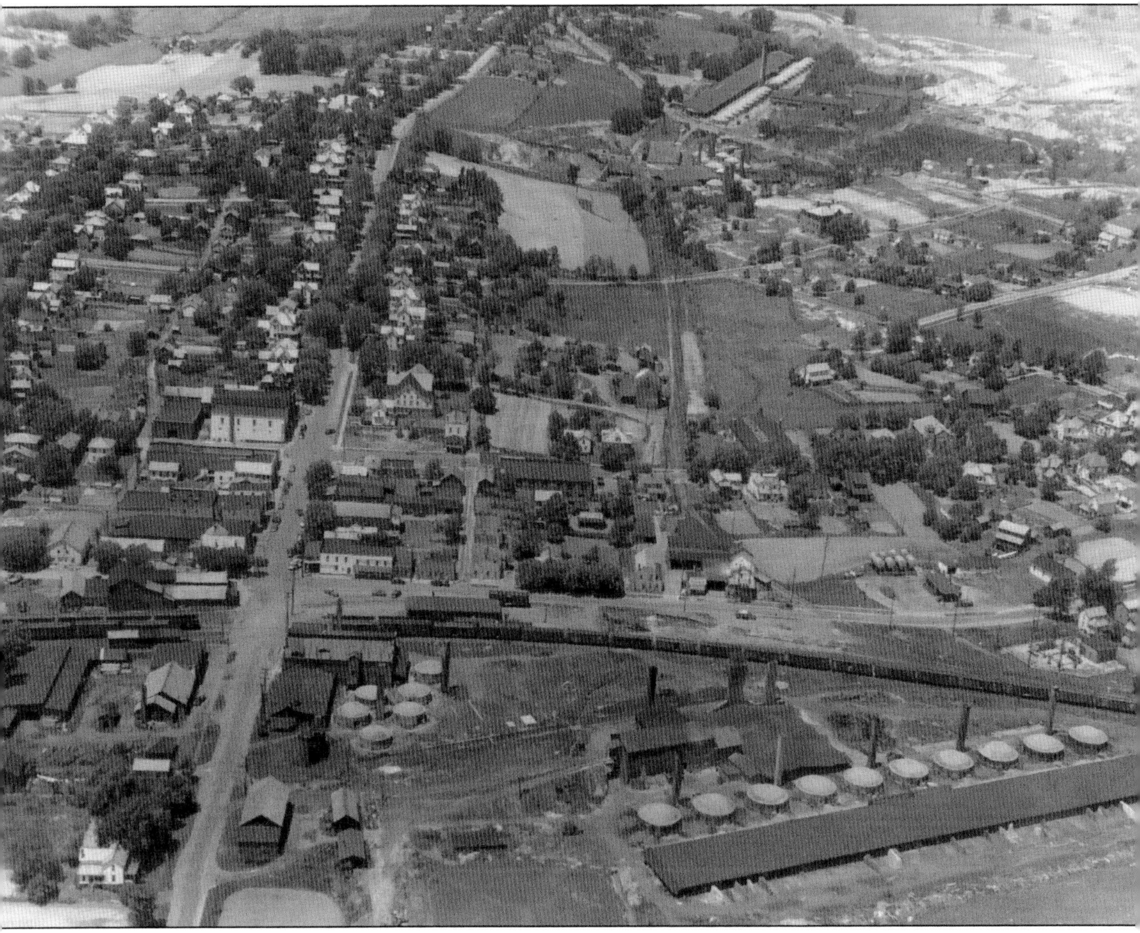

SUGARCREEK, OHIO, 1950. Immigrants of German and Swiss origin founded the Village of Sugarcreek in early 1882. The village has held a Swiss Festival every fall since 1953. Known for its Swiss cheese and the annual Swiss Festival, it is also known as the place where the world-famous Amish-Mennonite newspaper, the *Budget*, has been and continues to be published since the early 1880s. The town has prospered and is one of the largest tourist centers in the state of Ohio. When this photograph was taken, the town had 889 residents.

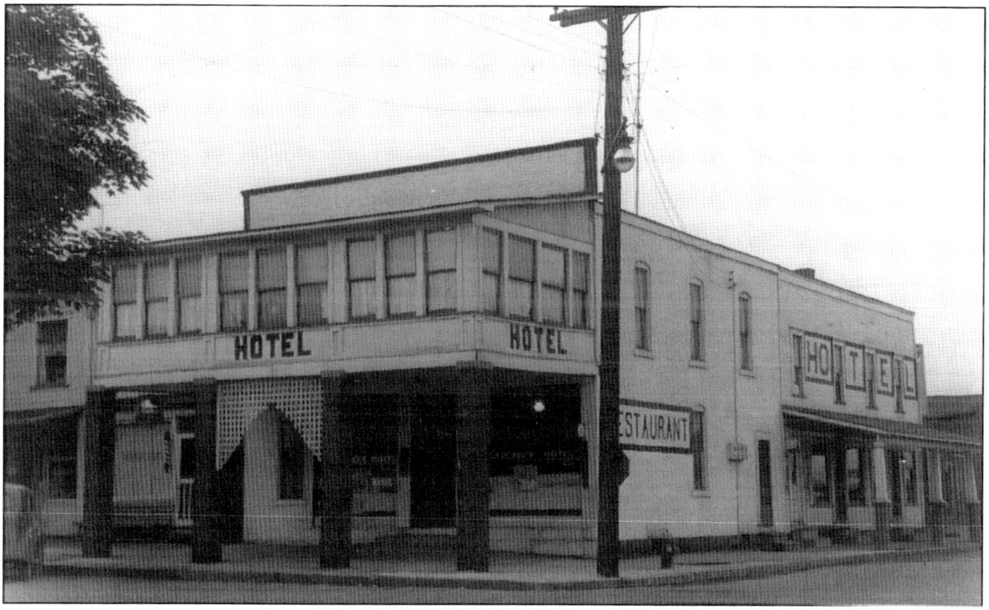

SUGARCREEK HOTEL 1949. The small towns in Tuscarawas County fortunate enough to have a passenger railroad, canal route, or bus line, soon found it necessary to have a hotel. This picture is representative of all the towns of Tuscarawas County in that regard. The hotel was located where currently there is a bank and parking lot, just across the street from the Sugarcreek Depot.

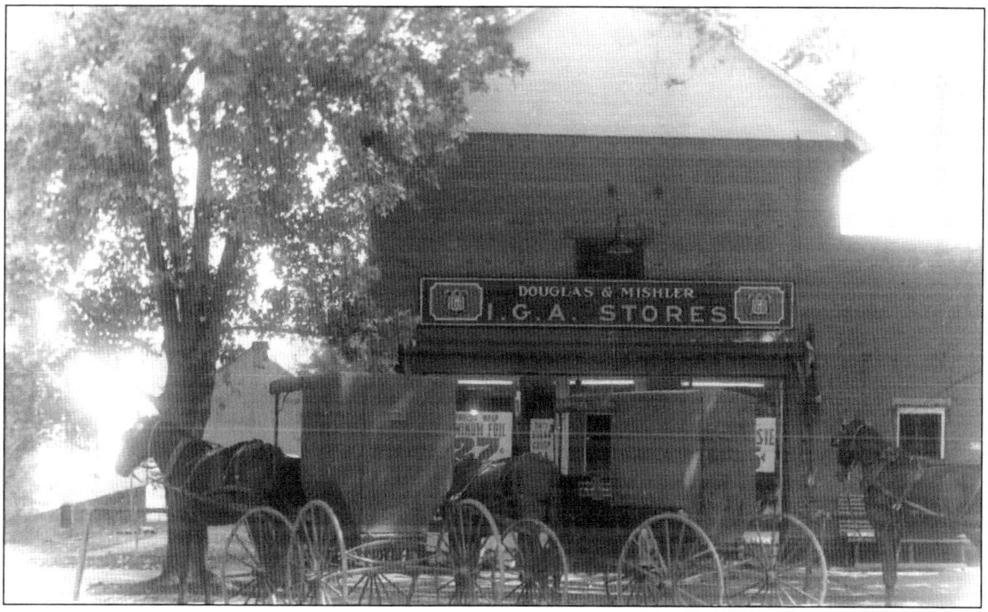

SUGARCREEK IGA 1950S. A pictorial book on Tuscarawas County without a picture of the Amish-Mennonite culture would be like a book on New York City without the skyscrapers. The Amish and Mennonite folk of Tuscarawas County remind residents and visitors of the joys of the simple life—a life that most of us have never experienced. Hardworking, industrious, family-oriented, and devoutly religious, the values this segment of society espouses are the principles that so many wish they had in the beginning of the twenty-first century.

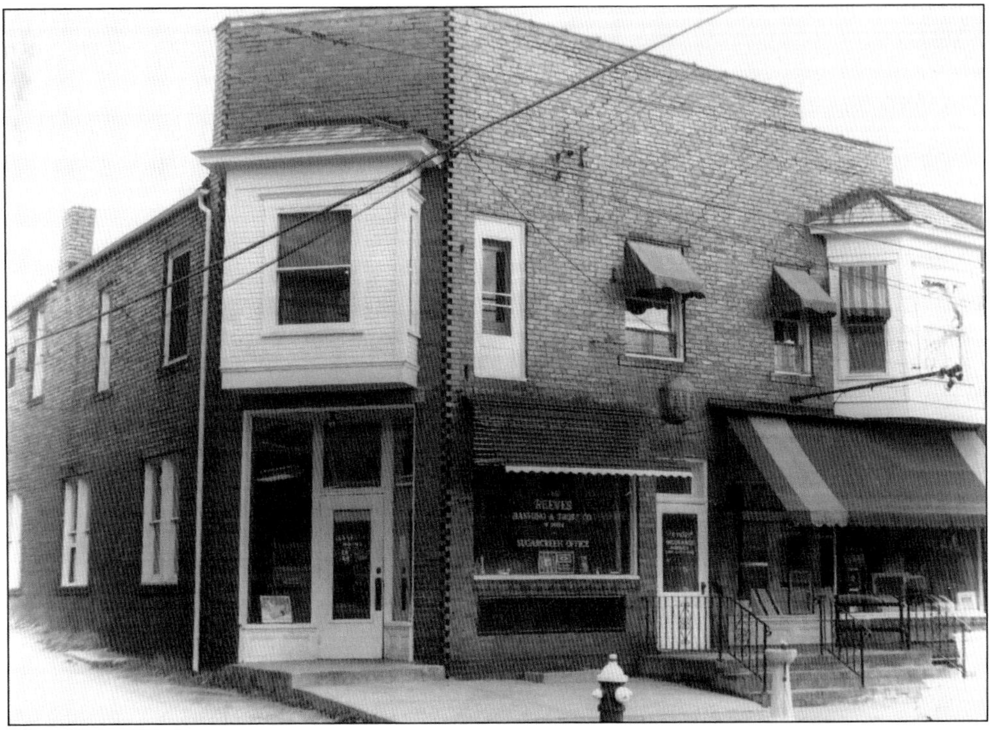

FUNCTIONAL USE OF A BUILDING, SUGARCREEK 1950S. This most interesting architectural style was completed not for the aesthetic eye but for functionality. This structure was built in 1916 to house the Citizens Bank. When the picture was taken, it was a branch of the Reeves Bank. The first thought that came to my mind when observing this picture centered on the door on the second floor—quite a first step and not for the faint at heart.

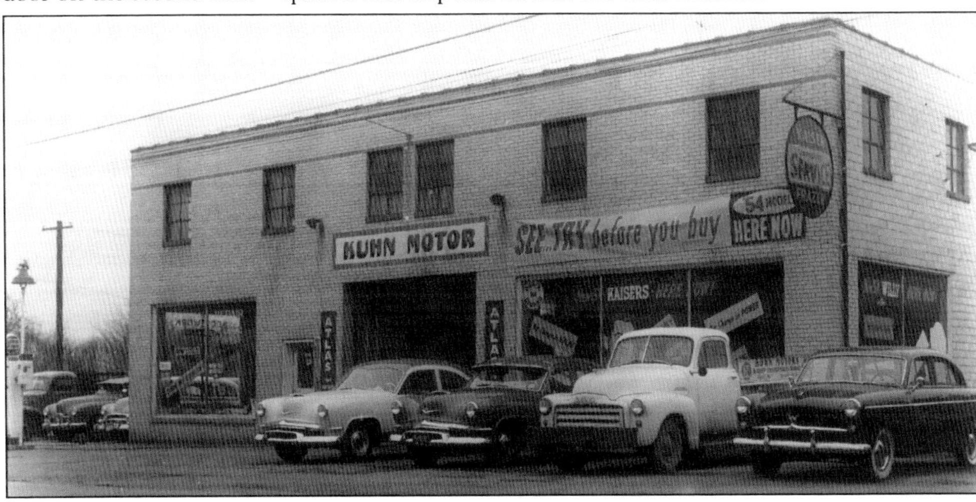

KUHN MOTOR BROTHERS, SUGARCREEK, OHIO, 1954. Every small town contained its own car dealership in the middle of the twentieth century. This photograph is reflective of how the small town dealers would stay competitive with their large city counterparts—personal service with many different models from which the customer could choose. Check out the names of products and cars on the various signs. The gas pump is now a collector's item, likely worth much more today than when actually in use by the customers.

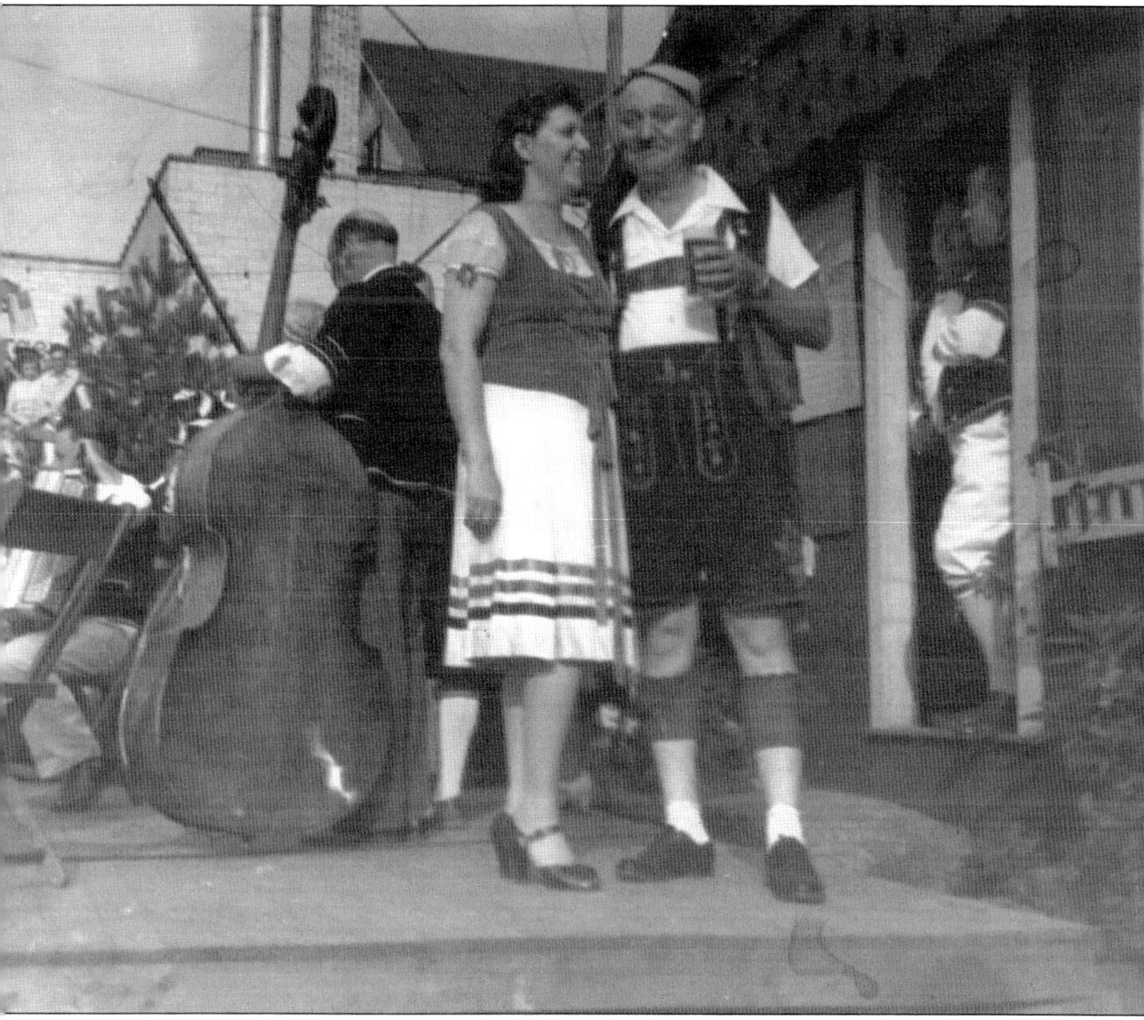

SWISS FESTIVAL, SUGARCREEK, OHIO, 1953. The world-famous Swiss Festival has been held the last weekend in September for the past half-century. Beautiful costumes, yodeling, dancing in the streets to live polka bands, lots of German food, two parades, and a queen's contest are but a small sampling of activities generously presented to visitors and residents alike. A national gathering of the Wally Byam Airstreams Group arrives each year and settles in at Winklepleck Grove to enjoy the festival and tour the area. Most residents are not able to see much of the activities, because they are so involved with making sure everyone has a good time. The author has enjoyed the distinct privilege of judging the parade and the queen's contest. Writing this book was a much easier task!

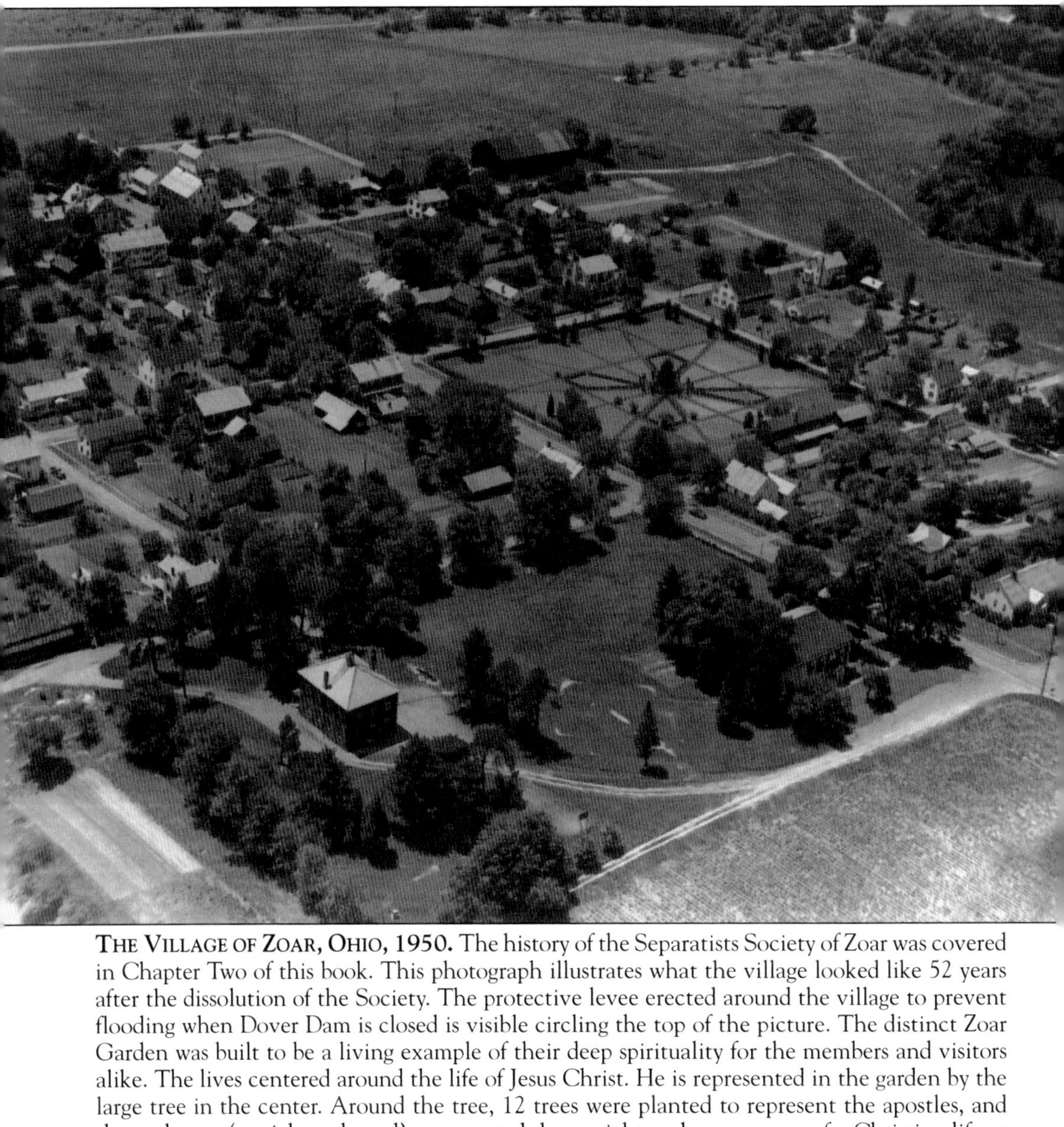

THE VILLAGE OF ZOAR, OHIO, 1950. The history of the Separatists Society of Zoar was covered in Chapter Two of this book. This photograph illustrates what the village looked like 52 years after the dissolution of the Society. The protective levee erected around the village to prevent flooding when Dover Dam is closed is visible circling the top of the picture. The distinct Zoar Garden was built to be a living example of their deep spirituality for the members and visitors alike. The lives centered around the life of Jesus Christ. He is represented in the garden by the large tree in the center. Around the tree, 12 trees were planted to represent the apostles, and the pathways (straight or boxed) represented the straight and narrow way of a Christian life or a worldly path (boxed) for those whose lives were not in tune with the Christian way of life. If you were on the worldly path you would just keep going around and around, as the world would lead you. The garden was also used to provide the many vegetables and herbs that the Society utilized in their daily diets.

Five

Social Institutions of Tuscarawas County

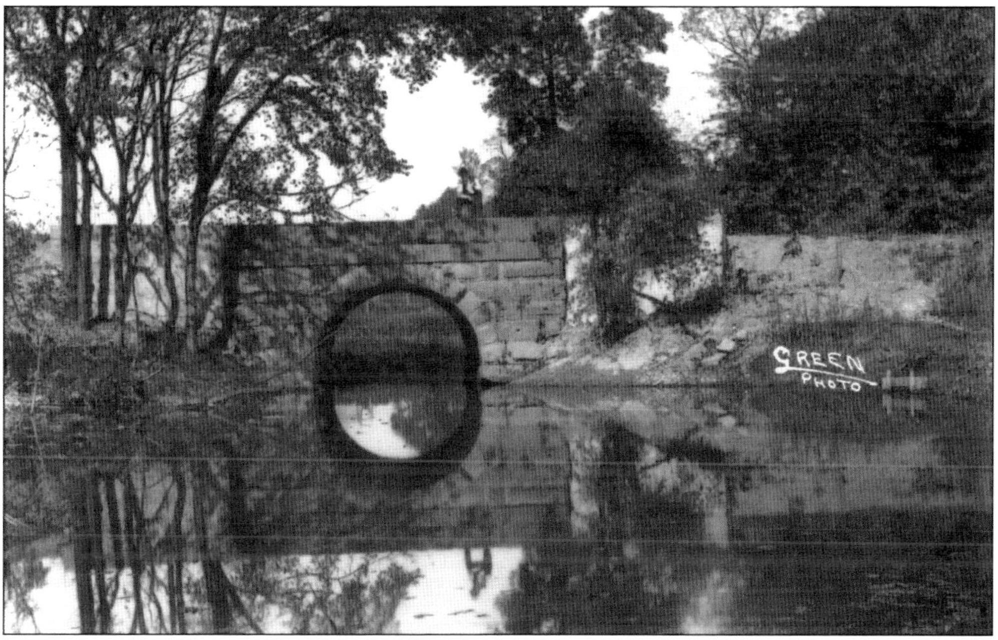

Springers Park, New Philadelphia, Ohio 1890s. The photographs associated with this chapter range from recreation and meeting the basic needs to being informed. The picture of Springer's Park, which was located on the west end of New Philadelphia, was selected because many folks long for a place to retreat after a long, hard work week. People would come to this park to enjoy a summer picnic, skip stones in the river, fish, or take a much-deserved nap in a beautiful setting.

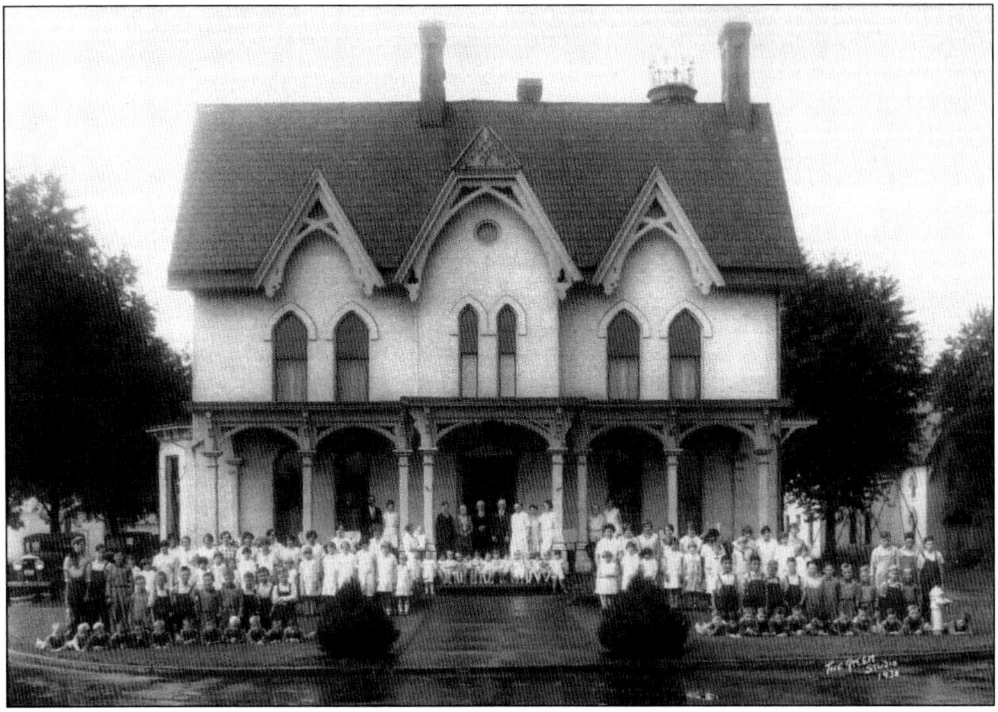

CHILDREN'S HOME OF TUSCARAWAS COUNTY 1938. The Children's Home was a working farm, which provided the basic needs for children whose families could no longer provide proper care. Many times the father was killed at work, and in those days of large families and no insurance or Social Security benefits, the only way to protect their children was to turn them over to the care of the home.

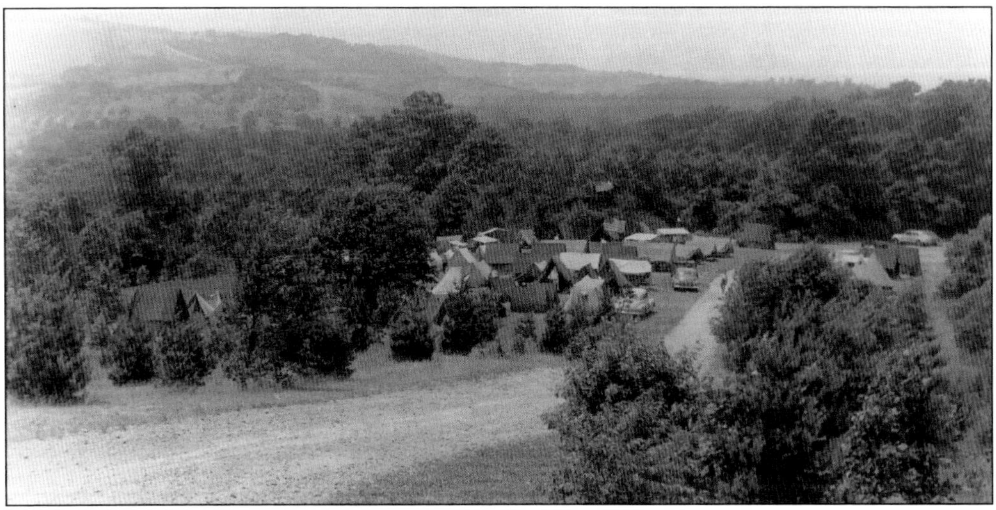

CAMP TUSCAZOAR BOY SCOUT CAMP. The Boy Scouts of America program in Tuscarawas County began in the early 1920s. Camp Tuscazoar was built, and the young men and their adult scoutmasters took a week-long camping trip into the hills alongside the Tuscarawas River in Fairfield Township. Most times the adult scoutmasters would sacrifice a week of their own vacation time to help teach the young men under their supervision a strong moral code and how to become a man.

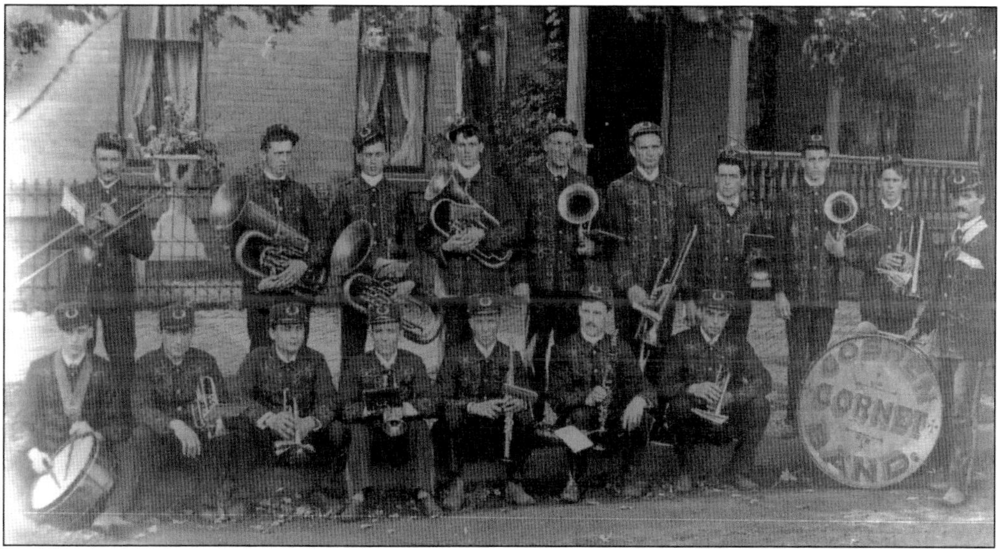

GOSHEN CORNET BAND. Before the advent of radio, television, and the computer, the leisure-time activities were associated with the arts or perhaps sporting events. Music was very important to the life of a community, and just like the story in the movie *Music Man*, the towns organized their own bands or orchestras in which to enjoy a lazy summer evening. This picture of the Goshen Cornet Band was taken in the late 1900s.

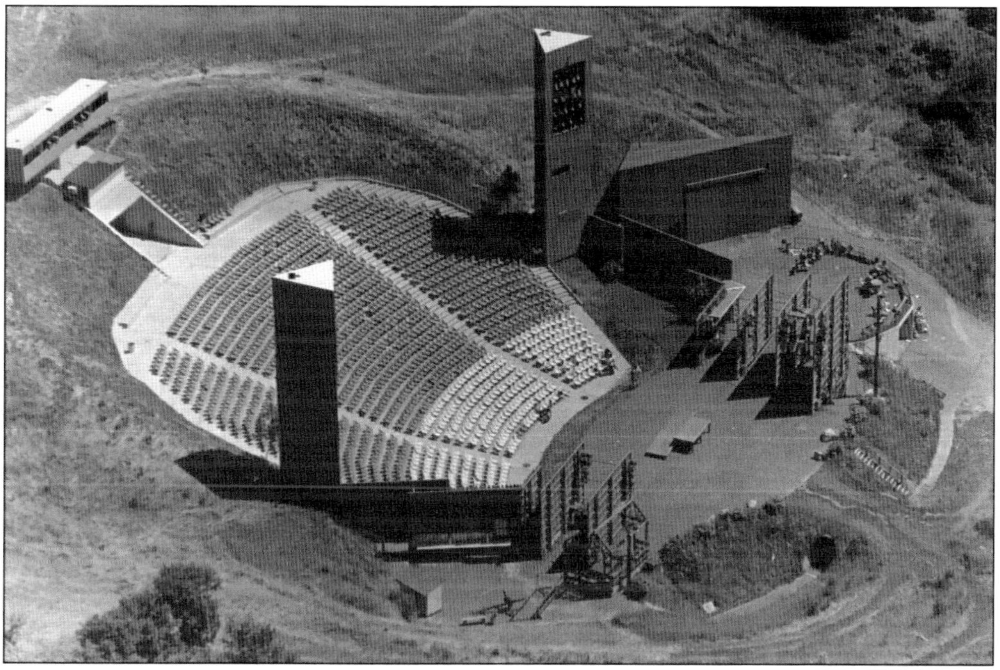

TRUMPET IN THE LAND AMPITHEATER 1970. *Trumpet in the Land* is an outdoor musical play, which dramatically tells the early story of the founding of the Ohio Country—especially the life of David Zeisberger and his cohorts. Written by nationally-known playwright, the late Paul Green, the drama has played to thousands of visitors every summer since 1970. It originated from the inspiration of Rachel Redinger, who spearheaded the committees to provide this excellent drama on the history of Tuscarawas County.

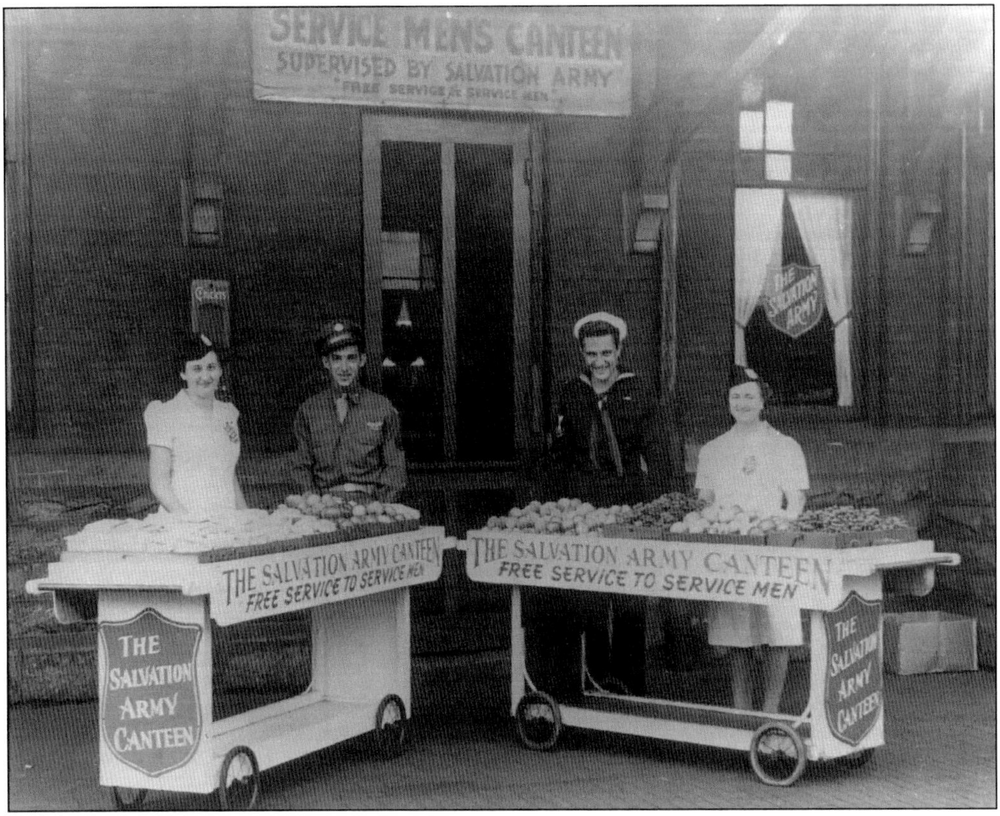

DENNISON CANTEEN, DENNISON, OHIO. During World War II, thousands of U.S. soldiers made their way from camp to battleground and traveled through Dennison Depot in Dennison, Ohio. The Salvation Army and women of the churches of Tuscarawas County devised a plan to provide refreshments to the soldiers on their layover. From 1942 through 1943, 1.3 million service personnel received this loving care. They nicknamed the town Dreamsville, Ohio.

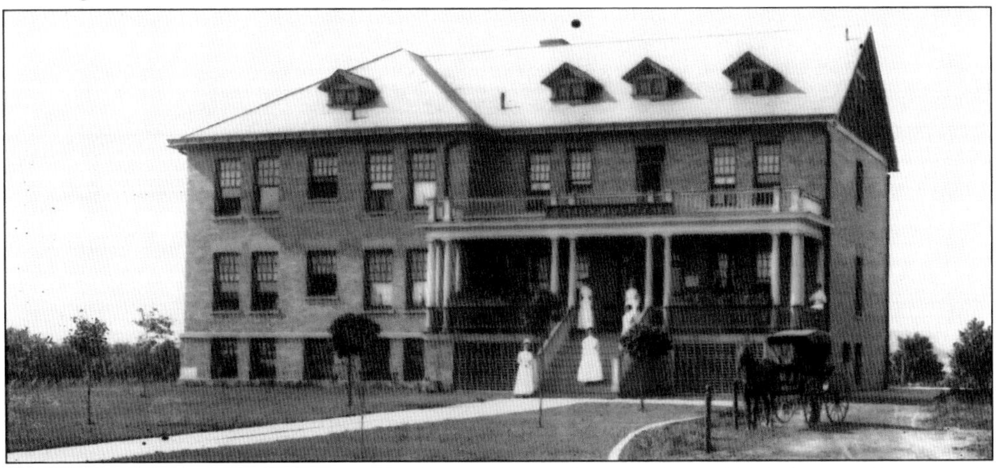

UNION HOSPITAL 1908. The original Union Hospital was built in 1908. During the Spanish flu outbreak of 1918–1919, there were so many sick that the doctors and nurses set up regional hospital sites in Dover and New Philadelphia and continued to remain abreast of the most modern advances in health care.

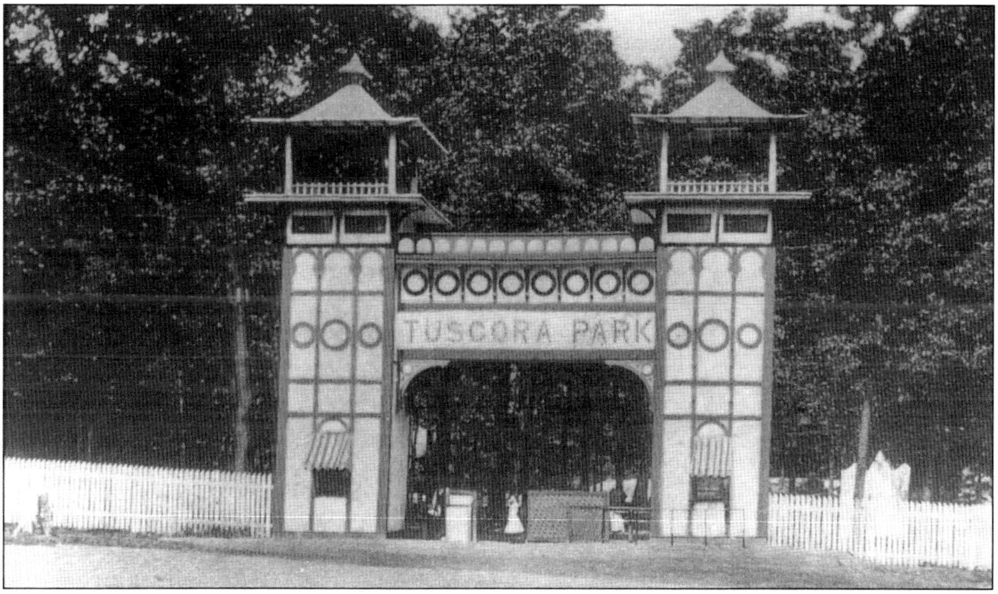

ENTRANCE TO TUSCORA PARK, NEW PHILADELPHIA, OHIO. Millions of folks have enjoyed passing through these portals since the opening of Tuscora Park on a rainy June 1, 1907. On special holidays, anywhere from 15,000 to 25,000 people will come to the park to enjoy a 25¢ ride on the merry-go-round, kiddie cars, train, to watch a ball game or a free concert at the amphitheater, and then to watch the fireworks.

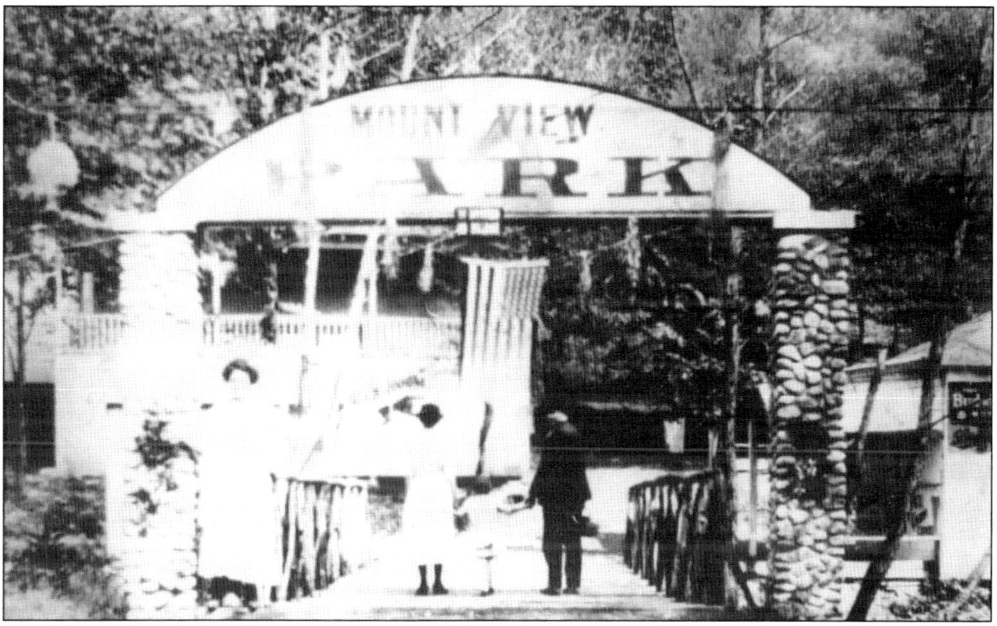

MOUNT VIEW PARK, NEW PHILADELPHIA, OHIO. Many people remember recreation sites other than Tuscora Park—Springer's Park, Winklepleck Grove, Heck's Grove, Riverside Park, Dies Hill, Schlegel's Park, and the pictured Mount View Park on the near-east side of New Philadelphia. Dances and many small amusement rides were offered at this park in the 1930s and 1940s. At the same time, folks were also taking streetcars to Meyer's Lake in Canton, Ohio, and to Cedar Point—some by lake steamer.

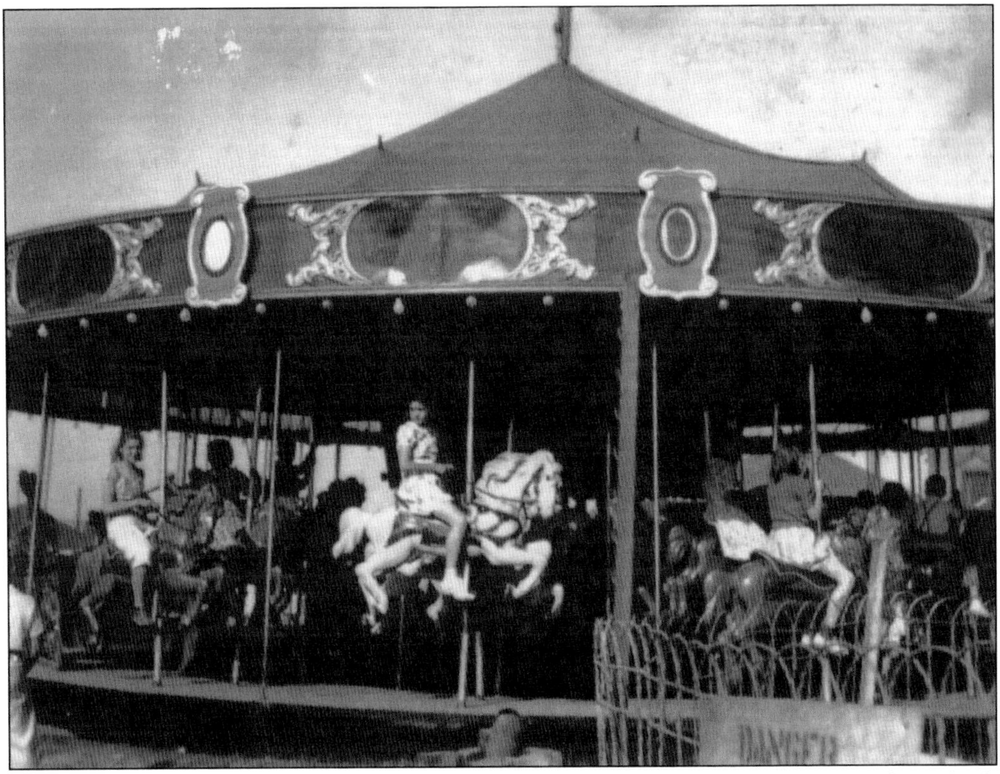

THE SPILLMAN CAROUSEL TUSCORA PARK 1942. The nostalgic Spillman Carousel was built in 1928. In 1940, the City of New Philadelphia was offered a chance to purchase this treasure. The picture was taken just two years after the carousel had been purchased and assembled at Tuscora Park. Thanks to the city park officials and the men and women of RTY, Inc., the grand lady has been completely restored, and a marvelous trip back in time can again be experienced for only 25¢.

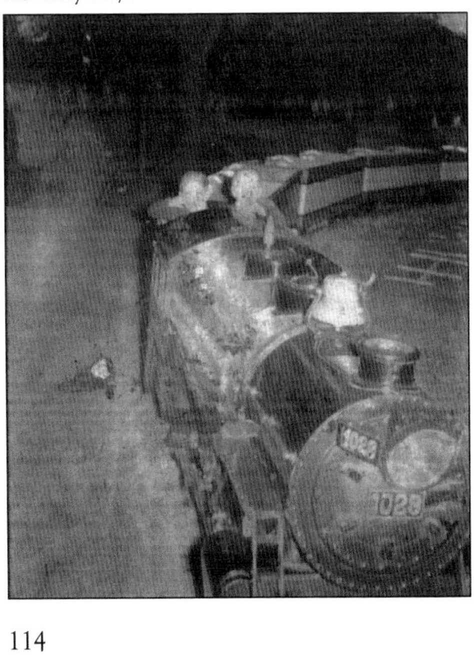

TRAIN RIDE AT TUSCORA PARK. Rich Geib Jr. gave this picture of the original train at Tuscora Park to the Society. We believe the photograph was taken in the mid-1940s. Those who come to the park today can recreate that ride once again.

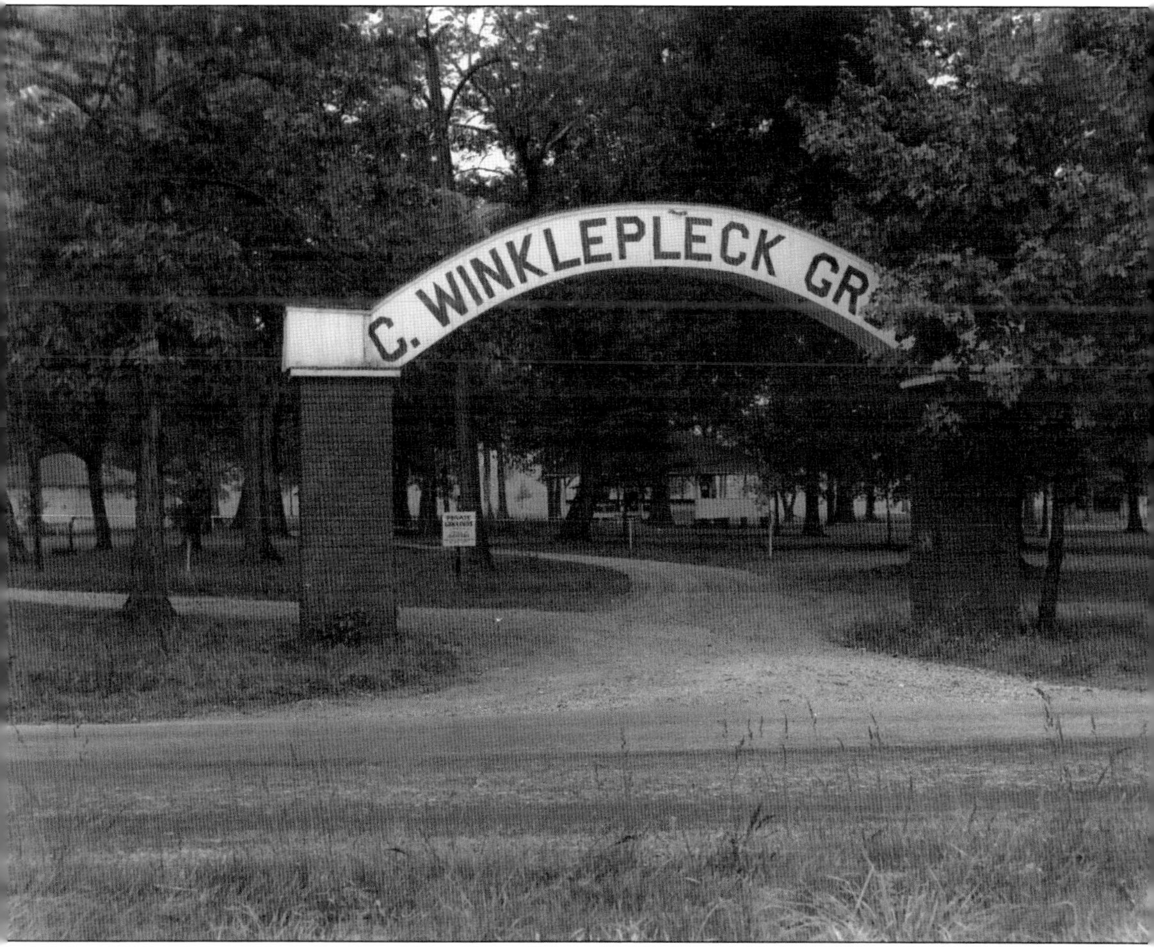

WINKLEPLECK GROVE NEAR SUGARCREEK, OHIO. In the year 1923, a plot of ground about a mile east of the town of Sugarcreek was leased to the village by Cornelius Winklepleck to be used as a site for reunions and picnics. The Wally Byam Club, a group of Airstream trailer enthusiasts, has used this site each year for the annual Swiss Festival. As one crests over the rolling hills, the gleam off of these campers can be seen for miles. Several of the large industries in the county have used the grove for their annual picnics.

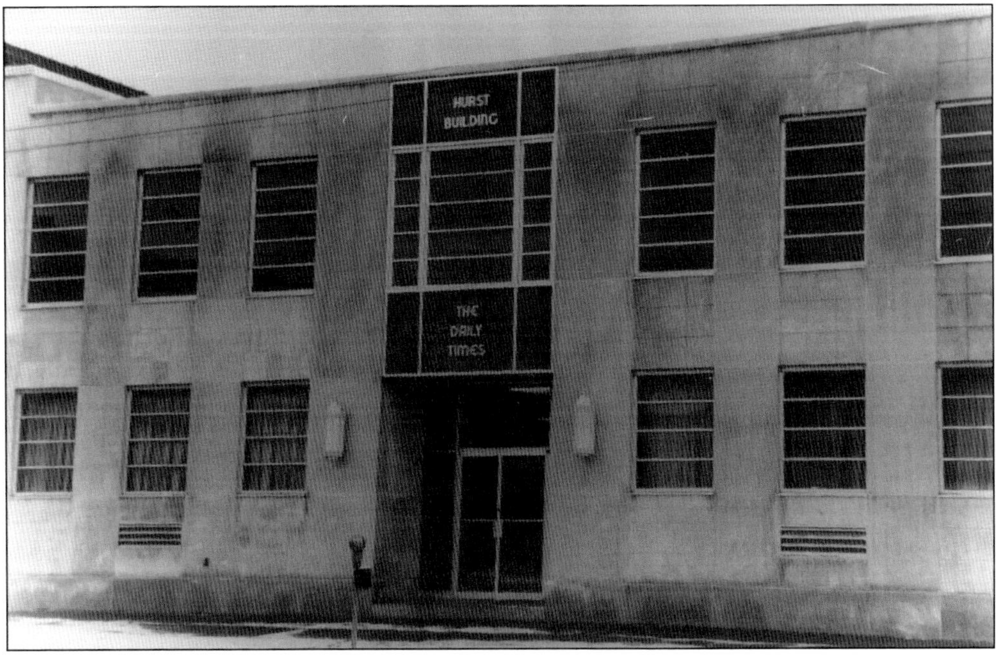

DAILY TIMES NEWSPAPER BUILDING NEW PHILADELPHIA, OHIO.

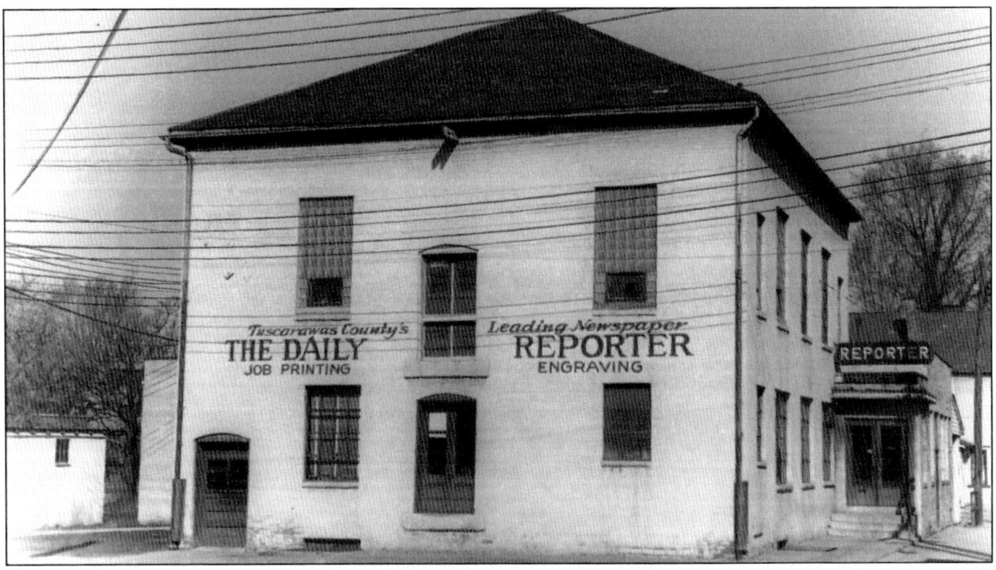

DAILY REPORTER NEWSPAPER BUILDING DOVER, OHIO. Tuscarawas County has operated numerous newspapers, which have kept the people informed of the events and happenings of the local communities as well as national and international stories. Today Tuscarawas County is served by just one daily newspaper, the *Times Reporter*. This was a result of the merger of the New Philadelphia *Daily Times*, begun in the year 1907, with the Dover *Daily Reporter*, begun in 1900. The merger took place in March 1968. The Uhrichsville *Chronicle* served the Uhrichsville and Dennison citizens until the 1970s, when it closed its doors for good. Newcomerstown has maintained a weekly newspaper that is still publishing today. Sugarcreek and the worldwide Amish and Mennonite communities have been served by the *Budget*, a weekly publication.

Six

A FEW SCHOOLS OF TUSCARAWAS COUNTY

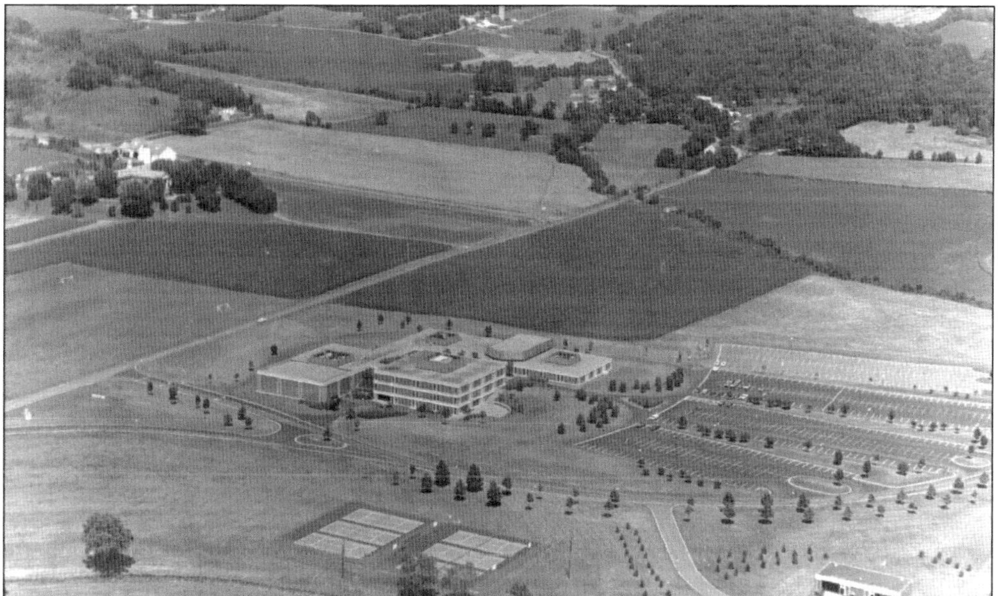

TUSCARAWAS CAMPUS KENT STATE UNIVERSITY. A common thread in almost every resident's life has been the school. The Tuscarawas Campus of Kent State University began in the 1960s with night classes held in New Philadelphia High School. In the late 1960s, this building was constructed. The campus currently provides educational opportunities for a little more than 1,700 students. This campus is unique in that the citizens of Tuscarawas County own the building and grounds. The progressive dean and staff possess great vision for the needs of not only the students but also the business and industry of the area.

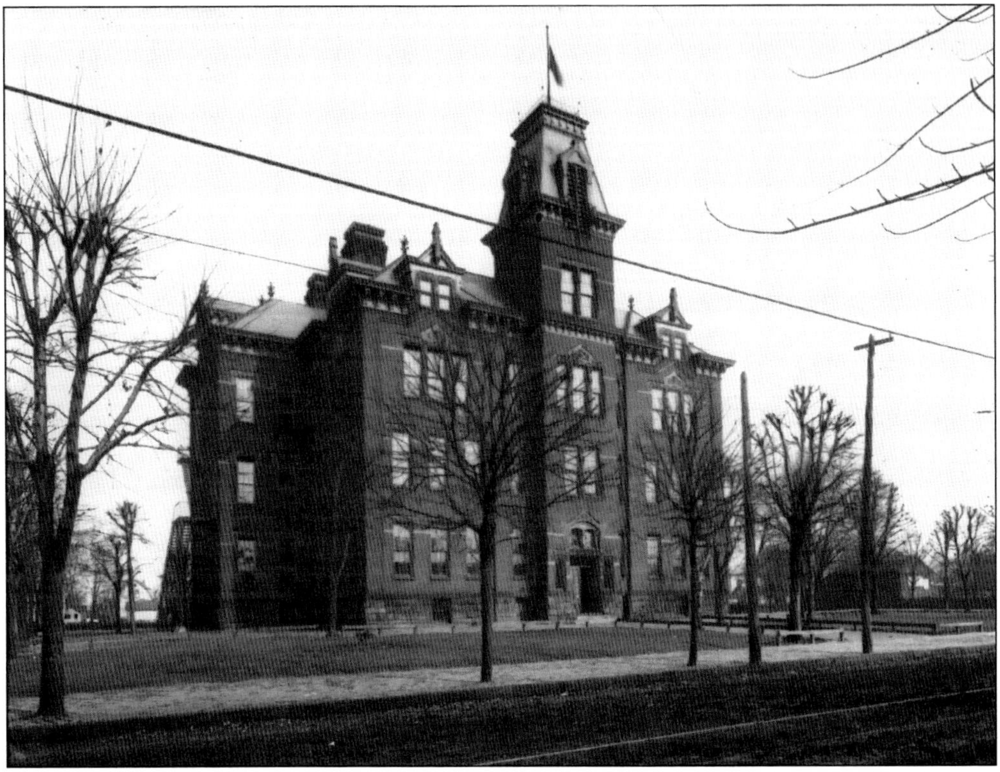

CENTRAL HIGH NEW PHILADELPIA, OHIO. Central High was replaced in 1914 by the new high school on the corner of Ray and 4th Streets. Most people today will only remember the present high school. Central School now serves as an elementary school and does not resemble this building in any manner.

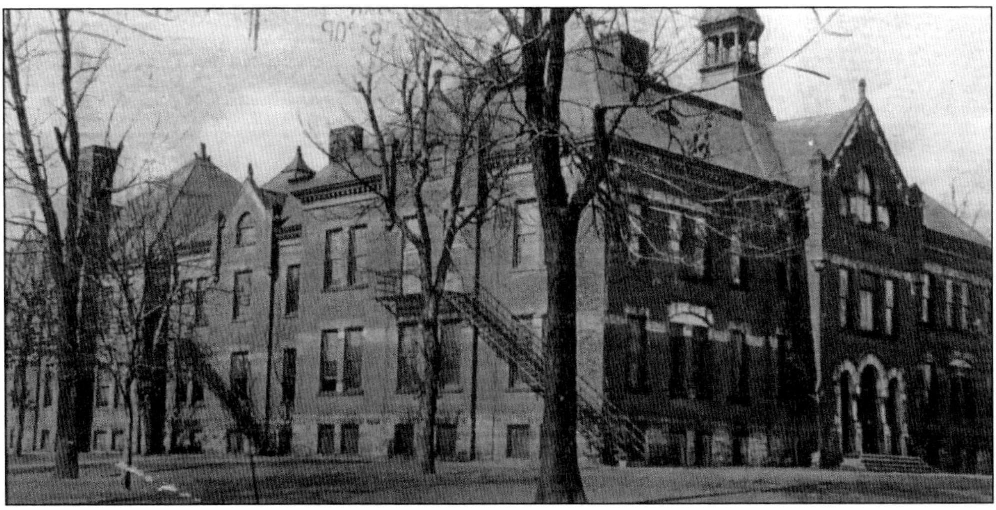

OAK GROVE SCHOOL DOVER, OHIO. A portion of this school was retained when the new Dover High School was built. Today it is situated alongside Fifth Street. The first county fairs were held on this site before the city fathers decided to build a new school, which was called Oak Grove School.

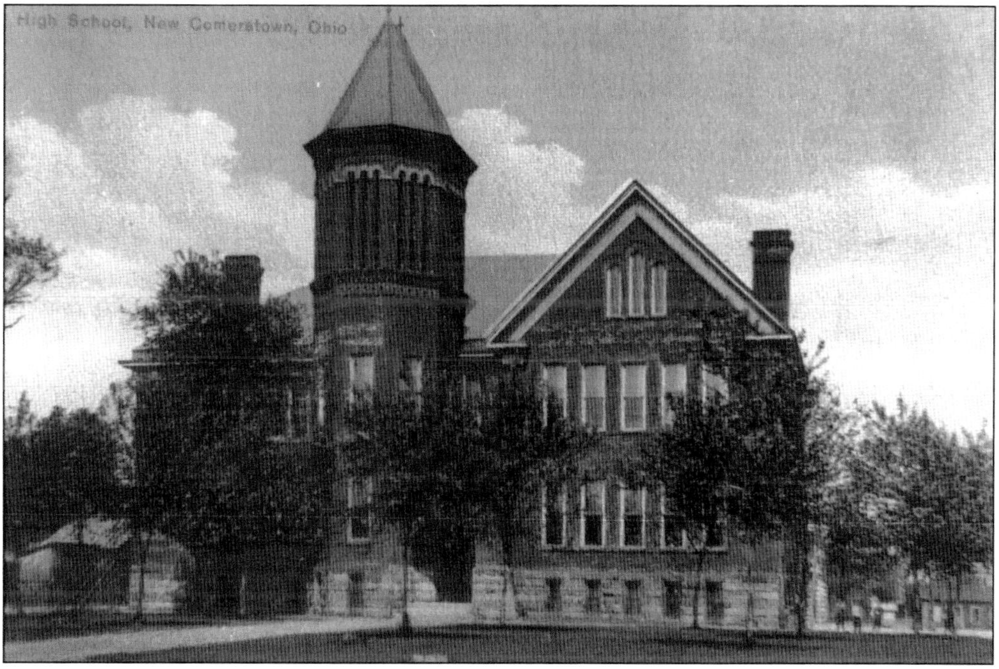

MAPLEWOOD SCHOOL NEWCOMERSTOWN, OHIO. The Maplewood School building served those in grades 1–8 who lived on the west side of the town. This building was constructed in 1900, and was razed after the 1957 school term.

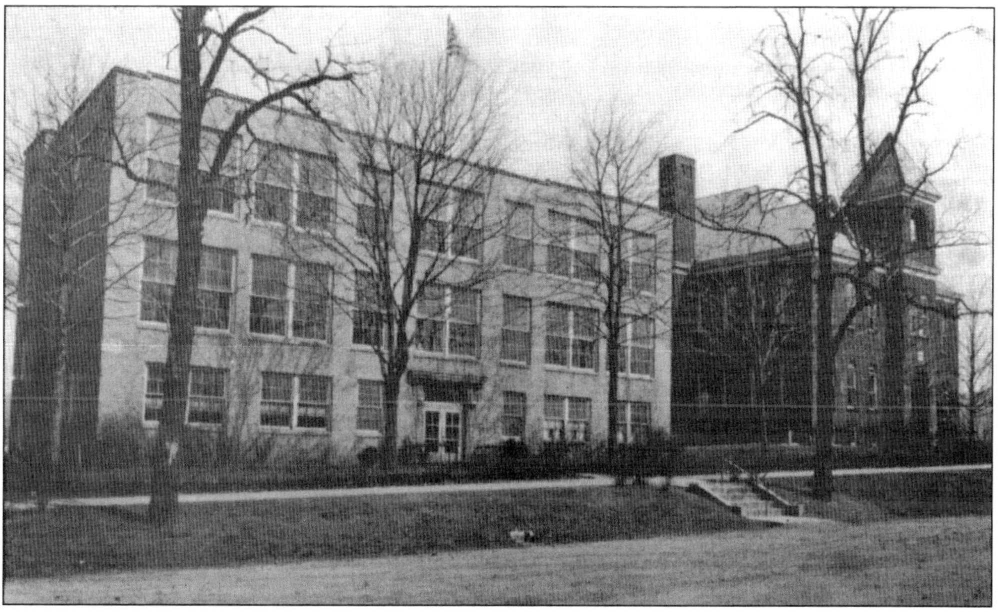

GNADENHUTTEN HIGH SCHOOL GNADENHUTTEN, OHIO. The old high school is pictured on the right of the new high school. The old high school was built in 1896, and the new high school was constructed in 1924 for junior and senior high students. Today the school is known as the Indian Valley School District and serves students from the Port Washington, Tuscarawas, Midvale, Barnhill, and Gnadenhutten areas.

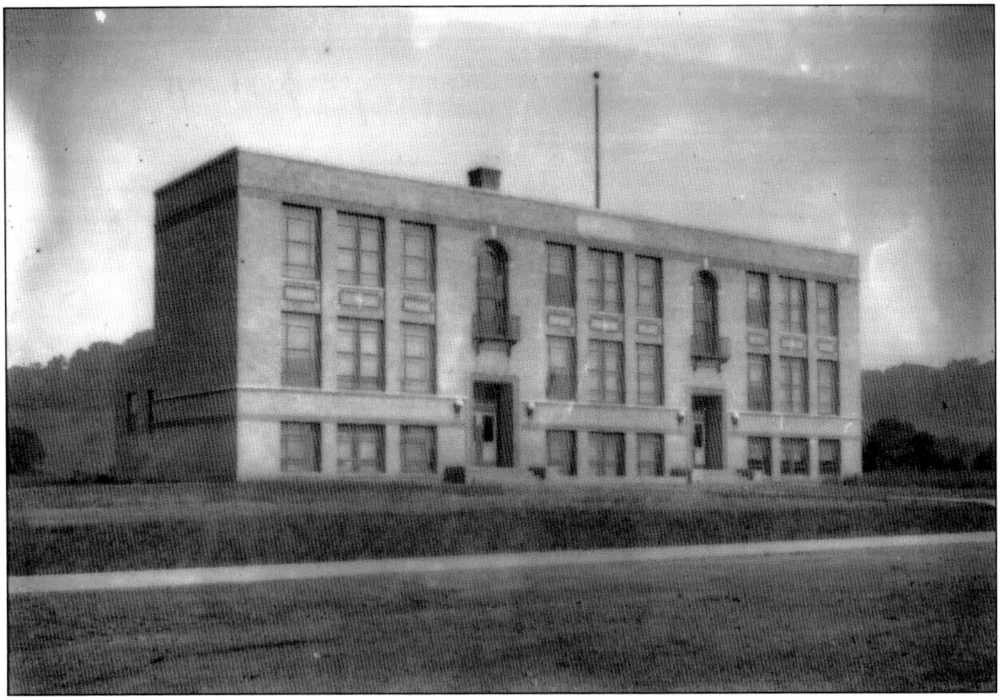

Port Washington High School Port Washington, Ohio. In 1926, this structure was built for grades 1–12. It consisted of ten classrooms, a library, and an auditorium-gymnasium. The first graduating class from this school in May of 1927 contained six girls and one boy.

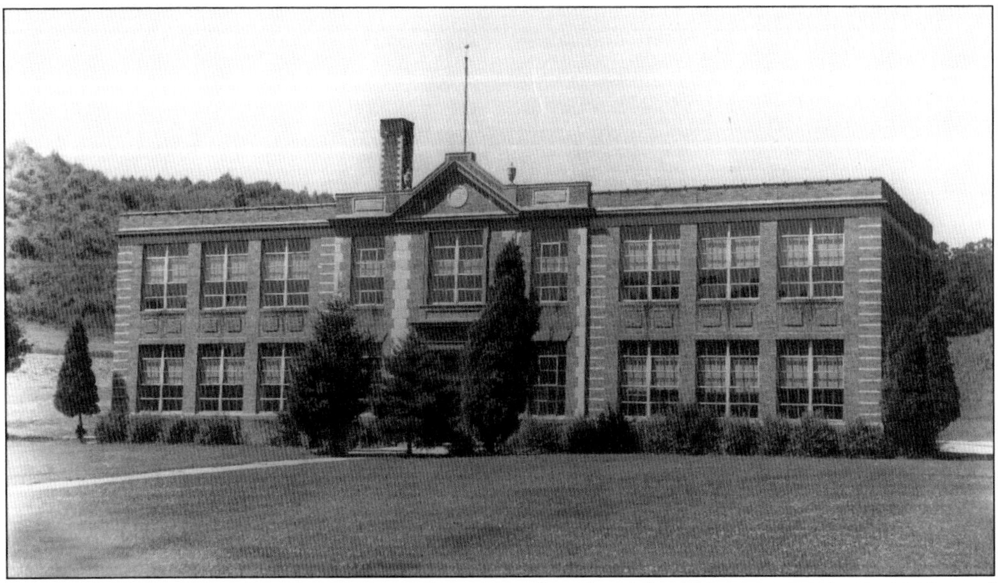

Roswell School Roswell, Ohio. The Roswell School building was built in 1932, and opened for the 1932–33 school year. There were 199 students in grades 1–12 in the building on its opening day. In 1966, the building was closed but was used as the site for the Tuscarawas Valley 6–1–77 Resource Center. The center served the teachers in six counties bordering Interstate 77. After a few years, the funding dwindled for the Resource Center, and it was then moved to the Tuscarawas County Board of Education offices in New Philadelphia.

Seven

Government Buildings and Services of Tuscarawas County

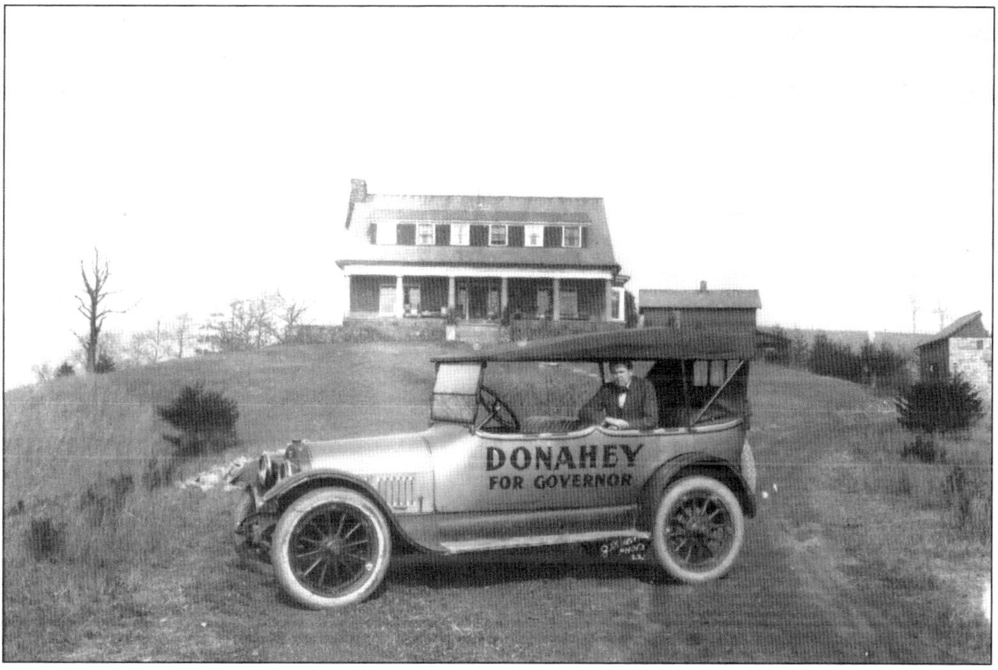

Donahey in his Campaign Car, 1922. A.V. (Vic) Donahey was the only governor of Ohio born and raised in Tuscarawas County. He served Tuscarawas County as county auditor in the late 1900s and early 1910s, and then was elected auditor of the State of Ohio. He ran unsuccessfully for governor in 1920, but was elected in 1922, 1924, and 1926. He served one term as senator from Ohio from 1934 to 1940.

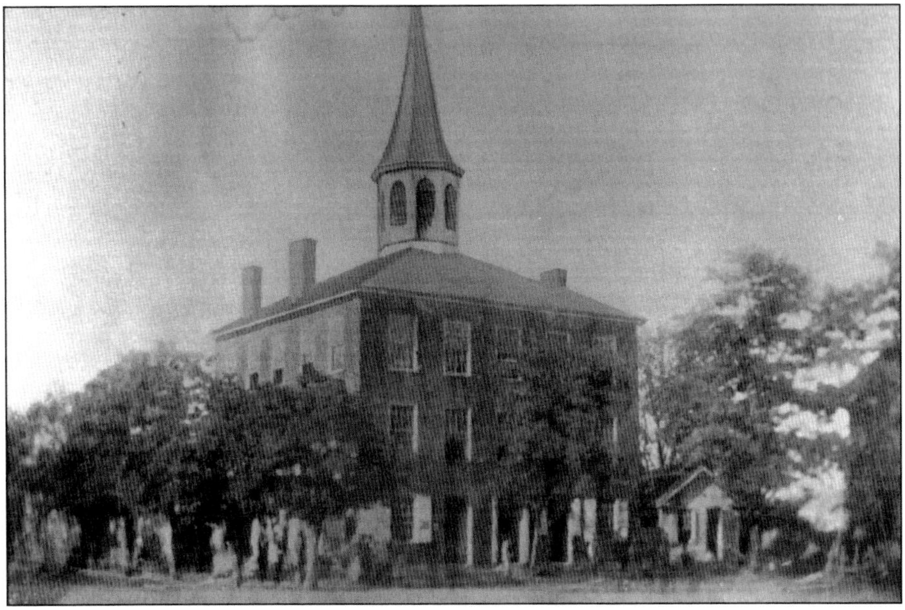

FIRST COURTHOUSE OF TUSCARAWAS COUNTY 1818–1882. Tuscarawas County was established as a county by an act of the Ohio Legislature in 1808. The commissioners would meet in the upstairs of Leininger's tavern on Front Street to enact their business for ten years. However, this was not a satisfactory site, so the commissioners had this structure erected.

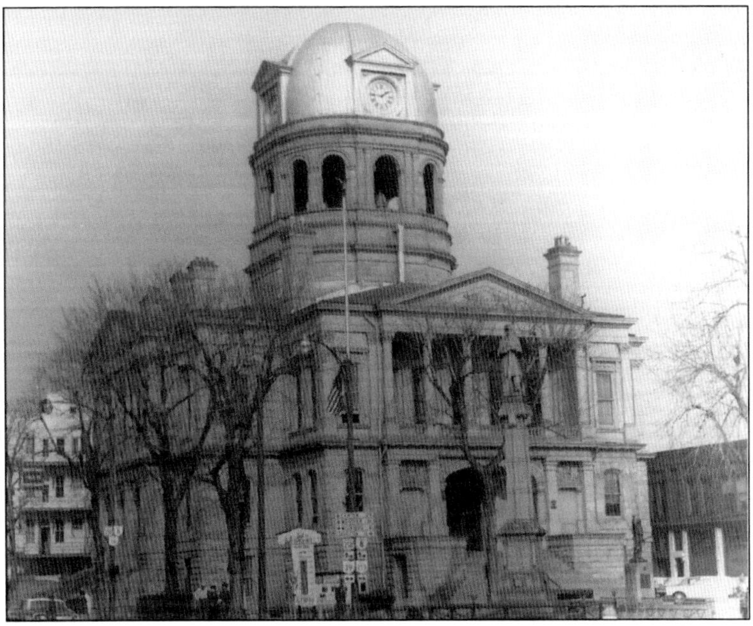

PRESENT COURTHOUSE OF TUSCARAWS COUNTY 1960S. We include this picture of the present courthouse to illustrate where the Reeves Hotel was located (the lower left building), the old courthouse annex (to the lower right of the picture), and to show that the dome was bald for a period of time. In the 1980s, the commissioners and citizens of Tuscarawas County provided the necessary funds to completely renovate this great structure and to add additional spaces for the business of serving the citizens of Tuscarawas County.

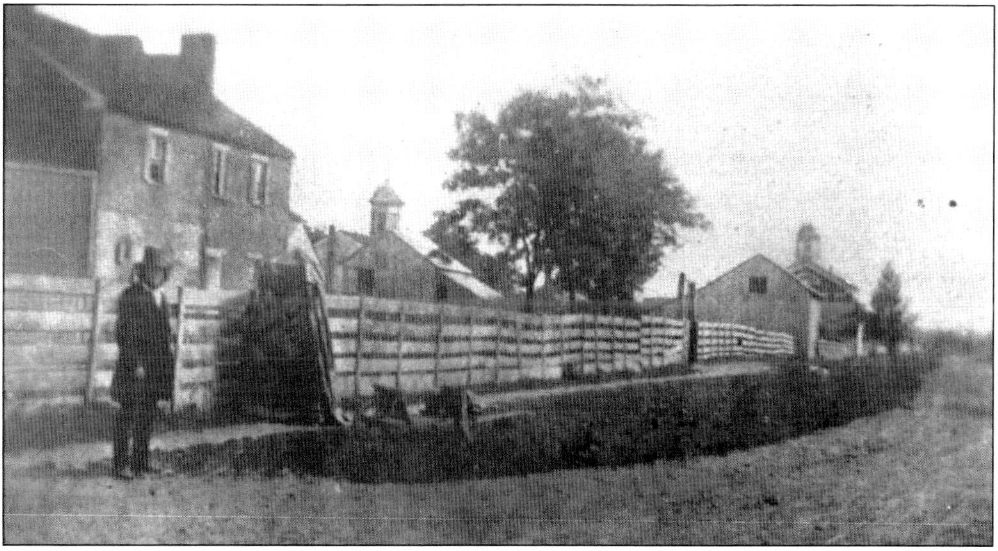

EARLY TUSCARAWAS COUNTY JAIL, NEW PHILADELPHIA, OHIO. Unfortunately, every town and county had to provide a place for those who refused to obey the laws of the land. The upper floors were used for the courtroom and offices for the county government. The building no longer stands.

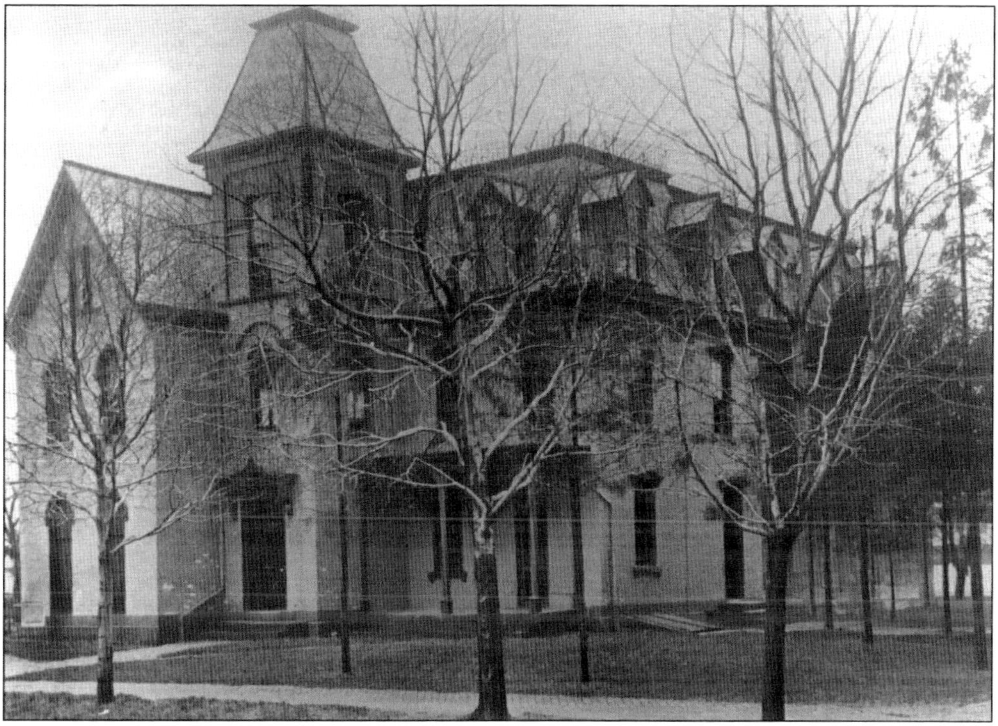

TUSCARAWAS COUNTY JAIL 1870–1990S. The second county jail, pictured here, was built on the northeast corner of Second Street and Fair Avenue in 1870. During many of the years in which the jail was located here, the elected sheriff and his family resided on the second floor. The wife was employed to provide the meals for the residents. Every grand jury would visit the jail to check on it efficiency and cleanliness.

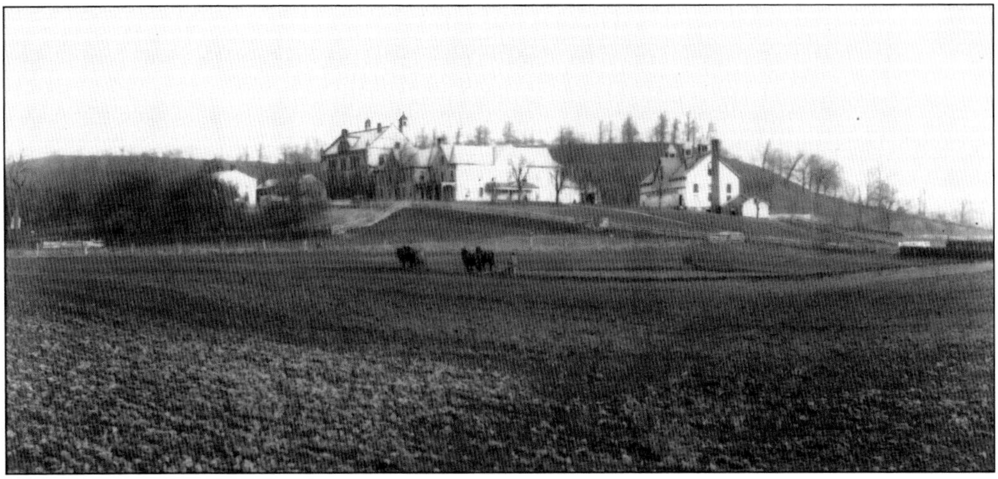

TUSCARAWAS COUNTY INFIRMARY NEW PHILADELPHIA, OHIO. In the late 1900s, the county began providing for those who could not take care of themselves or who had no relatives to provide proper care. In 1927, the county voted a $195,000 bond to build a new infirmary. Today the facility is called Colonial Manor and is located on University Drive in New Philadelphia.

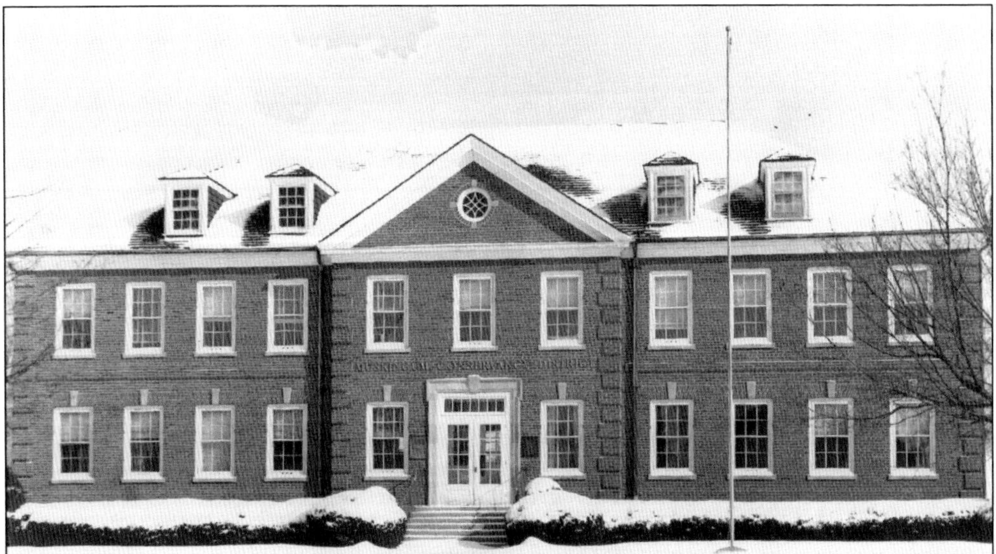

MUSKINGUM CONSERVANCY DISTRICT NEW PHILADELPHIA, OHIO. After the disastrous flood of 1913, a plan was devised to provide flood prevention dams and reservoirs. In the 1930s, the Muskingum Watershed Conservancy District was formed as the governing body for 14 dams and reservoirs. The U.S. Army Corps of Engineers has been responsible for each of the dams, and the conservancy district manages the lakes and the lands adjoining them.

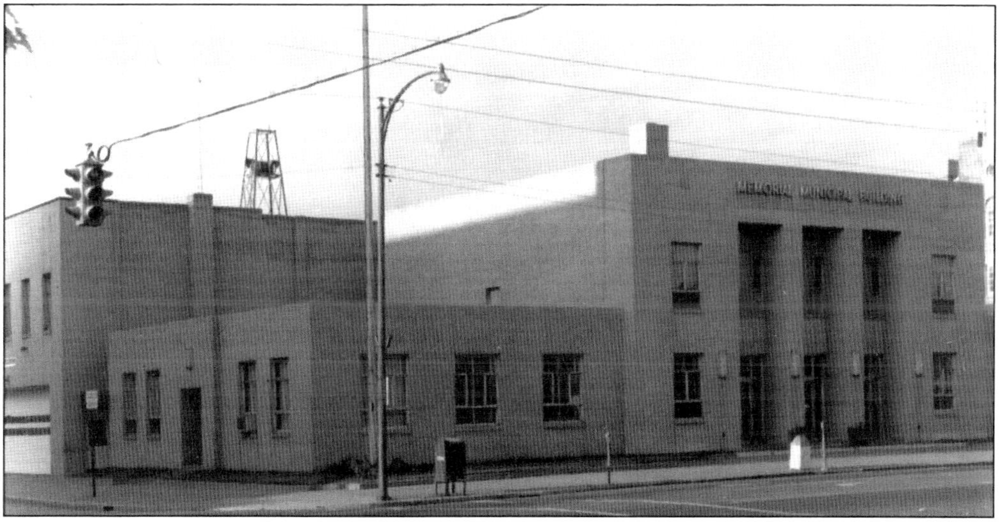

New Philadelphia Municipal Hall. Many people remember old Eagle Hall as the municipal building for the town of New Philadelphia. Since 1950, this building has been host to the offices for the City of New Philadelphia. The building attached to the left of the picture houses the New Philadelphia Fire Department.

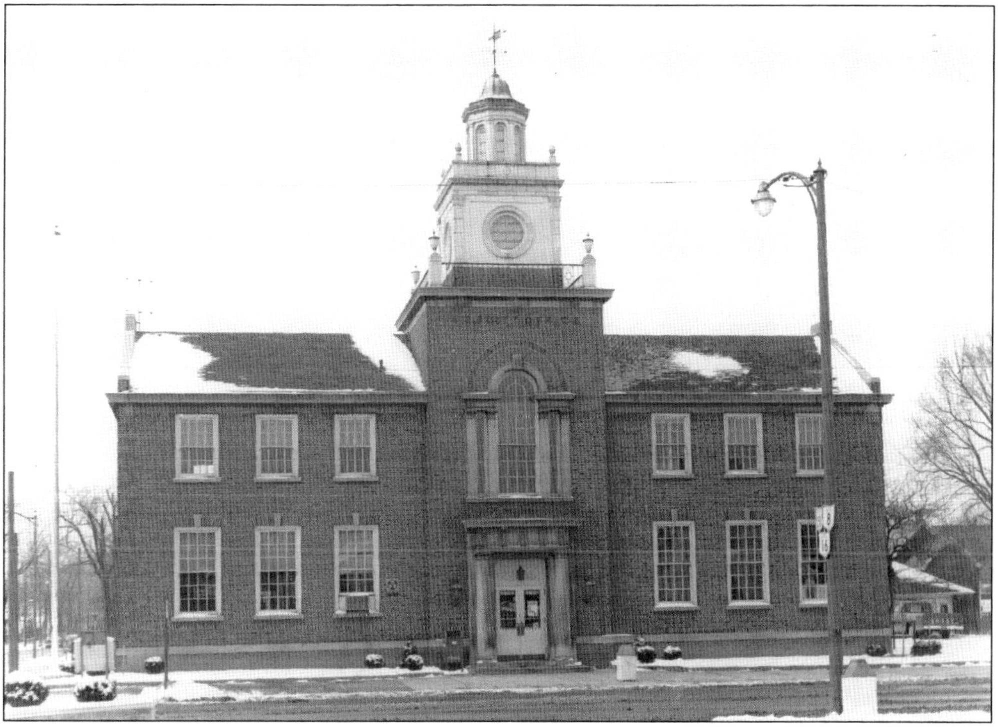

New Philadelphia Post Office. In 1929, a new post office building was needed in New Philadelphia, and the architects who had been selected for the project decided to build a structure which would reflect an image of the city that New Philadelphia was named after, Philadelphia, Pennsylvania. They decided to build a replica of Independence Hall. The general contractor for the building was a grandson of a slave who had operated a successful contracting business in Louisville, Kentucky, Samuel Plato.

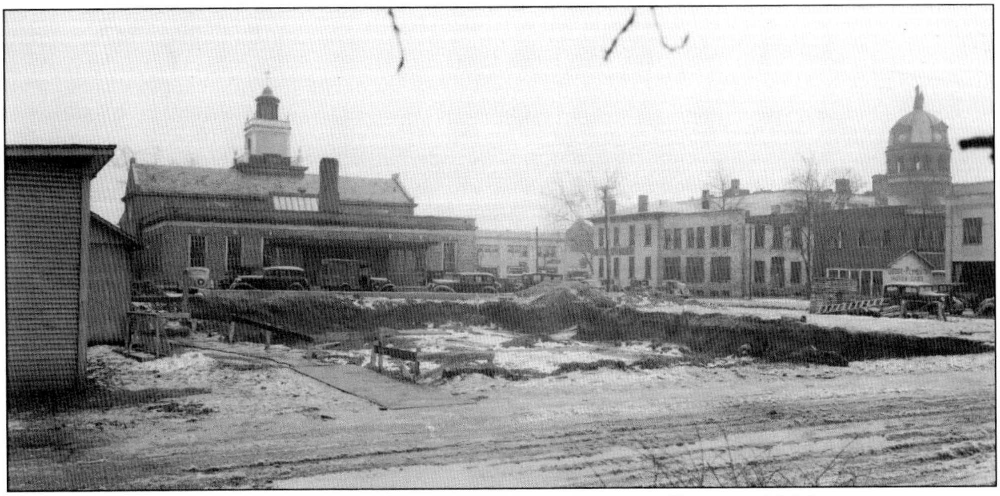

NEW PHILADELPHIA TUSCARAWAS COUNTY PUBLIC LIBRARY BEFORE 1936.

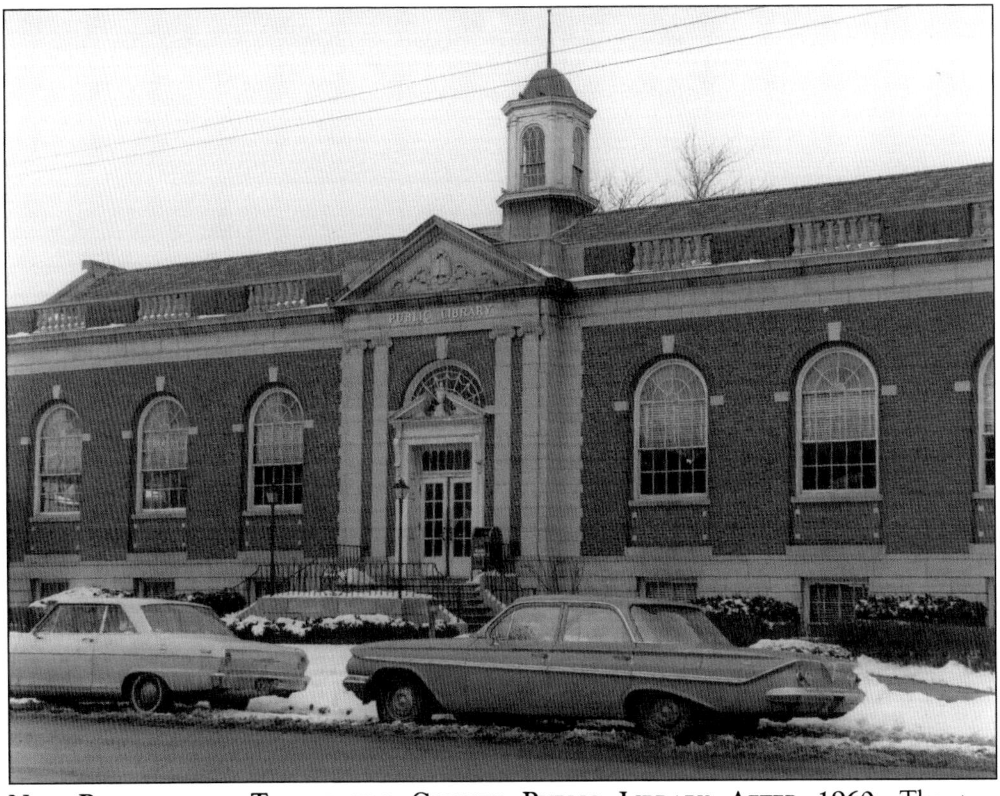

NEW PHILADELPHIA TUSCARAWAS COUNTY PUBLIC LIBRARY AFTER 1960. The two photographs above help to illustrate the citadel of enlightenment in every community—the public library. During the height of the Depression, money was made available to construct this magnificent building. During the same period, many churches in the county also began building their grand structures. There was little money, but the people had faith and hope. With these pictures, the story of Tuscarawas County comes full circle. The words expressed through these pictures reflect those that were in the thoughts of the settlers of the county in 1750s—faith and hope. Without either, society cannot survive.

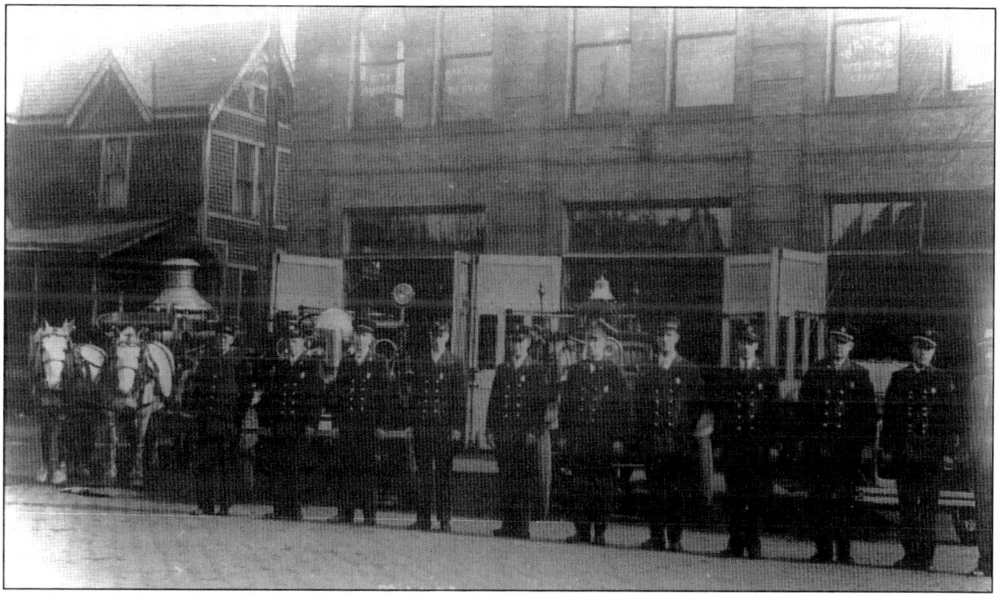

DOVER FIRE DEPARTMENT DOVER, OHIO, EARLY 1900S. This is an impressive picture, which we dedicate to all firefighters who have ever served their communities. This photograph of the Dover firemen of the early 1900s represents every village, town, and city fire department and its personnel who have dedicated their lives to assisting their fellow citizens. Many firefighters and emergency personnel in Tuscarawas County serve without pay. Whether paid or serving as a volunteer, saving a structure or giving lifesaving assistance is reward enough for these men and women.

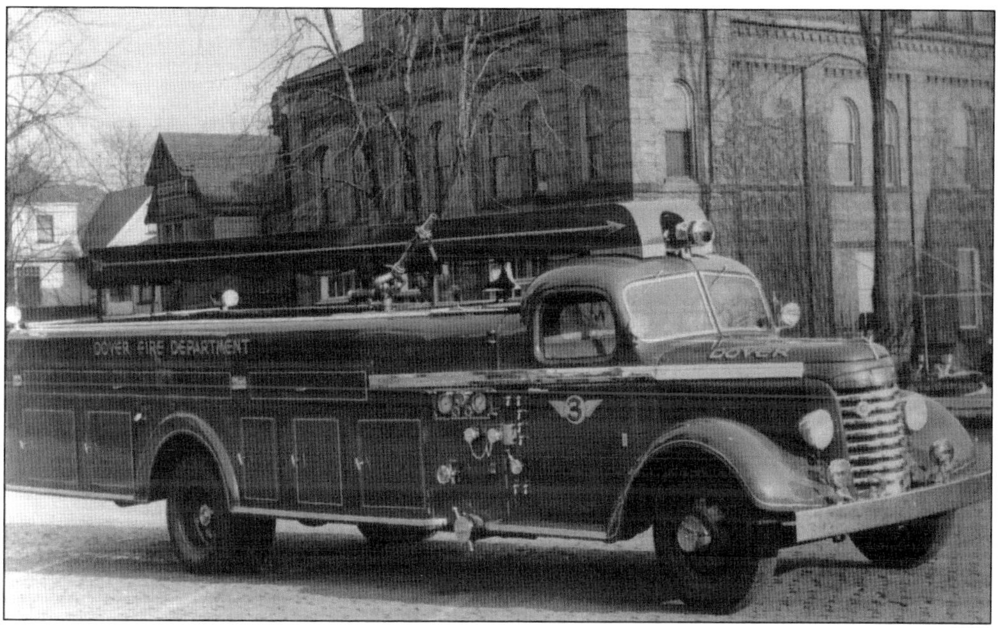

DOVER FIRE DEPARTMENT'S 1939 HENLEY PUMPER. When this photograph was taken, this was one of the finest pieces of equipment available to the fire departments of the county. Today it is merely a museum piece. The original Dover City Hall and Fire Department can be seen in the background of the picture.

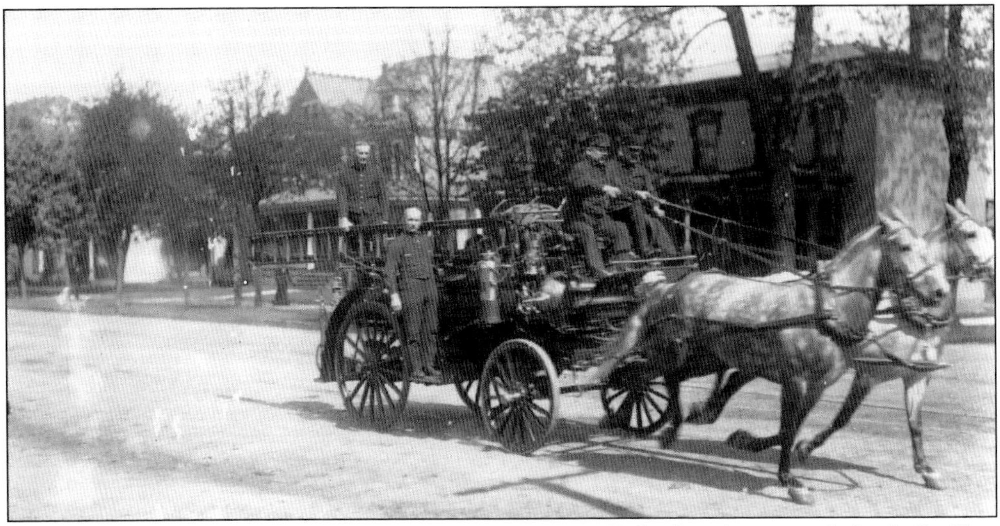

NEW PHILADELPHIA FIREMEN ANSWERING A CALL. With the clanging of the bell, Eliza Stocksdale, Harvey Wilson, Driver George Knisely, and Luther Bechold begin their run to extinguish a fire in New Philadelphia. Today, in the cities and towns of Tuscarawas County, some traffic lights turn red, and the cars and trucks pull to the side of the road at the sound of the sirens in order to let the emergency vehicles pass.

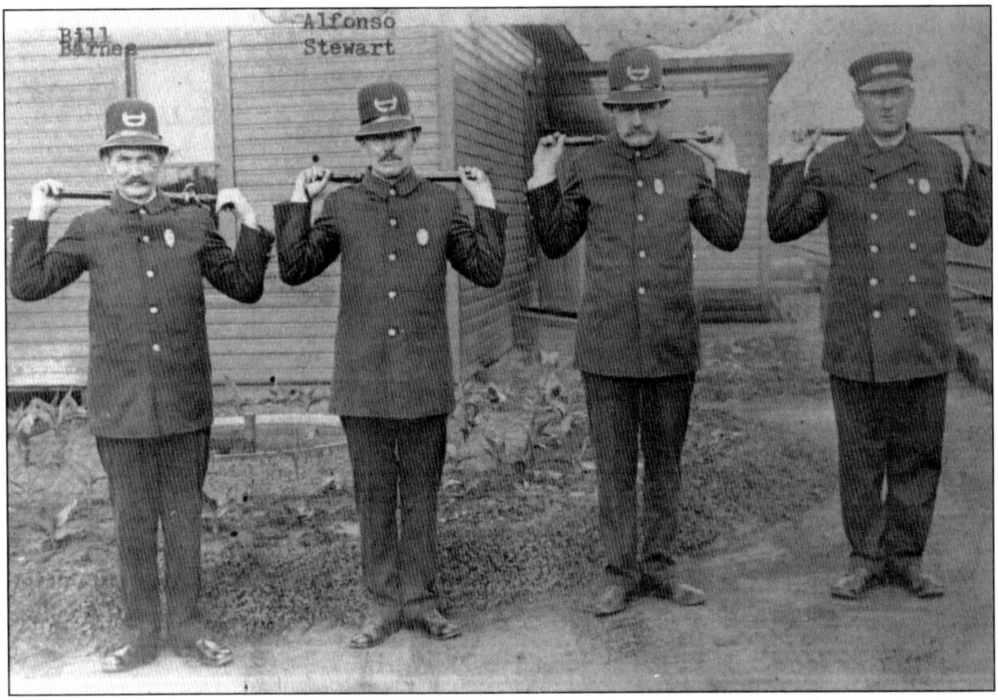

LOCKPORT'S FINEST 1900. We have been able to identify just two of these Lockport policemen—Bill Barnes on the left and Alfonso Stewart, second from the left. Much beleaguered and often assailed, the men and women who take an oath to preserve order in the villages, town, cities, and the countryside of Tuscarawas County have never had an easy task. Since the formation of the county in 1808, men and women have never failed to step forth to accept that task.